ADVANCES IN BUSINESS AND MANAGEMENT

ADVANCES IN BUSINESS AND MANAGEMENT

VOLUME 14

ADVANCES IN BUSINESS AND MANAGEMENT

Additional books in this series can be found on Nova's website under the Series tab.

Additional e-books in this series can be found on Nova's website under the eBooks tab.

ADVANCES IN BUSINESS AND MANAGEMENT

ADVANCES IN BUSINESS AND MANAGEMENT

VOLUME 14

WILLIAM D. NELSON
EDITOR

Copyright © 2017 by Nova Science Publishers, Inc.

All rights reserved. No part of this book may be reproduced, stored in a retrieval system or transmitted in any form or by any means: electronic, electrostatic, magnetic, tape, mechanical photocopying, recording or otherwise without the written permission of the Publisher.

We have partnered with Copyright Clearance Center to make it easy for you to obtain permissions to reuse content from this publication. Simply navigate to this publication's page on Nova's website and locate the "Get Permission" button below the title description. This button is linked directly to the title's permission page on copyright.com. Alternatively, you can visit copyright.com and search by title, ISBN, or ISSN.

For further questions about using the service on copyright.com, please contact:
Copyright Clearance Center
Phone: +1-(978) 750-8400   Fax: +1-(978) 750-4470   E-mail: info@copyright.com.

NOTICE TO THE READER

The Publisher has taken reasonable care in the preparation of this book, but makes no expressed or implied warranty of any kind and assumes no responsibility for any errors or omissions. No liability is assumed for incidental or consequential damages in connection with or arising out of information contained in this book. The Publisher shall not be liable for any special, consequential, or exemplary damages resulting, in whole or in part, from the readers' use of, or reliance upon, this material. Any parts of this book based on government reports are so indicated and copyright is claimed for those parts to the extent applicable to compilations of such works.

Independent verification should be sought for any data, advice or recommendations contained in this book. In addition, no responsibility is assumed by the publisher for any injury and/or damage to persons or property arising from any methods, products, instructions, ideas or otherwise contained in this publication.

This publication is designed to provide accurate and authoritative information with regard to the subject matter covered herein. It is sold with the clear understanding that the Publisher is not engaged in rendering legal or any other professional services. If legal or any other expert assistance is required, the services of a competent person should be sought. FROM A DECLARATION OF PARTICIPANTS JOINTLY ADOPTED BY A COMMITTEE OF THE AMERICAN BAR ASSOCIATION AND A COMMITTEE OF PUBLISHERS.

Additional color graphics may be available in the e-book version of this book.

Library of Congress Cataloging-in-Publication Data

ISSN: 2159-9335
ISBN: 978-1-53612-615-0

Published by Nova Science Publishers, Inc. † New York

CONTENTS

Preface   vii

Chapter 1   Modern Research on Work Motivation   **1**
Constantine I. Tongo

Chapter 2   The Cost of Poor Sleep for Employees and the
Workplace: A Review and Call for Intervention   **59**
*Victoria A. Felix, Mercedes Gremillion
and Walt Buboltz*

Chapter 3   The Resilience of the Informal Sector in the
Context of Major Widespread Crises in
Developing Countries: Evidence from an
African Country's Informal Sector   **93**
Alidou Ouedraogo

Chapter 4   Open Innovation: A Virtuous Process of
Inbound and Outbound Knowledge Flows   **127**
Diego Matricano

Chapter 5   Occupational Injuries from a Finnish Perspective   **155**
Simo Salminen

Chapter 6	Firms as Policy Advocates and Institutional Framers: Understanding the Impact of Ethnic and Political Stratification on BRICS MNEs *Luis Alfonso Dau, Elizabeth M. Moore,* *James Figgins and Joshua K. Ault*	**181**
Chapter 7	Social Entrepreneurship in Rural Development of Lithuania: Potential of Young Entrepreneurs *Jolita Greblikaite*	**207**
Index		**231**

PREFACE

Chapter One by Constantine I. Tongo, PhD categorizes contemporary work motivation philosophies into three wide-ranging classifications, with the goal to concisely present gray areas that research yet to examine. In Chapter Two, Victoria A. Felix, Mercedes Gremillion, and Walt Buboltz, PhD provide readers with a thorough overview of recent literature concerning sleep health and workplace efficiency. Next, Chapter Three by Alidou Ouedraogo, PhD seeks to answer the question, "What are the factors that determine the ability of the informal sector to endure large scale crises?" In Chapter Four, Diego Matricano recommends a method of open innovation while outlining the main facets of inbound and outbound knowledge flows. Simo Salminen provides a Finnish perspective on occupational injuries, risk factors, risk groups, and consequences in Chapter Five. Following this, Luis Alfonso Dau proposes a research program directed at comprehending the influence of ethnic and political arrangements on MNE growth and activity in the BRICS countries in Chapter Six. Lastly, Chapter Seven explores the challenges encountered i rural areas of Lithuania and presents social entrepreneurship as opportunity to develop the country.

Chapter 1 - Although several theories on work motivation h recently been formulated, the literature has not reported any attemp systematically categorizing them, reviewing their empirical studies, evaluating the extent to which they cover extant fundamental rese gaps. Albeit, fulfilling these objectives should help chart the course of future work motivation research. Consequently, this chapter classifies modern work motivation theories into three broad categories. Moreover, empirical studies resonating with the key assumptions of the different theories were reviewed in order to succinctly show grey areas that research has not yet explored. It was found that a few nascent individualistic theories which potentially encourage egocentrism fell short of empirical support in certain areas. However, all the key assumptions of the team based and transcendent theories were empirically validated. Based on these findings, it is believed that the burgeoning interest in empirical studies focusing on these latter theories (i.e., team based and transcendent theories) is most likely predicated on scholarly attempts to resolve the managerial challenges of motivating people towards achieving the common good in contemporary organizations and societies. Overall, the theories analyzed herein have synergistically been able to occupy the virgin territories that were once identified in the field.

Chapter 2 - According to the National Sleep Foundation's Sleep in America Poll (2008), 65% of a sample of 1,000 employed adults reported experiencing sleeping difficulties at least a few nights per week, while 44% report experiencing sleep difficulties every night or almost every night. When asked about the impact of sleepiness in the workplace, 29% reported they have fallen asleep or became very sleepy while working, and 12% reported that they were late to work due to sleepiness. Poor sleep among employees in the workplace has been supported to negatively impact employees' overall performance and well-being, while also impacting the gains for the businesses (Burton, Chen, Schultz, & Xingquan, Poor sleep reported by employees is significantly associated with cognitive performance, increased probability of accidents or injury in the workplace, increased risk for physical and/or mental health issues, and productivity (Gaultney & Collins-McNeil, 2009). As for the cost, it has been estimated that companies lose approximately in productivity costs per employee annually due to poor sleep (Burton et al., 2010). Based on these research findings, it is suggested that employers promote and prioritize healthy sleep among their employees. Recommendations are made in keeping with this. Further, readers are provided with a comprehensive review of the literature which currently exists regarding sleep health and workplace productivity overall.

Chapter 3 - Very small companies including informal sector, are confronted with recurrent crises, sometimes-brutal ones such as floods that menace their survival, growth, and development thereby necessitating the capacity to be resilient. In fact, without unemployment benefits, insurance, or even family or institutional support, certain entrepreneurs disappear while others rebound from disasters and become even stronger. Such a reality leads to the authors' research question: "What are the factors that determine the ability of the informal sector to endure large scale crises?" This is the core of the authors' research, which, by using a qualitative methodology, the authors seek to understand the factors that define business resilience in the face of large-scale crises. The main results are considered as follows: (i) business resilience depends in part upon the level of resources prior to the crisis, (ii) the dynamism of the entrepreneur, (iii) the vitality of the activity sector, (iv) the importance of the resources allocated after the crisis, and (v) the solidarity of family and friends when it comes to moral support.

Chapter 4 - Open innovation processes – OIPs are very common practices on which worldwide companies are leveraging in order to innovate (Chesbrough & Crowther 2006). When dealing with OIPs, managers, practitioners, and scholars mainly pay attention to inbound knowledge flows, i.e., the processes through which companies get innovative ideas and insights from the crowd. Very scarce attention, instead, is paid on outbound knowledge flows, i.e., intellectual property rights and brand out-licensing or new products and services offered onto markets (Gassmann et al. 2010; Schroll & Mild 2011). The choice to focus mainly on inbound knowledge flows, to the detriment of outbound knowledge flows, cannot be meant only as a practical choice made by managers and practitioners according to their interests and then followed by scholars. The above choice, in fact, implies something more.

By caring less about outbound knowledge flows, in fact, it seems that managers, practitioners, and scholars risk missing half of the process through which innovation can nurture and favour itself and be fostered. If they do not consider the whole OIP, then it is not possible to assess what happens to innovative ideas and insights collected by companies, how they are embodied in intellectual property rights, brand out-licensed or transformed into new products/services, how they are offered to final markets and – above all – how they move forward the frontiers of innovation both in practical terms (as a new technological standards) and in consumers' mind. According to the above, the present chapter aims to propose a whole process of open innovation.

In order to achieve the just-cited aim, the chapter is structured as it follows. After defining the main aspects of inbound and outbound knowledge flows, attention is focused on the whole process through which innovation nurtures and favours itself. Theoretically, the whole process can be divided into eight stages: 1) launch of open innovation processes; 2) proposal of insights and ideas by the crowd; 3) collection and selection of proposed insights/ideas; 4) internalization of the most fitting insights/ideas in intellectual property rights/brand out-licensing or in new products/services; 5) their offer to the market; 6) purchase by other companies or by the crowd; 7) collection of feedback; 8) moving of frontiers of innovation both in practical terms (as a new technological standards) and in consumers' mind.

According to the theoretical speculation, only if OIPs are considered as a whole, then companies can aspire to move forward the frontiers of innovation.

Chapter 5 - The aim of this review is to look at occupational injuries, their risk factors, risk groups and consequences from Finnish perspective. The author examined risk factors like age, experience, stress, sleeping problems, haste and handedness. Some working conditions like fixed-term contracts and subcontracting increased the risk of occupational injury. Then different occupations with high risk of occupational injury (agriculture, construction, fire fighters) were examined. In every chapter the author first presented Finnish studies on the topic and then compared them on studies from other countries. Finally, some conclusions about the situation and perspectives of Finnish study on occupational safety will be given.

Chapter 6 - The purpose of this chapter is to invigorate a research program aimed at understanding the impact of ethnic and political stratification on MNE growth and activity in the BRICS countries. Using contextual data from India, this inter-disciplinary chapter highlights the link between systemic political conditions and MNE strategy and success. Through the lens of intergroup contact theory, from international relations, and institutional theory, the authors argue that it is advantageous for BRICS MNEs to adopt a strategy of social activism, to avoid their profit being curtailed by ethnic and political conflict. By examining BRICS MNEs at the firm level, in conjunction with national-level political and ethnic factors that must be overcome before these firms can expand beyond their respective borders, this study aims to understand and highlight unique characteristics that propagate the proliferation and success of these MNEs in a globalizing world.

Chapter 7 - The chapter analyses the problems and challenges of social entrepreneurship in rural areas of Lithuania in order to further the development of this part of the country. The research problem of this chapter is based on the importance of social entrepreneurship for and its role in the rural development of Lithuania, emphasising social cohesion and job creation. Special attention is paid to other activities besides the agriculture in rural areas of Lithuania because of specific situation in villages and small towns. Raising unemployment, emigration, socially disintegrated groups, poor small business development are the main problems in these areas. In this chapter, recent changes in Lithuanian rural areas in terms of social entrepreneurship are presented. Situational analysis reveals both specific problems and some insight on young entrepreneurs in Lithuania. Workable solutions and recommendations on how to improve the situation for better development of rural areas are presented. The main findings reveal that Lithuania still lacks the implementation of social innovation, especially in rural areas. Some conditions and aspects such as culture of social innovation and entrepreneurship, appropriate legislation, different financial sources, national and international networking of social innovators, partnership between public sector, private sector and NGOs, involvement of target social groups, infrastructure for social innovation, effective control and monitoring of social innovation, sufficient administrative skills should be developed in appropriate way in favour of social entrepreneurship.

In: Advances in Business and Management
Editor: William D. Nelson

ISBN: 978-1-53612-615-0
© 2017 Nova Science Publishers, Inc.

Chapter 1

MODERN RESEARCH ON WORK MOTIVATION

Constantine I. Tongo[*]
Department of Business Administration,
Joseph Ayo Babalola University, Ikeji- Arakeji, Osun State, Nigeria

ABSTRACT

Although several theories on work motivation have recently been formulated, the literature has not reported any attempt at systematically categorizing them, reviewing their empirical studies, and evaluating the extent to which they cover extant fundamental research gaps. Albeit, fulfilling these objectives should help chart the course of future work motivation research. Consequently, this chapter classifies modern work motivation theories into three broad categories. Moreover, empirical studies resonating with the key assumptions of the different theories were reviewed in order to succinctly show grey areas that research has not yet explored. It was found that a few nascent individualistic theories which potentially encourage egocentrism fell short of empirical support in certain areas. However, all the key assumptions of the team based and transcendent theories were empirically validated. Based on these findings, it is believed that the burgeoning interest in empirical studies focusing on

---

[*] Corresponding Author Email: constongo@yahoo.com.

these latter theories (i.e., team based and transcendent theories) is most likely predicated on scholarly attempts to resolve the managerial challenges of motivating people towards achieving the common good in contemporary organizations and societies. Overall, the theories analyzed herein have synergistically been able to occupy the virgin territories that were once identified in the field.

INTRODUCTION

Undoubtedly, motivating people at work is central to achieving cutting edge organizational performance. Hence, work motivation has been described as "one of the most pivotal concerns of modern organizational research" (Baron, 1991:1) and an integral component of the performance equation at all organizational levels (Steers, et al., 2004). It is construed as the forces that initiate and determine the direction, amplitude and persistence of an individual's work- related behavior (Locke and Latham, 2004; Seo, Barrett and Bartunek, 2004).

Initially, research interest in work motivation led to development of theoretical models/frameworks that helped practicing managers gain useful insights about the various ways of motivating their employees towards increased productivity. More precisely, during the 1960s and 1970s, a sizable number of work motivation theories were propounded. Nevertheless, by the 1990s, work motivation researchers became more preoccupied with validating the veracity of extant theories than formulating new theories (Steers, et al., 2004).

Consequently, at the dawn of the 21st century, many scholars and researchers in the field of organizational behavior expressed their concerns about the dearth of contemporary work motivation theories that can considerably explicate behaviour in the new forms of organizational settings. Particularly, in 2001, the *Academy of Management Review* (AMR) made a clarion call for the formulation of 21st century theories on work motivation that can positively influence employees' behaviour towards the attainment of higher levels of performance in modern organizations (Steers, et al., 2004).

Just before and after the AMR's call for fundamental research in work motivation, few scholars developed renewed interest towards the formulation of new theories/models on the subject. However, the literature has not reported any attempt at systematically categorizing these theories, reviewing their empirical studies and evaluating the degree to which they have been able to fill fundamental research gaps. It is believed that achieving these objectives should help chart the future direction of work motivation research.

Therefore, through a review of the work motivation literature dating from 1998 to 2013; this chapter aims at documenting contemporary advancements in the field of work motivation theory and research. The year 1998 became a reference point in order to avoid duplicating the extensive literature review conducted by Ambrose and Kulik (1999). These authors reviewed empirically based articles of work motivation published between the periods of 1990 and 1997.

Even though more recent reviews of the work motivation literature had been done by various scholars (e.g., Latham and Pinder 2005; Kanfer, et al., 2008; Ryan, 2012); these reviews did not really capture the essence of modern theories in the field. Rather, their focus was more on the traditional theories of work motivation (e.g., expectancy theory, social cognitive theory, etc.). These theories are already well known to organizational behaviour scholars. Hence this current review became important because of its emphasis on highlighting the import of contemporary theories in the field, which is likely to be borne out of the current global business environmental exigencies.

It is important to note that historically, the evolution of work motivation theories is occasioned by the need to resolve certain work motivation related problems that confronted practicing managers during different epochs of economic development in a few industrialized countries. For instance, the theory on scientific management which derives from Adam Smith's concept of rational-economic man emerged at a time in which industrial managers had to respond to the challenge of soldiering that characterized workers' behaviour during the industrial revolution in Britain and the United States of America.

The primary assumption of scientific management was that man would rationally and positively respond to monetary rewards. The theory helped us appreciate the relevance of financial incentives in motivating people towards the boosting of their productivity in organizations. The need for people to affiliate with themselves so as to ensure organizational performance was brought to the fore by Elton Mayo's social man concept. The concept was subconsciously formed in order to mitigate the effects of the deep state of individualism that most workers were plunged into during the scientific management era.

Nevertheless, the exigencies that ushered in the reign of Adam Smith and Elton Mayo's philosophical concepts of human nature are quite different from those faced by contemporary managers. Presently, information technology has radically altered the ways in which work is being carried out, as well as the location of work activities. According to Steers, et al. (2004), "new organizational forms (such as those found in e-commerce) are now common place. Teams are re-defining the notion of hierarchy, as well as traditional power distributions. Motivating knowledge workers continues to perplex experienced managers across divergent industries. Globalization and the challenges of managing across borders are now the norm instead of the exception" (Steers, et al., 2004: 383).

Furthermore, for the very first time in management history, the moral basis or ethical dimension of managing businesses has been brought to the fore. Prior to this time, managerial ethics which addresses the potential conflict between managerial actions, organizational practices, and moral judgments were neglected (Goodrich and Rossiter, 2009). Until recently, in the aftermath of continuing national business scandals, business ethics had been grossly ignored in business curricula. However, incorporating ethical issues into business decisions adds to the complexities of motivating people in organizations.

Given these current management challenges, there is need to review modern work motivation theories that can unveil the relevant factors needed for uplifting employees' performance in today's organizations. It is also important to know how far these theories have been able to fill extant gaps in fundamental research on work motivation. Moreover, reviewing different research findings related to these theories directs scholarly attention to various research gaps that need to be covered. Consequently, an agenda for future research was set in motion after reviewing these research findings. The next section provides deeper insights into the criteria for selecting articles included in this study.

CRITERIA FOR SELECTING ARTICLES

Apprehensions had been expressed on the possible inability of contemporary work motivation theories being able to attract sufficient volume of research undertakings (Latham and Pinder, 2005). These apprehensions are based on the premise that extant work motivation theories had already been able to account for a wide variety of work behaviours in organizations (Ambrose and Kulik, 1999). Therefore, work motivation scholars tend to cast aspersions on the future impact of contemporary theories in the field.

Given that theory based articles published in peer reviewed journals are likely to be more impactful than those published in journals that are not peer reviewed; it became expedient to select only contemporary work motivation theories published in peer reviewed journals in order to conduct this review.

Table one specifically depicts the authors of the various theories and the Association of Business Schools (ABS) ranking of the journals in which they were published. The table reveals that five out of the nine contemporary work motivation theories were published by the most rated management journal i.e., Academy of Management Review (AMR). Nonetheless, four other highly rated journals (i.e., Journal of Organizational Behaviour, Applied Psychology: An International Review, Journal of Public Administrative Research and Theory, and Journal of Business Ethics) within the academic disciplines of Organizational Behaviour, Psychology, Public Administration and Business Ethics were responsible for publishing the remaining theories.

Table 1. Theories, Authors, and Journal Ranking

Serial Number	Theory of Work Motivation	Author	Journal Name	Journal Ranking
1	Affective Work Motivation	Seo, Barrett and Bartunek (2004)	Academy of Management Review	Four star
2	Life Span Developmental Theory of Work Motivation	Kanfer and Ackerman(2004)	Academy of Management Review	Four star
3	Self Determination Theory of Work Motivation	Gagne and Deci (2005)	Journal of Organizational Behaviour	Four star
4	Compensatory Model of Work Motivation and Volition	Kehr (2004)	Academy of Management Review	Four star
5	Temporal Motivational theory	Steel and Konig (2006)	Academy of Management Review	Four star
6	Social Identity Theory of Work Motivation	Van Knippenberg (2000)	Applied Psychology: An International Review	Two star
7	Joint Production Motivation	Lindenberg and Foss (2011)	Academy of Management Review	Four star
8	Theory of Public Service Motivation	Perry (2000)	Journal of Public Administration: Research and Theory	Four star
9	Meaningful Work Motivation	Lips-Wiersma and Morris (2009)	Journal of Business Ethics	Three star

Table 2. Theories and empirical articles

Theories	Number of Empirical Studies
(i) Affective Work Motivation.	20
(ii) Life Span Developmental Theory of Work Motivation.	14
(iii) Self Determination Theory of Work Motivation.	17
(iv) Compensatory Model of Work Motivation and Volition.	2
(v) Temporal Motivation Theory	8
(vi) Social Identity Theory of Work Motivation.	15
(vii) Joint Production Motivation.	9
(viii) Theory of Public Service Motivation	15
(ix) Meaningful Work Motivation.	6

Searching for work motivation theories in highly impactful journals was quite a straight forward process. The search was conducted by focusing on those international peer reviewed journals that published articles on work motivation between the periods 1998 and 2013. These theory based articles were then extensively read and selected.

Sequel to the selection of the theories, empirical studies that are primarily linked to their key assumptions were searched for in all international peer reviewed journals that publish articles on work motivation. Intensive search involving the key words of each work motivation theory was conducted in EBSCO host and other electronic data bases (e.g., JSTOR and Emerald insight). This search effort produced 106 empirical articles. A breakdown of the distribution of these articles to the nine different theories is shown in Table two. The articles included 23 longitudinal studies, 62 cross sectional studies, 16 experimental studies, and 5 meta-analytical studies.

CATEGORIZATION OF MODERN THEORIES

Based on literature review, three broad categories of work motivation theories that instigate contemporary research in the field were generated. These categories are the nascent individualistic theories, team based theories and transcendent theories of work motivation.

The nascent individualistic theories are entirely devoted to explaining the causes of productivity variances amongst individuals strictly from an individualistic perspective. These theories either implicitly or explicitly assume that individuals are egocentric in nature and that work performance can be boosted when individuals are treated as separate entities. It is important to note that this underlying assumption has immensely influenced the direction of extant theories on work motivation (Ellemers, et al., 2004; Bridoux, et al., 2011).

In this study, five nascent individualistic theories of work motivation were gleaned from the literature. These are: affective work motivation, compensatory model of work motivation and volition, life span developmental theory of work motivation, temporal motivation theory, and self- determination theory of work motivation.

Team based theories of work motivation account for the psychological factors that induce the individual to accept and be driven by group/organizational goals without necessarily sacrificing personal goals. These theories shift work orientation of self in individualistic terms to a work orientation of self in collectivistic terms. Two types of team based theories/models were obtained from the literature. These are the social identity theory (SIT) of work motivation and joint production motivation (JPM).

Transcendent theories of work motivation are geared towards defining the internal and external forces that propel the individual to think beyond the "self" while responding to the needs of others in different organizations and societies. Two transcendent theories on work motivation were located in the literature. These are: theory of public service motivation (PSM), and meaningful work motivation (MWM). The essential ingredients of sub-theories encapsulated by the three broad categories were first of all presented before delving into research findings that are relevant to them in the following sessions.

NASCENT INDIVIDUALISTIC THEORIES OF WORK MOTIVATION

Affective Work Motivation (AWM)

The term "affective work motivation" refers to the role that emotions play in shaping work motivation. Seo, Barrett and Bartunek (2004) decried the extant neglect of the impact that emotions have on employees' work motivation. According to them, it is imperative to move beyond the implicit adopted assumption held by goal setting and expectancy theorists that work motivational processes are always cognitively based, discrete choice processes. In fact, AWM presupposes that core affective experiences may have direct impact on behavioural processes and outcomes in ways that are unmediated by cognitively based processes (Seo, Barrett and Bartunek, 2004).

The theory simply states that core affective experiences defined in terms of the pleasantness and activation of an individual's hedonic state are responsible for the direction, intensity and persistence of work motivation in organizations. Pleasantness refers to how well an individual is doing with respect to hedonic valence of pleasant/unpleasant, good/ bad, or appetitive/aversive feelings. Activation connotes the degree of arousal or tension that an individual experiences in a particular hedonic state (Seo, Barrett and Bartunek, 2004).

Moreover, core affect influences the direction of behaviourial choices. These could either be generatively or defensively oriented. While generativeness is a behaviourial orientation towards exploring and achieving anticipated outcomes by taking risks and willing to incur loss in the process; defensiveness is a behaviourial orientation geared towards avoiding potential negative outcomes, in spite of feasible opportunities to achieve better outcomes (Seo, Barrett and Bartunek, 2004). The table below shows the distribution of empirical studies that are essentially linked to the key assumptions of the theory.

Table three shows that three empirical studies were aimed at verifying whether the impact of effect on work motivation is either mediated or unmediated by cognitive based processes. Two of these studies found that the cognitive based processes associated with Vroom's (1964) expectancy theory mediated the impact of emotions on work motivation (Erez and Isen, 2002; Seo, et al., 2010). The third empirical study also revealed that continuance commitment (i.e., a cognitive component of organizational commitment) impacted on the relationship between affect and work motivation (Naquin and Holton 111, 2002).

These findings contradict the assumption which posits that the impact of emotions on work motivation is not mediated by cognitive based processes. Therefore, it may be needful for future work motivation research to disclose the mediating impact of cognitive based processes on employees' emotions.

Table 3. Empirical Studies on Affective Work Motivation

Key Assumptions	Empirical Studies
(i) Impact of effect on work motivation is either mediated or unmediated by cognitive based processes.	Erez and Isen (2002); Seo, et al. (2010); Naquin and Holton 111 (2002).
(ii) Pleasantness and Activation of an individual's hedonic state are responsible for work motivation/performance.	Wright and Staw (1999); Grandey (2003); Seo, et al. (2010); Tsai, et al. (2009); Wegge, et al. (2010); Amabile and Gramer (2007); Janssen, et al. (2009); Brundin, et al. (2008); Mignonac, and Herrbach (2004); Harris, et al. (2003); Scott and Barnes (2011); Wiese and Freund (2005); Seery and Corrigall (2009).
(iii) Affect that is either induced generatively or defensively influences the direction of behavioural choices.	Binnewies and Wornlein (2011); George and Zhou (2002); Amabile, et al. (2005); Seo, et al. (2010).

Table three shows that empirical support for the second assumption of the theory abounds. Seven empirical studies showed that negative affect produced lower levels of work motivation/performance (Grandey, 2003; Wegge, et al., 2010; Janssen, et al., 2009; Brundin, et al., 2008; Mignonac and Herrbach, 2004; Scott and Barnes, 2011; Seery and Corrigall, 2009).

It is important to note that negative affect was conceptualized differently by some of these studies. Concepts such as emotional dissonance, emotional exhaustion, surface and deep acting were adopted in lieu of negative affect. Only one of these studies showed that activation of an individual's negative emotions could probably result in work motivation reduction. In this particular study, Mignonac and Herrbach (2004) observed that negative job related events produced negative affective states. This in turn negatively affected employees' job satisfaction and organizational commitment.

Furthermore, seven empirical studies indicated that positive emotions increased work motivation/ performance (Wright and Staw, 1999; Seo, et al, 2010; Tsai, et al., 2009; Amabile and Gramer, 2007; Brundin, et al., 2008; Mignonac and Herrbach, 2004; Harris, et al., 2003).

Three of these studies showed that activation of positive affect led to enhancement of work motivation/performance. However, Wright and Staw (1999) found that activating managers' positive emotions did not result to increases in their supervisory performance ratings. Due to these findings, further research could seek to extensively explore the unique ways by which activated emotional states of employees influence work motivation/performance.

The four empirical studies resonating with the assumption that affect which is either induced generatively or defensively influences the direction of behavioural choices are shown in the table. Three of the studies found that positive affect increased the creative performance of employees (Binnewies and Wornlein, 2011; Seo, et al., 2010; Amabile, et al., 2005). Thus implying that positive affect generatively influenced the direction of employees' behavioural choices. Nonetheless, George and Zhou (2002) indicated that negative feelings were positively related to employees' creativity when perceived recognition and rewards for creative performance as well as clarity of feelings were high.

Future empirical evidence is therefore needed to unpack the circumstances under which negative affect may become detrimental to creative performance. Apparently, none of the four empirical studies accounted for defensive direction of behavioural choices. It therefore becomes expedient for findings of future research undertakings to fill this knowledge gap.

Life Span Developmental Theory (LSDT) of Work Motivation

The LSDT of work motivation was formulated by Kanfer and Ackerman (2004) in a bid to account for the impact of aging on individuals' motives and values. Before now, aging had generally been viewed as a correlate of redundancy and many believed that older workers constitute a huge cost to organizations (NG and Feldman, 2012). This pessimistic nuance of aging that is somewhat associated with low productivity has been reviewed by the LSDT of work motivation; as it maintains that the motivational drives of younger workers are quite different from those of older workers. Thus, jobs that motivate younger workers towards actualizing high performance may not produce similar results with older workers.

Firstly, Kanfer and Ackerman (2004) averred that the perception which an adult has about the efforts required to perform a task is always affected by the very nature of the task or job. Traditionally, tasks or jobs that managers allocate to adults place demand on two sets of intellectual abilities. The first set is known as fluid intellectual abilities (Gf), while the second set is called crystallized intellectual abilities (Gc) (Cattell, 1943).

Gf resources are required for abstract reasoning, processing of novel information and working memory (Kanfer and Ackerman, 2004). However, Gc resources pertain to broad dimensions of experiential or educational knowledge (Cattell, 1987) and are linked to general knowledge, verbal comprehension, use of vocabulary and always needed for the performance of high knowledge tasks. Such tasks are referred to as "effort-insensitive tasks" (Kanfer and Ackerman, 2004).

Kanfer and Ackerman (2004) conclude that since adult development is negatively related to Gf, but positively related to Gc; adults would tend to pessimistically perceive that efforts should lead to performance if placed on jobs that demand the exhibition of high levels of Gf. Nevertheless, they would optimistically perceive that efforts should correlate with performance if assigned to jobs that require the display of high levels of Gc.

Secondly, unlike younger workers that are attracted by varied forms of extrinsic and intrinsic rewards (e.g., pay, sense of achievement, recognition, and career advancement); older workers do not necessarily increase their performance when these rewards are present. This is occasioned by the reorganization of motives and values that characterize adulthood. Consequently, the theory assumes that as adulthood looms, the strength of some motives (e.g., need for achievement, demonstration of mastery) that younger workers seek to satisfy gradually wanes, while the strength of other motives related to protecting self concept and promoting positive affect becomes stronger (Kanfer and Ackerman, 2004). Table four presents empirical studies that can be linked to the key assumptions of the theory.

As shown in the table, four empirical studies verified whether older employees perform better when placed on jobs that demand the use of Gc resources rather than Gf resources. Findings from these studies showed that while older workers produce inferior performance when confronted with complex jobs that are mentally demanding; they perform better on jobs that enable them leverage on their experience and general knowledge.

For instance, De Lange, et al. (2010) found that there was a reciprocal causal relationship between job control (defined as the tendency for a job to require creativity) and the learning related behaviour of older employees. However, Stamov-Robnagel and Biemann (2012) revealed that older employees perform better on generatively related tasks (i.e., tasks pertaining to teaching, training and sharing skills with younger generation) than when they handle growth related tasks (i.e., tasks that aggravate the need for achievement and improvement of one's social status).

Results from the other two empirical studies implied that older employees need extra supports in form of job enrichment programs and organizational stimulation i.e., training and re-training (Van Den Berg, 2011); as well as successful aging strategies (e.g., setting goals and deciding on goal priorities, coordinated use of personal resources to achieve important goals, acquisition and utilization of alternative means to reach goals) that could help them cope with mentally demanding jobs (Zacher and Frese, 2011). These results give credence to the first assumption of the theory presented in Table four.

Research had also been undertaken for the purpose of ascertaining whether aging is characterized by re-organization of motives and values. Table three shows that eleven empirical studies verified the authenticity of this key assumption. The impact of aging on different forms of motives was investigated. Several studies discovered that while aging was positively related to the growth of intrinsic motivation (Twenge, et al., 2010; Van Den Berg, 2011; Orth, et al., 2012); it had a negative relationship with extrinsic motivation (Twenge, et al., 2010; Kooij, et al., 2011; Inceoglu, et al., 2012).

Table 4. Empirical Studies on LSDT

Key Assumptions	Empirical Studies
(i) Older employees perform better when placed on jobs that demand the use of Gc rather than Gf.	De lange, et al. (2010); Stamov-Robnagel and Biemann (2012); Zacher and Frese (2011); Van Den Berg (2011).
(ii) Aging is characterized by a re-organization of motives and values.	Kooij, et al. (2011); Nakai, et al. (2011); Bertolino, et al. (2011); Van Vianen, et al. (2011); Twenge, et al. (2010); NG and Feldman (2012); Orth, et al. (2012); Inceoglu, et al. (2012); Kooij and Van De Voorde (2011); Von Bonsdorff (2011); Van Den Berg (2011).

Albeit, Nakai, et al. (2011) and Von Bonsdorff (2011) found that aging positively correlated with the rise of extrinsic motivation amongst some categories of older employees. Based on the motives of mature job seekers over forty years old, Nakai, et al. (2011) identified three clusters of job seekers. These are: those who work primarily for family and monetary reasons (satisfiers), those who seek employment for a wide variety of reasons (maximizers), and some others who seek personal satisfaction and learning opportunities from employment (free agents). Also, Von Bonsdorff (2011) found that older and more experienced nurses tended to prefer financial rewards more than younger nurses. The above contradictory findings on the relationship between aging and extrinsic motivation provide an opportunity for conducting a meta-analysis of past empirical studies on the subject in future.

Three empirical studies explored the relationship between aging and motivation to engage in training and development activities. Results from these studies indicated that older workers were less motivated to engage in training and development activities than their younger counterparts (Bertolino, et al., 2011; Van Vianen, et al., 2011; NG and Feldman, 2012). These results may stem from the fact that training and development activities place demands on employees' Gf resources; and older employees are less motivated to engage in jobs that require the exhibition of such abilities.

Two other empirical studies examined the nexus between aging and altruistic motivation. Kooij and Van De Voorde (2011) investigated the relationship between future time perspective (i.e., an individual's perceptions of his or her remaining time to live) and generativity motives (i.e., desire to engage in tasks that involve teaching, training and transfering knowledge to younger generations). They found a positive relationship between limited future time perspective and generativity motives. Thus, implying that aging somewhat correlate positively with altruistic motivation. The study conducted by Twenge, et al. (2010) aligns with this submission because its findings revealed that past generations favoured altruistic work values (e.g., helping) more than millennials.

Given the above research findings on the LSDT of work motivation, it is recommended that future research involving samples of older employees can be undertaken for the purpose of extensively analyzing jobs that are most suited to boosting their productivity. Findings from such research should direct managerial attention to the peculiarities of certain jobs and industries that allow older employees produce effective performance.

Towards helping organizations successfully manage older employees, it will be needful for researchers to embark on longitudinal studies that explicitly shed light on the particular range of age that the work motivational differences between young and old employees become pronounced. Moreover, qualitative research endeavours should also be undertaken with a view to knowing the major reasons behind re-organization of motives and values during adulthood.

Self Determination Theory (SDT) of Work Motivation

The SDT can be regarded as a polemic on the cognitive evaluation theory and aims to guide against the general belief that all forms of extrinsic motivation attenuate autonomous motivation (Deci and Ryan, 2000). The main thrust of the SDT is hinged on the possibility of influencing human behavior through certain extrinsic motivational factors that can produce a close semblance of intrinsic motivational outcomes of job autonomy and competence (Deci and Ryan, 2000; Gagne and Deci, 2005).

The theory maintains that even though autonomous motivation (i.e., acting with a sense of volition) is somewhat the natural behavioural consequence of individuals that find themselves performing intrinsically motivating jobs; it can also be produced if extrinsic rewards that are contingent on job performance initiate and sustain an external process of regulation that gets fully internalized within the individual.

Nonetheless, external regulation that stems from extrinsic motivation does not always get fully internalized within the person. In extreme cases, external regulation could actually produce controlled motivational behaviour (i.e., acting with a sense of pressure instead of volition (Gagne and Deci, 2005).

The SDT buttresses that autonomous and controlled motivations vary in terms of both their regulatory processes and their accompany experiences, and the theory further states that behaviours can be placed between two ends of a continuum that typify autonomous and controlled motivations respectively. According to Gagne and Deci (2005), internalization is a generic term that can refer to three different processes. These are: introjection, identification, and integration.

A regulation that has been internalized by someone, but has not been accepted as his or her own is said to be introjected and provides the basis for *introjected regulation.* Introjected regulation is particularly interesting because the regulation is within the person but is a relatively controlled form of internalized extrinsic motivation (Gagne and Deci, 2005).

The second form of external regulation is termed *identified regulation.* Identified regulation enhances individual freedom and autonomy because the behaviour that is produced from the external regulation is more in sync with personal goals and identities. In other words, identified regulation direct the cause of human behaviour to an aspect of a person's self concept (i.e., internal perceived locus of causality).

Modern Research on Work Motivation   17

However, the most matured type of internalization (i.e., integrated regulation) allows extrinsic motivation to be truly autonomous or volitional. It involves a full integration of the externally regulated behaviour into several aspects of oneself. With integrated regulation, individuals have a full conviction that the behaviour is an integral component of who they are and that it originates from their sense of self and it is self- determined (Gagne and Deci, 2005).

Integrated regulation requires nutriments so as to function properly. Satisfying the basic needs for competence, relatedness and autonomy provides the nutriments for experiencing integrated extrinsic motivation (Gagne and Deci, 2005). Table five depicts empirical studies that are associated with the theory's key assumptions/concepts.

Table 5. Empirical Studies on SDT

Key Assumptions/Concepts	Empirical Studies
(i) Introjected regulation can be produced by extrinsic motivation.	Chen and Bozeman (2013); Roche and Haar (2013); Broeck, et al. (2011); Gillet, et al. (2013); Van Beek, et al. (2012); Grant, et al. (2011)
(ii) Identified regulation can be the consequence of extrinsic motivation.	Chen and Bozeman (2013); Van Beek, et al. (2012)
(iii) Integrated regulation can be the outcome of extrinsic motivation	Chen and Bozeman (2013); Roche and Harr (2013); Broeck, et al. (2011); Gillet, et al. (2013); Van Beek, et al. (2012); Hardre and Reeve (2009); Grant, et al. (2011)
(iv) Satisfying the basic needs for competence, relatedness and autonomy provides the nutriments for experiencing integrated regulation.	Roche and Haar (2013); Kovjanic, et al. (2012); Gregarus, et al. (2009); Kuvaas (2009); Heather, et al. (2007); De Cooman, et al. (2013); Dysvik, et al. (2013); Gagne, et al. (2000); Baard, et al. (2004).

Table five shows that six empirical studies were aimed at investigating the first assumption. Chen and Bozeman (2013) found that public sector managers experienced higher levels of introjected regulation than non-profit sector managers when both classes of managers were exposed to extrinsic motivational factors. Thus, suggesting that managers in the public sector were less motivated by extrinsic rewards than their non-profit sector counterparts.

Introjected regulation that emanates from extrinsic motivation was also shown to be negatively related to organizational citizenship behaviours (Roche and Haar, 2013), but positively related to compulsive work (Broeck, et al., (2011) and turnover intentions (Gillet, et al., 2013). Moreover, greater experiences of introjected regulation have been linked to higher levels of workaholism- a bad way of working hard (Van beek, et al., 2012); and lower levels of exercising initiative (Grant, et al., 2011). The above results reveal that the manifestation of negative work behaviours could be borne out of the introjected regulation that employees experience while working.

Only two empirical studies examined whether identified regulation stems from extrinsic motivation. One of these studies concluded that in the presence of extrinsic motivational factors, public sector managers exhibited stronger levels of identified motivation than managers in the non-profit sectors (Chen and Bozeman, 2013). This implies that public sector managers were better able to direct the cause of extrinsic motivation to an aspect of their personal identities.

However, the findings of Van Beek, et al. (2012) tend to cast some doubts on the capacity of identified regulation yielding positive work behaviours; as they showed that workaholism was highly associated with identified regulation. Future research could therefore explore the conditions under which identified regulation produces positive work behaviours.

With regards to integrated regulation, six empirical studies implied that it can be linked to positive work behaviours. These studies conclude that integrated regulation is positively related to organizational citizenship behaviours (Roche and Harr (2013); work vigour (Broeck, et al., 2011); work satisfaction (Gillet, et al., 2013); work engagement (Van Beek, et al., 2012; Hadre and Reeve, 2009) and exercise of initiative (Grant, et al.,

2011). Furthermore, the study conducted by Chen and Bozeman (2013) indicated that integrated regulation was more experienced by public sector managers than their non-profit counterparts.

While many empirical studies in varying degrees tend to support the assumption that satisfying the basic needs for competence, relatedness and autonomy provides the nutriments for experiencing integrated regulation (Roche and Harr, 2013; Kuvjanic, et al., 2012; Gregarus, et al., 2009; Heather, et al., 2007; De Cooman, et al., 2013; Baard, et al., 2004); one study reported that satisfying the needs for autonomy and relatedness, but not the need for competence actually correlates with integrated regulation (Dysvic, et al., 2013). However, Kuvaas (2009) revealed that supervisors' support for autonomy and competence was fully mediated by integrated regulation. This latter finding suggested that managers should pay sufficient attention to autonomy supportive work environments, as this was found to facilitate the acceptance of organizational change (Gagne, et al., 2000).

Based on the above empirical findings, it will be correct to conclude that the four key assumptions of the SDT have been well authenticated by research. Nevertheless, it is recommended that future research on the theory could dwell on the effect that personality traits have on individuals' ability to successfully engage in integrated regulation when they are subjected to extrinsic forms of motivation.

Compensatory Model of Work Motivation and Volition (CMWMV)

According to Kehr (2004), some motives that we harbour are quite explicit to us and may even be accessible by other individuals because these explicit motives are occasionally discussed, analyzed and reviewed with some other persons. Yet, beneath our consciousness, there may be some other motives, termed "implicit motives" that we cannot easily articulate (Kehr, 2004). Unfortunately, it is possible for explicit and implicit motives to be diametrically opposed to one another. When this happens, intrapersonal conflict arises within the individual (Kehr, 2004).

These conflicts may result in performance deficits, preference reversals, health problems and impaired well- being (McClelland et al., 1989; Sheldon and Kasser, 1995; Brunstein, et al., 1998; Ryan and Deci, 2000).

Apart from implicit and explicit motives, perceived ability is also a structural component of Kehr's CMWMV. Perceived ability is a person's perception of the amount of actual control he or she can exert over the environment and job tasks (Kehr, 2004). It is generally believed that successful performance of certain difficult job tasks should logically lead to the perception that similar tasks can be successfully executed (Bandura, 1977). Many work motivation researchers hold that perceived ability is one of the most important determinants of work motivation (Bandura, 1977; Tubbs and Ekeberg, 1991; Ajzen, 1991; Ambrose and Kulik, 1999).

Given the three structural components (i.e., implicit motives, explicit motives and perceived ability) of the CMWMV; how do they impact on work motivation in organizations?

Firstly, Kehr (2004) asserts that volitional strategies would be utilized when an individual's explicit motives conflict with his or her implicit motives. Volition was defined as an array of self- regulatory strategies that support explicit action tendencies which are at variance with implicit behavioural impulses (Kehr, 2004). However, like similar psychological processes, volitional regulation could have some deficiencies (Baumeister and Heatherton, 1996). The most important deficiency stems from the fact that volition consumes limited psychological resources (Kehr, 2004). Various work motivation scholars hold that after some acts of volition, subsequent volitional acts are more likely to fail (Baumeister, et al., 1998; Muraven and Baumeister, 2000).

Secondly, Kehr (2004) opined that when an individual perceives that his or her ability is not strong enough to allow for performance of certain job tasks; the individual resorts to problem solving. Problem solving was defined as conscious processes utilized to overcome impediments to performing difficult job tasks (Kehr, 2004).

Thirdly, Kehr (2004) posited that when an individual experiences congruency between implicit and explicit motives, he or she would confront low intrapersonal conflict, successful performance and intrinsic motivation. Apparently, these are the preconditions for psychological well-being, good health and happiness (Deci and Ryan, 2000; Sheldon and Elliot, 1999).

Fourthly, congruence of explicit motives, implicit motives and perceived abilities is associated with what was referred to as "flow experiences" (Kehr, 2004). Flow experiences connote intrinsic motivation that is characterized by absence of both extra-personal and intra-personal conflicts, undivided attention to tasks and complete lack of distracting thoughts (Csikszentmihalyi, 1988). An individual does not need the support of problem solving or volitional regulation when perceived abilities are in tandem with implicit and explicit motives (Karoly, 1995).

Table six reveals that the CMWMV lacks empirical support for three of its key assumptions. It is pertinent to state that empirical studies that had been undertaken to investigate the interactions between implicit and explicit motives did not take the subject of work motivation into cognizance (e.g., Job, et al., 2009; Laws and Rivera, 2012). This implies that the fourth assumption in Table five which states that the congruency between employees' explicit and implicit motives produces intrinsic motivation/successful work performance needs to be scrutinized by future research. Similarly, it will be necessary to conduct research that verifies the third assumption (i.e., employees engage in problem solving when they perceive that their abilities cannot allow them achieve effective tasks' performance).

Even though many empirical studies (e.g., Fullugar and Mills, 2008; Rodriguez- Sanchez, et al., 2011; Ceja and Navarro, 2012; Lavigne, et al., 2012) had been conducted on the antecedents and consequences of flow experiences at work; none was directly aimed at knowing whether congruency between explicit motives, implicit motives and perceived ability accounted for these experiences. In other words, no research has been undertaken to find out the veracity of the fifth assumption in Table five. This therefore provides a window of opportunity for future researchers to explore.

With respect to the first assumption in the table, Kehr (2004) confirmed that volition is exercised whenever there is a conflict between employees' explicit and implicit motives. Kehr (2004) also showed that volition consumes the limited psychological resources of employees. However, Job, et al. (2010) found that reduction in volitional strength after it has been utilized in carrying out a demanding work task reflects individuals' beliefs about the availability of willpower rather than true resource depletion.

Table 6. Empirical Studies on CMWMV

Key Assumptions	Empirical Studies
(i) Volition will be exercised when there is a conflict between employees' explicit and implicit motives.	Kehr (2004)
(ii) Volition consumes the limited psychological resources of employees.	Kehr (2004); Job, et al. (2010)
(iii) Employees engage in problem solving when they perceive that their abilities cannot allow them achieve effective tasks' performance.	None
(iv) Congruency between employees' explicit and implicit motives produces intrinsic motivation/successful work performance.	None
(v) Congruence of explicit motives, implicit motives and perceived ability is associated with flow experiences.	None

This finding violates the theory's assumption on the general exhaustive tendencies of volitional strength. Consequently, the mysteries surrounding the resourcefulness of volitional strength when employees confront incongruent implicit and explicit motives should be further unpacked, since current research has not sufficiently resolved this issue.

Temporal Motivational Theory (TMT)

TMT was synthesized from the common features of other extant cognitively based motivation theories that many disciplines in the social sciences have offered in explicating work motivation (Steel and Konig,

2006). TMT incorporates time into work motivation equations by building on Ainslie's (1992) theory on hyperbolic discounting and Vroom's (1964) expectancy theory of motivation.

While Ainslie's theory states that people have innate tendency to exchange tasks leading to distant but valuable rewards for those that are more immediate, though associated with lesser rewards; Vroom's theory presumes that people will be motivated to perform job tasks if they perceive that their efforts will lead to performance and that performing these tasks would attract rewards that they appreciate.

Integrating the commonalities of the two theories yielded four salient features of the TMT. These are value, expectancy, time, and different functions for losses and gains. Value represents how much satisfaction or drive reduction that an outcome is believed to realize. Expectancy connotes the perceived probability that an outcome will occur (Steel and Konig, 2006). Time refers to people's sensitivity to delay and the delay itself (i.e., the time needed to realize an outcome). The positive and negative perceptions that people have about an outcome represent their differences for gains and losses respectively (Steel and Konig, 2006). TMT proposes that value, expectancy and time depend on both the situation and individual differences.

Table 7. Empirical Studies on TMT

Key Assumptions	Empirical Studies
(i) Work Motivation/Performance is positively related to Value.	Shu and Gneezy (2010); Pittman, et al. (2008); Sanchez, et al. (2000); Fuller, et al. (2012).
(ii) Work Motivation/Performance is positively associated with Expectancy.	Sanchez, et al. (2000).
(iii) Work Motivation/Performance is negatively related to time.	Ariely and Wertenbroch (2002).
(iv) Work Motivation/Performance is associated with differences for gains and losses about an outcome.	None
(v) Any one of these variables (i.e., value expectancy and time) depends on either the situation or individual Differences.	Steel (2007); Judge and Ilies (2002); Shu and Gneezy (2010); Fuller, et al. (2012); Bott, et al. (2010).

In summary, TMT states that motivation can be understood by the positive effects of expectancy and value, weakened by time and differences for gains and losses (Steel and Konig, 2006). Table seven displays the key assumptions and empirical studies of the theory.

Four empirical studies (i.e., Steel, 2007; Shu and Gneezy, 2010; Ariely and Wertenbroch, 2002; Pittman, et al., 2008) in the table linked procrastination to the TMT. The reason being that procrastination is regarded as a quintessential temporal motivational problem (Steel and Konig, 2006), and it is attributable to certain situational and personality factors. For instance, Steel (2007) found that task aversiveness, task delay, self- efficacy, impulsiveness, conscientiousness and achievement motivation were strong and consistent predictors of procrastination.

This empirical finding suggests that procrastination is influenced by some task situations and individual differences. However, procrastination is also likely to be a function of one of these variables i.e., value, expectancy and time (Shu and Gneezy, 2010; Ariely and Wertenbroch, 2002; Pittman, et al., 2008). One empirical study captured in the sixth row of the table tends to support this assumption because it found that procrastination is related to the value people derive from positive experiences with immediate benefits (Shu and Gneezy, 2010). The other empirical studies highlighted in this row authenticate the last assumption in the table.

Although three empirical studies (i.e., Sanchez, et al. 2000; Pittman, et al., 2008 and Fuller, et al., 2012) supported the first assumption which states that work motivation/performance is positively related to value; results obtained from the Shu and Gneezy's study reflect the fact that when people have unlimited time available, the tendency to procrastinate is applicable not only to aversive tasks but also to delightful work experiences. It could therefore be inferred that the relationship between work motivation/performance and value may be moderated by the available time required to satisfy oneself from a particular outcome. It will be useful for future research to verify the authenticity of this inference.

In support of the third assumption; Ariely and Wertenbroch (2002) found that people are willing to impose meaningful (i.e., costly) deadlines to overcome procrastination and that these deadlines are effective in improving task performance. One empirical study sought to investigate the second assumption. In this study, Sanchez, et al. (2000) found that test performance of job applicants correlated with their expectancy. Unfortunately, there was no empirical investigation of the fourth assumption. This leaves much to be desired and so it is recommended that future research should cover this research gap.

TEAM BASED THEORIES OF WORK MOTIVATION

Social Identity Theory (SIT) of Work Motivation

The fundamental assumption that underscores SIT is that while in some social situations individuals think of themselves as separate entities who interact with each other on the basis of personal characteristics or preferences; there are many social settings in which individuals primarily think of themselves and others in terms of their particular group memberships Ellemers, et al., 2004; Meyer, et al., 2006).

Social identity is the individual's self- concept derived from perceived membership of social groups (Hogg and Vaughan, 2002). Therefore, it is an individual based perception of what defines "us" associated with any internalized group membership. This should be distinguished from the notion of personal identity which refers to self- knowledge that derives from the individual's personality attributes.

Three social identity processes underlie an individual's motivation to perform work tasks (Van Knippenberg, 2000). These are social categorization, social comparison, and social identification. Social categorization is based on the premise that individuals tend to categorize themselves and others into various categories, such as organizational membership, religious affiliation, gender and age cohort (Tajfel and Turner, 1985; Hogg, et al., 1995; Chattopadhyay, et al; 2004).

Individuals that have been socially categorized as members of a group seek to achieve positive self-esteem by differentiating their in-group from a comparison out-group based on some valued dimensions. Social comparisons with other groups determine which features help to define the group in a particular situation. Typically, these features are those that distinguish the group from relevant comparison groups (Van and Ellemers, 2002).

It is important to note that besides comparing their in-group with other referent out-groups; individual members of an in-group also tend to assess the extent to which they are either similar or different from each other. Their differences or similarities are accentuated when they get involved with the social identification process, otherwise known as self-categorization (Pratt, 1998; Hogg, et al., 1995; Ellemers, et al., 2004; Meyer, et al., 2006). As soon as members of a group can cognitively identify their personal selves as parts of a social group; their need for homogeneity (i.e., need to see oneself as similar to others) becomes satisfied.

It is generally assumed that each of the above social identity processes (i.e., social categorization, social comparison and social identity) is related to work motivation/performance (Van Knippenberg, 2000; Ellemers, et al., 2004). An analysis of the empirical studies in table eight provides the directions of this relationship.

Table 8. Empirical Studies on SIT and Work Motivation

Key Assumptions	Empirical Studies
(i) Social Categorization is related to Work Motivation/Performance.	Blader and Tyler (2009); Haslam, et al. (2000); Haslam, et al. (2006); Van Knippenberg and Van Shie (2000); Hirst, et al. (2009); Liu, et al. (2011); Ngo, et al. (2013); Van Dick, et al. (2009); Van Dick and Wagner (2002); Helem (2013); Derks, et al. (2009)-ref.
(ii) Social Comparison correlates with Work Motivation/Performance.	Reinhard, et al. (2014); Hersby, et al. (2011); Lount and Phillips (2007).
(iii) Social Identification is associated with Work Motivation/Performance.	Haslam, et al. (2000); Chattopadhyay and George (2001); Fuller, et al. (2003); Tanghe, et al. (2010).

Empirical findings indicate that social categorization is positively related to work motivation/performance in certain unique ways. Specifically, it was found to be positively associated with work motivation (Van Dick and Wagner, 2002); increased performance (Van Dick, et al., 2009; Derks, et al., 2009); extra role behaviour (Blader and Tyler, 2009); organizational citizenship behaviour (Haslam, et al., 2000; Liu, et al., 2011); continued commitment to faltering organizational projects (Haslam, et al., 2006); job satisfaction (Van Knippenberg and Van Shie, 2000; Ngo, et al., 2013; Helem, 2013); and employee creativity (Hirst, et al., 2009). These empirical findings tend to justify the import of social categorization in prodding work motivation/performance.

Similarly, three empirical studies in the table also showed that social comparison is positively related to work motivation/performance. For instance, Reinhard, et al. (2014) revealed that high status group members (i.e., men) were more motivated to achieve the normative goal of the low status group (i.e., women) when their performance was compared with those of the low status group.

In another study, Hersby, et al. (2011) found that women were willing to engage in mentoring when they perceived that gender discrimination was illegitimate and pervasive. This implies that women's enhanced motivation to embark in mentoring was occasioned by social comparison. Notably, Lount and Phillips (2007) provide empirical support for the motivating tendencies of social comparison. They discovered that in-group members dissipated more efforts towards actualizing work goals when being out-performed by out-group members.

Four empirical studies unveiled the nature of the relationship between social identification and work motivation/performance. Studies conducted by Fuller, et al. (2003) indicate that social identification (viewed as the sense of value and appreciation ascribed to employees) mediates the relationship between perceived organizational support and long term work motivation (i.e., organizational commitment). Haslam, et al. (2000) also found that group based respect that is occasioned by social identification was positively associated with employees' willingness to engage in organizational citizenship behaviour.

Moreover, the empirical findings from Chattopadhyay and George's (2001) study depict the negative influences that work status dissimilarity has on team performance. Apparently, work status dissimilarity stifles social identification because it may tend to produce different affective states amongst team members. Thus leading to unfulfillment of their homogeneity needs and concomitant declines in work motivation/ performance. Conversely, convergence of members' affective states via social identification facilitates team effectiveness (Tanghe, et al., 2010).

In spite of the abundant empirical support for SIT of work motivation, current research does not specifically account for the elemental impacts of social categorization, social comparison and social identification on motivation of group members. Knowledge of their relative impacts would help managers efficiently and effectively allocate organizational scarce resources towards facilitating these SIT processes for the purpose of inducing work motivation/performance in teams. It will therefore be needful for future research to fill this knowledge lacuna.

Joint Production Motivation (JPM)

The term "joint production motivation" was invented by Lindenberg and Foss (2011) to explain human capacity to actively engage in collaborative activities. It is based on the notion that the motivation to engage in collective work is intricately related to cognitions about tasks, interdependencies, and common goals (Tomasello, et al., 2005). According to Lindenberg and Foss (2011), joint production is similar to Alchain and Demsetz (1972) concept of team production. Unlike their view of team production, Lindenberg and Foss (2011) saw human beings as naturally equipped with coordinated cognitive and motivational faculties that are dedicated to participating in joint production.

Joint production was defined as any productive activity that involves different but complementary resources and with a high degree of task and outcome interdependence for actualization of common goals (Lindenberg and Foss, 2011). Since common goals are so important, how do managers ensure that team members get committed to them? Lindenberg and Foss (2011) utilized the goal framing theory in order to provide an answer to this critical question.

The goal framing theory has three core elements. These are: normative goals, hedonic goals and gain goals (Lindenberg and Foss, 2011). Normative goals are best understood by the individual's desire to act appropriately in the service of the team or organization. Conversely, hedonic goals are related to an intense desire to improve the way an individual presently feels and gain goals express the individual's desire to improve his or her resources, e.g., improvement in personal income or status.

The goal framing theory has two essential components that are pertinent for understanding the conditions necessary for fostering JPM. These are the precariousness of the normative frame and the difference between foreground and background goals (Lindenberg and Foss, 2011).

From an evolutionary perspective, the normative goal frame is the weakest of the three goal frames since it makes sense for both hedonic and gain goals to occupy higher positions of priority in individuals' scale of preference. In the absence of organizational supportive arrangements (e.g., the administration of positive and negative sanctions) the normative goal becomes highly precarious. Therefore, if the normative goal cannot be sustained by these supportive arrangements, the entire organization may be plunged into a culture that encourages myopic behaviours that are often geared towards satisfying the hedonic and gain goals of individuals (Lindenberg, 2004; Perlow, 1999). Empirical studies associated with the key assumptions/concepts of JPM are presented in Table nine.

The veracity of the key assumptions/concepts was confirmed by the three sets of studies in the table. Particularly, three empirical studies are in tandem with the first assumption; as they all support the premise that motivation to attain the normative goals of joint production is enhanced by organizational supportive arrangements.

In line with this argument, Grant, et al. (2008) found that organizational supportive programs that provided financial, material and educational assistance to employees strengthened their motivation towards attaining normative organizational goals. Similarly, leadership support that stems from leaders' procedural fairness and perceived charisma motivates employees to embrace the collective goals of organizations (De Cremer and Van Knippenberg, 2002). Wang, et al. (2009) also revealed that economic and relationship based governance mechanisms (i.e., granting employees stock ownership and building firm-employee relationships) support the motivation of employees to make specialized human capital investments that are difficult to redeploy to other organizational settings.

Table 9. Empirical Studies on JPM

Key Assumptions	Empirical Studies
(i) Motivation to attain normative goals of joint production is enhanced by organizational supportive arrangements.	Grant, et al. (2008); De Cremer and Van Knippenberg (2002); Wang, et al. (2009).
(ii) Motivation to pursue normative goals of joint production can be overshadowed by the need to attain gain goals	Dierdorff, et al. (2011); Kleingeld, et al. (2011); Zhang and Chiu (2012).
(iii) Motivation to achieve normative goals of joint production can be subjugated by the need to attain hedonic goals	Thau, et al. (2013); Tanghe, et al. (2010); Van Knippenberg, et al. (2010).

The second assumption was supported by three empirical studies. For example, Dierdorff, et al. (2011) concluded that differences in goal priority among team members (i.e., the level of disharmony amongst team members with respect to prioritizing the normative goals of teams over individual goals) negatively affected team performance. In the same vein, Kleingeld, et al. (2011) showed that egocentric individual goals aimed at promoting individual performance negatively impacted on group goals. Recent empirical findings from Zhang and Chiu (2012) imply that subjugation of group goals by personal goals can be prevented if the latter goals are shared in the group.

It was also found that their hedonic goals have the capacity to create the same impact. Three empirical studies agree with this assertion. Thus supporting the third assumption presented in the table. Empirical evidence suggested that group members who have leaders that are less considerate may not be sufficiently motivated to concentrate on group tasks/goals (Thau, et al. 2013). It has also been shown that positive moods led to lower quality decisions (Van Knippenberg, et al., 2010) that may presumably affect group goals; and low trusting group members were more willing to pursue group goals when they confronted others that displayed highly activated affective states of trust (Tanghe, et al., 2010).

Indubitably, the key assumptions of JPM have been supported by the above empirical findings. Nonetheless, JPM seemed to be achieved only when employees are extrinsically induced to accept the normative goals of their groups/organizations. However, it may be possible for JPM to be seen as an intrinsically derived process based on human nature or personality. Future theorizing and research in JPM may want to follow this perspective because it could help in distilling out the intrinsic human needs that have to be satisfied for people to perform well in joint productive undertakings.

TRANSCENDENT THEORIES OF WORK MOTIVATION

Public Service Motivation (PSM)

Although the PSM concept was introduced into the work motivation literature in 1990 (see Perry and Wise, 1990); it was only at the dawn of the 21st century that Perry (2000) developed a full blown theory of the concept. It was specifically brought into the literature so as to address the lack of attention that has been given to work motivation in the public sector. Consequently, it has been defined as a person's predisposition to respond to motives grounded primarily or uniquely in public sector organizations (Perry, 2000).

Vandenabeele (2007) also defines PSM as the beliefs, values and attitudes that go beyond self-interest and organizational interest, that concern the interest of the larger society and that motivate individuals to act accordingly whenever appropriate. While the first definition on one hand, seems to suggest that a person's public service motivation arises from the motives of external public institutions, the second definition on the other hand, highlights the internal motivation of a person which is directed towards serving people in the larger society; with organizations only serving as a means of satisfying the altruistic motives of the individual.

In its simplest form, Perry's (2000) theory provided the predisposing factors of PSM orientation. According to Perry (2000), there are three main antecedents of PSM. These are: the socio- historical context- representing influences from institutions of the larger society (e.g., family, churches, government and school); nature of motivational context- connoting situational factors that influence behaviour in organizations (e.g., job characteristics, organizational incentives and work environment); and individual characteristics- specifying the impact of individual identities and self-concepts on work behaviour. Perry's theory therefore assumes that the PSM orientation of an individual will be a function of the above factors. The empirical studies in Table ten investigate the correctness of these key assumptions.

Table 10. Empirical Studies on PSM

Key Assumptions	Empirical Studies
PSM orientation is associated with the socio-historical context.	Vandenabeele (2011); Moynihan and Pandey (2007); Davis (2013)
PSM orientation is related to an organization's motivational context.	Stazyk (2013); Camilleri (2007); Belle (2014); Ward (2014); Moynitan and Pandey (2007); Kjeldsen (2014); Braender and Andersen (2013); Wright (2007); Scott and Pandey (2005); Davis (2013)
PSM orientation corresponds with individual characteristics.	Kim (2012); Liu and Tang (2011); Bright (2005); Wright and Pandey (2008)

Three empirical studies support the first assumption in the table. Findings from Vandenabeele's (2011) study showed that identities formed through associations with the family, political parties, educational institutions and age cohorts correlate with PSM. While Davis (2013) found that employees' commitment to trade unions was positively associated with PSM; Moynitan and Pandey (2007) revealed that socio- historical variables (i.e., level of education and membership in professional organizations) were positively related to it.

Furthermore, results from ten empirical studies authenticate the second assumption of the theory; as it was shown that PSM had positive relationships with performance related pay (Stazyk, 2013); conducive organizational settings (Camilleri, 2007); transformational leadership (Belle, 2014); training (Ward, 2014); work tasks (Kjeldsen, 2014; Braender and Andersen, 2013); and organization's mission (Wright, 2007). However, other findings showed that PSM was negatively related to red tape (Scott and Pandey, 2005; Moynihan and Pandey, 2007, Davis, 2013); and organizational tenure (Moynihan and Pandey, 2007).

Empirical findings also align with the third assumption in the table. For instance, Bright (2005) concluded that PSM was significantly related to personal characteristics like gender, educational level, management level and monetary preferences of employees. Three other empirical studies found that congruency between the values of employees and their organizations (i.e., person- organization fit) correlated positively with PSM (Wright and Pandey, 2008; Kim, 2012). Moreover, Liu and Tang (2011) showed that the relationship between PSM and job satisfaction was significantly stronger for individuals with strong love of money.

The above empirical findings support the assumptions underlying Perry's (2000) theory of PSM. However, they do not provide sufficient justification for restricting the operations of the theory only to the public sector; since some of the findings suggest that the PSM orientation of public sector employees could be closely associated with fulfilling some egocentric motives (e.g., need for more money) characterizing their private sector counterparts. Therefore, the work motivation differences between public and private employees as purported by PSM theory could be made clearer if researchers conduct meta-analyses of contemporary findings on the subject matter.

Meaningful Work Motivation (MWM)

From time immemorial, humans endeavour to make some meaning out of the various work tasks that they engage in (Michaelson, et al., 2014). Work that is meaningful helps to answer the question, 'why am I here?' (Pratt and Ashforth, 2003). Hence meaningful work has been defined as 'the value of a work goal or purposes, judged to the individual's own ideals of standards' (May, et al., 2004). It also refers to work experienced as particularly significant and holding positive meaning for individuals (Rosso, et al., 2010).

Contemporary theorizing on meaningful work presents it as work that comprises self- transcendence, either "vertically" through an orientation towards something greater than the self, or "horizontally" through a concern for issues beyond one's immediate self- interests (Schnell, 2011). Based on this view, meaningful work arises when the "self" cannot be extricated from the "other". The "other" here signifies anything that is different from the self.

Michaelson (2005) sees meaningful work as an important work motivator and wonders why it has not been incorporated into work motivation theory. Based on Michaelson's perspective, motivation derived from engaging in meaningful work is herein referred to as meaningful work motivation (MWM). Lips-Wiersma and Morris (2009) developed a model that identifies its four main sources. These are: (i) developing and becoming self (ii) serving others (iii) unity with others and (iv) expressing full potential.

Developing and becoming self- encapsulate moral development, personal growth, and staying true to oneself. Moral development influences the experience of meaningful work through daily practicing of virtues. Meaningful work is also experienced through personal growth and "being true to oneself" by engaging in ongoing learning and maintaining one's personal identity respectively (Lips-Wiersma and Morris, 2009).

Serving others pertains to 'making a difference and meeting the needs of humanity". While the former is related to the positive contributions an individual makes within his/her organization, the latter connotes a transcendent cause that stems from a resolution to address the social, economic or environmental problems of society (Lips- Wiersma and Morris, 2009).

Unity with others involves sharing values, belonging and working together. Lips- Wiersma and Morris assert that MWM is experienced when others share similar values, people depend on each other while performing work tasks and a social bond is created in the process

Expressing full potential creates meaning for individuals at work because they feel empowered to exercise control over work outcomes (i.e., gain mastery) and gives them the ability to change their viewpoints or situations at any particular point in time (Lips-Wiersma and Morris, 2009). Table eleven presents empirical studies that can be traced to the testable assumptions of their MWM model.

Table 11. Empirical Studies on MWM

Key Assumptions	Empirical Studies
MWM stems from the need to develop and become self.	Bunderson and Thompson (2009); Soane, et al. (2013); Duchon and Plowman (2005); Saks (2011).
MWM can be traced to the need to serve others.	Grant, et al. (2007)
MWM is occasioned by the need to unite with others.	Nair and Vohra (2010)
MWM derives from the need to express one's full potential	Nair and Vohra (2010)

Results of four empirical studies tend to support the first assumption which presupposes that MWM stems from the need to "develop and become self". Findings from Bunderson and Thompson's (2009) study showed that MWM in the zoo keeping profession derives from the notion of personal calling. Two other studies revealed that spirituality at the workplace can be a major source of MWM (Duchon and Plowman, 2005; Saks, 2011).

The above findings support the sub theme of Lips- Wiersma and Morris' (2009) model which assumes that "being true to oneself" could be a source of MWM. However, one study somewhat aligns with the moral development facet of the model because its findings showed that low levels of work absenteeism were related to MWM (Soane, et al., 2013). There was only a piece of empirical evidence for the second assumption of the model. Findings from this empirical study indicate that MWM is induced when employees are made to have direct contact with beneficiaries of their work efforts (Grant, et al., 2007).

One empirical study authenticated the last two assumptions of the model. Nair and Vohra (2010) found that the strongest predictors of work alienation that is contingent on the lack of MWM amongst knowledge workers were poor quality of work relationships and inability of work to allow for self-expression.

Given the findings of these empirical studies, it will be expedient to know the actual benefits of MWM from both the employee and employer perspectives. Future research on the subject could therefore dwell on how MWM translates to the elevation of employees' quality of work life and its impact on overall organizational performance.

DISCUSSION

The contemporary theories of work motivation presented in this chapter have been able to highlight many aspects of human nature (e.g., emotions, aging, volition, self- concept, implicit motives, altruistic motives, etc.) that were previously ignored by extant theories in the field. Hence creating an eclectic approach to examining the subject of work motivation.

Table twelve depicts the extent to which they synergistically address the knowledge gaps that Locke and Latham (2004) identified in work motivation theory. These authors once craved for the formulation of contemporary theories that would help integrate valid aspects of extant work motivation theories; create a science on work motivation without disciplinary boundaries; identify how variables that determine our various work motivational states get applied to and are mediated by task and specific situations; study subconscious as well as conscious motivation and the relationship between them; and acknowledge the role of volition in work motivation.

The boxes labelled "yes" in the table indicate knowledge gaps that have been filled by a particular theory, while those with the "no" response show uncovered territories. It can be inferred from the table that the nine theories have holistically and adequately filled all the knowledge gaps identified by Locke and Latham (2004); as there are no more virgin territories left to be occupied. Each theory is further analyzed in another table below with a view to presenting how it fills the specific knowledge gap that is reflected in Table twelve. Proper understanding of the analysis would be facilitated by comparing the contents of Tables twelve and thirteen. Essentially, table 13 provides the justifications for the knowledge gaps that the theories filled in table 12. The other tables in the preceding sections of this article indicate that apart from two nascent individualistic theories (i.e., compensatory model of work motivation and volition and temporal motivation theory); they have been able to attract empirical studies that verify their key assumptions/concepts.

Table 12. Knowledge Gaps Covered by Contemporary Theories

	Contemporary Theory	Integrates valid Aspects of Extant Work Motivation Theories	Creates a Science on Work Motivation Without Disciplinary Boundaries	Determines various Work Motivational States and Apply Them To Tasks and Specific Situations	Studies Subconscious and Conscious Motivation	Investigates the Role of Volition in Work Motivation
1	Affective Work Motivation	No	No	Yes	No	No
2	Life Span Developmental Theory of Work Motivation	No	No	Yes	No	No
3	Self Determination Theory of Work Motivation	Yes	No	Yes	No	Yes
4	Compensatory Model of Work Motivation and Volition	No	No	Yes	Yes	Yes
5	Temporal Motivational Theory	Yes	Yes	Yes	No	No
6	Social Identity Theory of Work Motivation	No	No	Yes	No	No
7	Joint Production Motivation	Yes	No	Yes	No	No
8	Theory of Public Service Motivation	No	No	No	No	Yes
9	Meaningful Work Motivation	No	No	No	No	Yes

Table 13. Theories and Justifications for Filling Knowledge Gaps

Theories	Justifications For Filling Knowledge Gaps
Affective Work Motivation.	Examines the role of various affective states in the work motivation process and elucidates how these states influence the direction of behavioural choices that can either be generatively or defensively induced work situations.
Life Span Developmental Theory of Work Motivation.	Asserts that the motivational states of an individual is a function of his or her age and that older employees effectively carry out work tasks that demand crystallized intellectual resources, while their younger counterparts perform well in jobs requiring fluid intellectual abilities.
Self Determination Theory of Work Motivation.	Integrates the extrinsic and intrinsic forms of work motivation as captured by cognitive evaluation theory and avers that the extent to which an extrinsic motivational factor gets fully internalized depends on certain processes of regulation. The regulatory processes of introjection, identification and integration determine the motivational state of the individual. The concepts of autonomous and controlled motivations bring the significance of acting with a sense of volition to the fore.
Compensatory Model of Work Motivation and Volition.	Investigates the role of implicit motives, explicit motives and perceived ability in the work motivation process and how these affect the performance of work tasks in varying situations. It studies the subconscious conflicts that occur between explicit and implicit motives and assumes that volitional resources need to be consumed in order to resolve these conflicts.
Temporal Motivation Theory.	Integrates the salient features of extant cognitively based motivational theories offered by disciplines in the social sciences. It distils work motivation equations from these different disciplines. It suggests that the motivational state of an individual in a given situation depends on expectancy, value, time and differences for gains and losses.
Social Identity Theory of Work Motivation.	Assumes that work motivation states are determined by the extent to which the social identity processes influence an individual's self-concept while functioning in groups.
Joint Production Motivation.	Integrates and utilizes valid aspects of goal framing theory and assumes that motivation to embark on the normative goal of joint productive endeavours could be determined by the structural and governance features of organizations.
Public Service Motivation.	Highlights the significance of altruistic work behaviours in the public sector which supposedly stems from volitional service orientation.
Meaningful Work Motivation.	Focuses on humans' volitional search for work meaningfulness.

It is interesting to note that while all the key assumptions of the team based and transcendent theories have somewhat been authenticated by empirical studies; those of certain nascent individualistic studies (e.g., affective work motivation, compensatory model of work motivation and volition) present some grey areas that require further investigation. This finding may imply that these former theories could be of more relevance to practicing managers in modern organizations.

CONCLUSION

The knowledge economy of the 21st century has created a competitive landscape in which organizations striving to be at the leading edge of performance must now form work teams that facilitate transfer of requisite knowledge amongst employees (Steers, et al., 2004). Application of such knowledge is aimed at beating market competition and improving overall organizational performance. This current management exigency which is predicated on the emergence of the knowledge economy call for the formulation of team based theories that can unveil the relevant motivational factors needed for uplifting employees' performance while they work in teams.

Furthermore, the moral basis or ethical dimension of managing businesses has recently been brought to limelight. Previously, managerial ethics dealing with potential conflict between managerial actions, organizational practices, and moral judgments were neglected (Goodrich and Rossiter, 2009). Nevertheless, integrating ethical issues into management decisions intensifies the challenges of motivating people in organizations.

These challenges could have influenced work motivation scholars' minds about human nature since business ethics is caught up in the middle of the road between the egocentric motives of organizations that strictly pursue profit maximization and the spirit of altruism that their stakeholders expect them to manifest for the common good of society. Hence necessitating the search for transcendent theories of work motivation that can somewhat account for the dialectics of selfishness and altruism manifested by modern employees/managers while they engage in their disparate work activities.

During the 20th century, work motivation scholars were influenced by the environmental exigencies of the century. This led to the development of individualistic theories that encouraged egocentric behaviours. Irrespective of the various twists that occurred in work motivation theory and research in the 20th century, scholars were entirely disposed to generating and verifying individualistic theories.

Despite the fact that the nascent individualistic theories analyzed in this chapter threw more light on the factors that motivate egocentric individuals at work; it is believed that the team based and transcendent theories would ascend to occupy a central position in future work motivation literature. This is because they are most likely to generate research findings that could be directly applied by practicing managers in order to resolve the challenges of motivating people towards achieving the common good in contemporary organizations and societies.

The possible attraction of future research undertakings by these theories would catalyze a departure of the devotion that work motivation scholars previously had for research in individualistic theories. Departure from this research tradition presents an unorthodox twist in modern work motivation studies. This unorthodox twist is occasioned by the fact that the team based and transcendent theories more aptly resonate with the challenges of motivating people in contemporary organizations. Therefore, it is expected that this unorthodox twist would become more and more impactful as the future looms. The only caveat is that its future impact rests squarely on the shoulders of business environmental vagaries.

REFERENCES

Ainslie, G. (1992). *Pico economics: The Strategic Interaction of Successive Motivational States within the Person*, New York: Cambridge University Press.

Ajzen, I. (1991). "The Theory of Planned Behaviour", *Organizational Behaviour and Human Decision Processes*, Vol. *50*, 179-211.

Alchain, A. & Demsetz, H. (1972). "Production, Information Costs, and Economic Organization", *American Economic Review*, Vol. *62*, 772-795.

Amabile, T. & Kramer, S. (2007). "Inner Work Life", *Harvard Business Review*, Vol. *85*, No. 5, 72-83.

Amabile, T., Barsade, S., Mueller, J. & Staw, B. (2005). "Affect and Creativity at Work", *Administrative Science Quarterly*, Vol. *50*, 367-403.

Ambrose, M. & Kulik, C. (1999). "Old Friends, New Faces: Motivation Research in the 1990s", *Journal of Management*, Vol. *25*, No. 3, 231-292.

Ariely, D. & Wertenbroch, K. (2002). "Procrastination, Deadlines and Performance: Self Control by Pre-commitment", *Psychological Science*, Vol. *13*, No. 3, 219-224.

Baard, P., Deci, E. & Ryan, R. (2004). "Intrinsic Need Satisfaction: A Motivational Basis of Performance and Well Being in Two Work Settings", *Journal of Applied Social Psychology*, Vol. *34*, No. 10, 2045-2068.

Bandura, A. (1977). "Self Efficacy: Toward a Unifying Theory of Behavioural Change", *Psychological Review*, Vol. *84*, 191-215.

Baron, R. (1991). "Motivation in Work Settings: Reflections on the Core of Organizational Research", *Motivation and Emotion*, Vol. *51*, 1-8.

Baumeister, R. & Heatherton, T. (1996). "Self- regulation Failure: An Overview", *Psychological Inquiry*, Vol. *7*, 1-15.

Baumeister, R., Bratslavsky, E., Muraven, M. & Tice, D. (1998). "Ego Depletion: Is the Active Self a Limited Resource?" *Journal of Personality and Social Psychology*, Vol. *74*, 1252-1265.

Belle, N. (2014). "Leading to Make a Difference: A Field Experiment on the Performance Effects of Transformational Leadership, Perceived Social Impact and PSM", *Journal of Public Administration Research and Theory*, Vol. *24*, No. 1, 109-136.

Bertolino, M., Truxillo, D. & Fraccaroli, F. (2011). "Age as Moderator of the Relationship of Proactive Personality with Training Motivation, Perceived Career Development from Training, and Training Behavioural Intentions", *Journal of Organizational Behaviour*, Vol. *32*, No. 2, 248-263.

Binnewies, C. & Wornlein, S. (2011). "What Makes a Creative Day? A Diary Study on the Interplay Between Affect, Job Stressors and Job Control", *Journal of Organizational Behaviour*, Vol. *32*, No. 4, 589-607.

Blader, S. & Tyler, T. (2009). "Testing and Extending the Group Engagement Model: Linkage Between Social Identity, Procedural Justice, Economic Outcomes and Extra Role Behaviour", *Journal of Applied Psychology*, Vol. *94*, No. 2, 445-464.

Bott, J., Snell, A., Dahling, J. & Smith, B. (2010). "Predicting Individual Score Elevation in an Applicant Setting: The Influence of Individual Differences and Situational Perceptions", *Journal of Applied Social Psychology*, Vol. *40*, No. 11, 2774-2790.

Braender, M. & Andersen, L. (2013). "Does Deployment To War Affect PSM? A Panel Study of Soldiers Before and After Their Service in Afghanistan", *Public Administration Review*, Vol. *73*, No. 3, 466-477.

Bridoux, F., Coeurderoy, R. & Durand, R. (2011). "Heterogeneous Motives and the Collective Creation of Value" *Academy of Management Review*, Vol. *36*, No. 4, 711-730.

Bright, L. (2005). "Public Employees With High Levels of Public Service Motivation Who Are They, Where are They and What Do They Want?", *Review of Public Personnel Administration*, Vol. *25*, No. 2, 138-154.

Broeck, A., Schreurs, B., De Witte, H., Vansteekiste, M., Germeys, F. & Schaufel, W. (2011). "Understanding Workaholics Motivation: A Self Determination Perspective", *Applied Psychology: An International Review*, Vol. *60*, No. 4, 600-621.

Brundin, E., Patzelt, H. & Shepherd, D. (2008). "Managers' Emotional Displays and Employees' Willingness to Act Entrepreneurially", *Journal of Business Venturing*, Vol. *23*, No. 2, 221-243.

Brunstein, J., Schultheiss, O. & Grassmann, R. (1998). "Personal Goals and Emotional Well Being: The Moderating Role of Motive Dispositions", *Journal of Personality and Social Psychology*, Vol. *75*, 494-508.

Bunderson, J. & Thompson, J. (2009). "The Call of the Wild: Zoo Keepers, Callings and the Double Edged Sword of Deeply Meaningful Work", *Administrative Science Quarterly*, Vol. *54*, No. 1, 32-57.

Camilleri, E. (2007). "Antecedents Affecting Public Service Motivation", *Personnel Review*, Vol. *36*, No. 3, 356-377.

Cattell, R. (1943). "The Measurement of Adult Intelligence", *Psychological Bulletin*, Vol. *40*, 153-193.

Cattell, R. (1987). "*Intelligence: Its Structure, Growth and Action*", Amsterdam: North Holland.

Ceja, L. & Navarro, J. (2012). "Suddenly I Get Into the Zone: Examining Discontinuities and Nonlinear Changes in Flow Experiences at Work", *Human Relations*, Vol. *65*, No. 9, 1101-1127.

Chattopadhyay, P. & George, E. (2001). "Examining the Effects of Work Externalization Through the Lens of Social Identity Theory", *Journal of Applied Psychology*, Vol. *86*, No. 4, 781-788.

Chattopadhyay, P., Tluchowska, M. & George, E. (2004). "Identifying the In-group: A Closer Look at the Influence of Demographic Dissimilarity on Employee Social Identity", *Academy of Management Review*, Vol. *29*, No. 2, 180-202.

Chen, C. & Bozeman, B. (2013). "Understanding Public and Nonprofit Managers' Motivation Through the Lens of Self Determination Theory", *Public Management Review*, Vol. *15*, No. 4, 584-607.

Csikszentmihalyi, M. (1988). "The Flow Experience and Its Significance for Human Psychology", In M. Csikszentmihalyi and I. Csikszentmihalyi (eds.), *Optimal Experience: Psychological Studies of Flow in Consciousness*, 15-35, New York: Cambridge University Press.

Davis, R. (2013). "Unionization and Work Attitudes: How Union Commitment Influences Public Sector Job Satisfaction", *Public Administration Review*, Vol. *73*, No. 1, 74-84.

Deci, E. & Ryan, R. (2000). "The "What" and "Why" of Goal Pursuits: Human Needs and Self Determination of Behaviour", *Psychological Inquiry*, Vol. *11*, 227-268.

De Cooman, R., Stynen, D., Van Den Broeck, A., Sels, L. & De Witte, H. (2013). "How Job Characteristics Relate to Need Satisfaction and Autonomous Motivation: Implications for Work Effort", *Journal of Applied Social Psychology*, Vol. *43*, No. 6, 1342-1352.

De Cremer, D. & Van Knippenberg, D. (2002). "How Do Leaders Promote Cooperation? The Effects of Charisma and Procedural Fairness", *Journal of Applied Psychology*, Vol. *87*, 858-866.

De Lange, A., Taris, T., Jansen, P., Kompier, M., Houtman, I. & Bongers, P. (2010). "On the Relationships Among Work Characteristics and Learning Related Behaviours: Does Age Matter?", *Journal of Organizational Behaviour*, Vol. *31*, 925-950.

Derks, B., Van Laar, C. & Ellemers, N. (2009). "Working for the Self or Working for the Group: How Self Versus Group Affirmation Affects Collective Behaviour in Low Status Groups", *Journal of Personality and Social Psychology*, Vol. *96*, No. 1, 183-202.

Dierdorff, E., Bell, S. & Belohlav, J. (2011). "The Power of "We": Effects of Psychological Collectivism on Team Performance Over Time", *Journal of Applied Psychology*, Vol. *96*, No. 2, 247-262.

Duchon, D. & Plowman, D. (2005). "Nurturing the Spirit At Work: Impact on Work Unit Performance", *Leadership Quarterly*, Vol. *16*, No. 5, 807-833.

Dysvik, A., Kuvaas, B. & Gagne, M. (2013). "An Investigation of the Unique Synergistic and Balanced Relationships Between Basic Psychological Needs and Intrinsic Motivation", *Journal of Applied Social Psychology*, Vol. *43*, No. 5, 1050-1064.

Ellemers, N., Gilder, D. & Haslam, S. (2004). "Motivating Individuals and Groups at Work: A Social Identity Perspective on Leadership and Group Performance", *Academy of Management Review*, Vol. *29*, No. 3, 459-478.

Erez, A. & Isen, A. (2002). "The Influence of Positive Affect on the Components of Expectancy Motivation", *Journal of Applied Psychology*, Vol. *87*, 1055-1067.

Fuller, B., Barnett, T., Hester, K. & Relyea, C. (2003). "A Social Identity Perspective on the Relationship Between Perceived Organizational Support and Organizational Commitment", *Journal of Social Psychology*, Vol. *143*, No. 6, 789-791.

Fuller, J., Marler, L. & Hester, K. (2012). "Bridge Building Within the Province of Proactivity", *Journal of Organizational Behaviour*, Vol. *33*, No. 8, 1053-1070.

Fullugar, C. & Mills, M. (2008). "Motivation and Flow: Toward An Understanding of the Dynamics of the Relation in Architecture Students", *Journal of Psychology*, Vol. *142*, No. 5, 533-556.

Gagne, M., Koester, R. & Zuckerman, M. (2000). "Facilitating Acceptance of Organizational Change: The Importance of Self Determination", *Journal of Applied Social Psychology*, Vol. *30*, No. 9, 1843-1852.

Gagne, M. & Deci, E. (2005). "Self Determination Theory and Work Motivation", *Journal of Organizational Behaviour*, Vol. *26*, No. 4, 331-362.

George, J. & Zhou, J. (2002). "Understanding When Bad Moods Foster Creativity and Good Ones Don't: The Role of Context and Clarity of Feelings", *Journal of Applied Psychology*, Vol. *81*, 474-482.

Gillet, N., Gagne, M., Sauvagere, S. & Fouquereau, E. (2013). "The Role of Supervisor Autonomy Support, Organizational Support and Autonomous and Controlled Motivation in Predicting Employees' Satisfaction and Turnover Intentions", *Journal of Work and Organizational Psychology*, Vol. *22*, No. 4, 450-460.

Goodrich, P. & Rossiter, N. (2009). "Remote Ownership Shareholders in the 21st Century: Theoretical Implications For Corporate Governance Profitability and Long Term Wealth Creation", *Journal of American Academy of Business Cambridge*, Vol. *14*, No. 2, 40-46.

Grandey, A. (2003). "When the Show Must Go on: Surface Acting and Deep Acting as Determinants of Emotional Exhaustion and Peer Rated Service Delivery", *Academy of Management Journal*, Vol. *46*, 86-96.

Grant, A., Campbell, E., Chen, G., Cottone, K., Lapedis, D. & Lee, K. (2007). "Impact and the Art of Motivation Maintenance: The Effects of Contact With Beneficiaries on Persistence Behaviour", *Organizational Behaviour and Human Decision Processes*, Vol. *103*, No. 1, 53-67.

Grant, A., Dutton, J. & Rosso, B. (2008). "Giving Commitment: Employee Support Programs and the Pro-social Sense making Process", *Academy of Management Journal*, Vol. *51*, 898-918.

Grant, A., Nurmohamed, S., Ashford, S. & Dekas, K. (2011). "The performance Implications of Ambivalent Initiative: The Interplay of Autonomous and Controlled Motivations", *Organizational Behaviour and Human Decision Processes*, Vol. *116*, No. 2, 241-251.

Gregarus, G. & Diefendorff, J. (2009). "Different Fits Satisfy Different Needs: Linking Person-Environment Fit to Employee Commitment and Performance Using SDT", *Journal of Applied Psychology*, Vol. *94*, No. 2, 465-477.

Hadre, P. & Reeve, J. (2009). "Training Corporate Managers to Adopt a More Autonomy-Supportive Motivating Style Toward Employees: An Intervention Study", *International Journal of Training and Development*, Vol. *13*, No. 3, 165-184.

Harris, C., Daniels, K. & Briner, B. (2003). "A Daily Diary Study of Goals and Affective Well Being at Work," *Journal of Occupational and Organizational Psychology*, Vol. *76*, No. 3, 401-410.

Haslam, A., Powell, C. & Turner, J. (2000). "Social Identity, Self Categorization and Work Motivation: Rethinking the Contribution of the Group to Positive and Sustainable Organizational Outcomes", *Applied Psychology: International Review*, Vol. *49*, No. 3, 319-339.

Haslam, A., Ryan, M., Postmes, T., Spears, R., Jetten, J. & Webley, P. (2006). "Sticking To Our Guns: Social Identity As a Basis For the Maintenance of Commitment to Faltering Organizational Projects", *Journal of Organizational Behaviour*, Vol. *27*, 607-628.

Hersby, M., Jetten, J., Ryan, M. & Schmitt, M. (2011). "Responding to Group Based Discrimination: The Impact of Social Structure on Willingness to Engage in Mentoring", *Group Processes and Intergroup Relations*, Vol. *14*, No. 3, 319-335.

Hirst, G., Van Dick, R. & Van Knippenberg, D. (2009). "A Social Identity Perspective On Leadership and Employee Creativity", *Journal of Organizational Behaviour*, Vol. *30*, No. 7, 963-982.

Hogg, M. & Vaughan, G. (2002). *Social Psychology*, 3rd Edition, London: Prentice Hall.

Hogg, M., Terry, D. & White, K. (1995). "A Tale of Two Theories: A Critical Comparison of Identity Theory with Social Identity Theory", *Social Psychology Quarterly*, Vol. *58*, No. 4, 255-269.

Inceoglu, I., Segers, J. & Bartram, D. (2012). "Age Related Differences in Work Motivation", *Journal of Occupational and Organizational Psychology*, Vol. *85*, No. 2, 300-329.

Janssen, O., Lam, C. & Huang, X. (2009). "Emotional Exhaustion and Job Performance: The Moderating Roles of Distributive Justice and Positive Affect", *Journal of Organizational Behaviour*, Vol. *31*, No. 6, 787-809.

Job, V., Langens, T. & Brandstalter, V. (2009). "Effects of Achievement Goal Striving on Well Being: The Moderating Role of the Explicit Achievement Motive", *Personality and Social Psychology Bulletin*, Vol. *35*, 983-996.

Job, V., Dweck, C. & Walton, G. (2010). "Ego Depletion- Is It All In Your Head? Implicit Theories About Willpower Affect Self Regulation", *Psychological Science*, Vol. *21*, No. 21, 1686-1693.

Judge, T. & IIies, R. (2002). "Relationship of Personality to Performance Motivation: Meta-Analytic Review, *Journal of Applied Psychology*, Vol. *87*, No. 4, 797-807.

Kanfer, R. & Ackerman, P. (2004). "Aging, Adult Development, and Work Motivation", *Academy of Management Review*, Vol. *29*, No. 3, 440-458.

Kanfer, R., Chen, G. & Pritchard, R. (eds.) (2008). *Work Motivation: Past, Present and Future*, New York: Taylor and Francis Group.

Karoly, P. (1995). "Self Control Theory", In W. O'Donoghue and L. Krasner (eds.), *Theories of Behaviour Therapy: Exploring Behaviour Change*, 259-285, Washington, DC: American Psychological Association.

Kehr, H. (2004). "Integrating Implicit Motives, Explicit Motives, and Perceived Abilities: The Compensatory Model of Work Motivation and Volition", *Academy of Management Review*, Vol. *29*, No. 3, 479-499.

Kehr, H. (2004). "Implicit/Explicit Motive Discrepancies and Volitional Depletion Among Managers", *Personality and Social Psychology Bulletin*, Vol. *30*, 315-327.

Kjeldsen, A. (2014). "Dynamics of PSM: Attraction-Selection and Socialization in the Production and Regulation of Social Services", *Public Administration Review*, Vol. *74*, No. 1, 101-112.

Kim, S. (2012). "Does Person-Organization Fit Matter in the Public Sector? Testing the Mediating Effect of Person-Organization Fit in the Relationship Between PSM and Work Attitudes", *Public Administration Review*, Vol. *72*, No. 6, 830-840.

Kleingeld, A.; Van Mierlo, H. & Arends, L. (2011). "The Effect of Goal Setting on Group Performance: A Meta Analysis", *Journal of Applied Psychology*, Vol. *96*, No. 6, 1289-1304.

Kooij, D., De Lange, A., Jansen, P., Kanfer, P. & Dikkers, J. (2011). "Age and Work Related Motives: Results of a Meta- analysis", *Journal of Organizational Behaviour*, Vol. *32*, No. 2, 197-225.

Kooij, D. & Van De Voorde, K. (2011). "How Changes in Subjective General Health Predict Future Time Perspective and Development and Generativity Motives Over the Life Span", *Journal of Occupational and Organizational Psychology*, Vol. *84*, No. 2, 228-247.

Kovjanic, S., Schuh, S., Jonas, K., Van Quaquebeke, N. & Van Dick, R. (2012). "How Do Transformational Leaders Foster Positive Employee Outcomes? A Self Determination Based Analysis of Employees' Needs as Mediating Links", *Journal of Organizational Behaviour*, Vol. *33*, No. 8, 1031-1052.

Kuvaas, B. (2009). "A Test of Hypotheses Derived From Self Determination Theory Among Public Sector Employees", *Employee Relations*, Vol. *31*, No. 1/2, 39-56.

Latham, G. & Pinder, C. (2005). "Work Motivation Theory and Research at the Dawn of the Twenty-First Century", *Annu. Rev. Psychol*, Vol. *56*, 485-516.

Lavigne, G., Forest, J. & Crevier-Braud, L. (2012). "Passion at Work and Burnout: A Study Test of the Mediating Role of Flow Experiences", *European Journal of Work and Organizational Psychology*, Vol. *21*, No. 4, 518-546.

Laws, V. & Rivera, L. (2012). "The Role of Self Image Concerns in Discrepancies Between Implicit and Explicit Self Esteem", *Personality and Social Psychology Bulletin*, Vol. *38*, 1453-1466.

Lindenberg, S. (2004). "Myopia's Price: Inefficiencies in Organizations", In A. Diekmann and T. Voss (eds.), Rational-Choice-theorie in den Sozialwissenschaften, 217-229, Munich: Oldenbourg.

Lindenberg, S. & Foss, N. (2011). "Managing Joint Production Motivation: The Role of Goal Framing and Governance Mechanisms", *Academy of Management Review*, Vol. *36*, No. 3, 500-525.

Lips-Wiersma, M. & Morris, L. (2009). "Discriminating Between 'Meaningful Work' and the "Management of Meaning", *Journal of Business Ethics*, Vol. *88*, No. 3, 491-511.

Liu, Y., Loi, R. & Lam, L. (2011). "Linking Organizational Identification and Employee Performance in Teams: The Moderating Role of Team-Member Exchange", *International Journal of Human Resource Management*, Vol. *22*, No. 15, 3187-3201.

Liu, B. & Tang, T. (2011). "Does the Love of Money Moderate the Relationship Between PSM and Job Satisfaction? The Case of Chinese Professionals in the Public Sector", *Public Administration Review*, Vol. *71*, No. 5, 718-727.

Locke, E. & Latham, G. (2004). "What Should We Do About Motivation Theory? Six Recommendations for the Twenty First Century", *Academy of Management Review*, Vol. *29*, No. 3, 388-403.

Lount, R. & Phillips, K. (2007). "Working Harder with the Out-group: The Impact of Social Category Diversity on Motivation Gains", *Organizational Behaviour and Human Decision Processes*, Vol. *103*, No. 2, 214-224.

May, D., Gilson, L. & Harter, L. (2004). "The Psychological Conditions of Meaningfulness, Safety and Availability and the Engagement of the Human Spirit at Work", *Journal of Occupational and Organizational Psychology*, Vol. *77*, 11-37.

McClelland, D., Koestner, R. & Weinberger, J. (1989). "How Do Self Attributed and Implicit Motives Differ? *Psychological Review*, Vol. *96*, 690-702.

Meyer, J., Becker, T. & Van-Dick, R. (2006). "Social Identities and Commitments at Work: Toward an Integrative Model", *Journal of Organizational Behaviour*, Vol. *27*, No. 5, 665-683.

Michaelson, C. (2005). "Meaningful Motivation for Work Motivation Theory", *Academy of Management Review*, Vol. *30*, No. 2, 235-238.

Michaelson, C. & Pratt, M. (2014). "Meaningful Work: Connecting Business Ethics and Organization Studies", *Journal of Business Ethics*, Vol. *121*, 77-90.

Mignonac, K. & Herrbach, O. (2004). "Linking Work Events, Affective States and Attitudes: An Empirical Study of Managers' Emotions", *Journal of Business and Psychology*, Vol. *19*, No. 2, 221-240.

Moynihan, D. & Pandey, S. (2007). "The Role of Organizations in Fostering PSM", *Public Administration Review*, Vol. *67*, No. 1, 40-53.

Muraven, M. & Baumeister, R. (2000). "Self Regulation and Depletion of Limited Resources: Does Self Control Resemble a Muscle?", *Psychological Bulletin*, Vol. 126, 247-279.

Nakai, Y., Chang, B., Snell, A. & Fluckinger, C. (2011). "Profiles of Mature Job Seekers: Connecting Needs and Desires to Work Characteristics", *Journal of Organizational Behaviour*, Vol. *32*, No. 2, 155-172.

Nair, N. & Vohra, N. (2010). "An Exploration of Factors Predicting Work Alienation of Knowledge Workers", *Management Decision*, Vol. *48*, No. 4, 600-615.

Naquin, S. & Holton, E. (2002). "The Effects of Personality, Affectivity, and Work Commitment on Motivation to Improve Work Through Learning", *Human Resource Development Quarterly*, Vol. *13*, No. 4, 357-376.

NG, T. & Feldman, D. (2012). "Evaluating Six Common Stereotypes About Older Workers With Meta-Analytical Data", *Personnel Psychology*, Vol. *65*, No. 4, 821-858.

Ngo, H., Loi, R., Foley, S., Zheng, X. & Zhang, L. (2013). "Perceptions of Organizational Context and Job Attitudes: The Mediating Effect of Organizational Identification", *Asia Pacific Journal of Management*, Vol. *30*, No. 1, 149-168.

Orth, U., Robins, R. & Widaman, K. (2012). "Life Span Development of Self Esteem and Its Effects on Important Life Outcomes", *Journal of Personality and Social Psychology*, Vol. *102*, No. 6, 1271-1288.

Patrick, H., Canevello, A., Knee, C. & Lonsbary, C. (2007). "The Role of Need Fulfillment in Relationship Functioning and Well Being: A Self Determination Theory Perspective", *Journal of Personality and Social Psychology*, Vol. *92*, No. 3, 434-457.

Perlow, L. (1999). "The Time Famine: Toward a Sociology of Work Time", *Administrative Science Quarterly*, Vol. *44*, 57-81.

Perry, J. (2000). "Bringing Society In: Toward a Theory of Public Service Motivation", *Journal of Public Administration Research and Theory*, Vol. *10*, No. 2, 471-488.

Perry, J. & Wise, L. (1990). "The Motivational Bases of Public Service", *Public Administration Review*, Vol. *50*, 367-373.

Pittman, T., Tykocinski, O., Sandman-Keinan, R. & Matthews, P. (2008). "When Bonuses Backfire: An Inaction Inertia Analysis of Procrastination Induced By a Missed Opportunity" *Journal of Behavioural Decision Making*, Vol. *21*, No. 2, 139-150.

Pratt, M. (1998). "To Be or Not to Be: Central Questions in Organizational Identification", in D. Whetten and P. Godfrey (eds.) *Identity in Organizations: Developing Theory Through Conversations*, Sage publications, Thousand Oaks, CA: 171-208.

Pratt, M. & Ashforth, B. (2003). "Fostering Meaningfulness in Working and At Work" In K. Cameron.; J. Dutton.; and R. Quinn (eds.), *Positive Organizational Scholarship: Foundations of a New Discipline* (pp. 308-327), San Francisco: Berrett-Koehler.

Reinhard, M., Schindler, S. & Stahlberg, D. (2014). "The Risk of Male Success and Failure: How Performance Outcomes Along With A High Status Identity Affect Gender Identification, Risk Behaviour and Self Esteem", *Group Processes and Intergroup Relations*, Vol. *17*, No. 2, 200-220.

Roche, M. & Haar, J. (2013). "A Meta-model Approach Towards Self Determination Theory: A Study of New Zealand Managers' Organizational Citizenship Behaviours", *International Journal of Human Resource Management*, Vol. *24*, No. 18, 3397-3417.

Rodriguez-Sanchez, A., Schaufeli, W., Salanova, M., Cifre, E. & Sonnenschein, M. (2011). "Enjoyment and Absorption: An Electronic Diary Study on Daily Flow Patterns", *Work and Stress*, Vol. *25*, No. 1, 75-92.

Rosso, B., Dekas, K. & Wrzesniewski, A. (2010). "On the Meaning of Work: A Theoretical Integration and Review", *Research in Organizational Behaviour*, Vol. *30*, 91-127.

Ryan, R. & Deci, E. (2000). "Self Determination Theory and the Facilitation of Intrinsic Motivation", Social Development and Well Being", *American Psychologist*, Vol. *55*, 68-78.

Ryan, R. (ed.) (2012). *The Oxford Handbook of Human Motivation*, Oxford: Oxford University Press.

Sanchez, R., Truxillo, D. & Bauer, T. (2000). "Development and Examination of an Expectancy Based Measure of Test Taking Motivation", *Journal of Applied psychology*, Vol. *85*, No. 5, 739-750.

Schnell, T. (2011). "Individual Differences in Meaning Making: Considering the Variety of Sources of Meaning, Their Density and Diversity", *Personality and Individual Differences*, Vol. *51*, 667-673.

Scott, P. & Pandey, S. (2005). "Red Tape and Public Service Motivation", *Review of Public Personnel Administration*, Vol. *25*, No. 2, 155-180.

Scott, B. & Barnes, C. (2011). "A Multilevel Field Investigation of Emotional Labour, Affect, Work Withdrawal and Gender", *Academy of Management Journal*, Vol. *54*, No. 1, 116-136.

Seo, M., Barrett, F. & Bartunek, J. (2004). "The Role of Affective Experience in Work Motivation", *Academy of Management Review*, Vol. *29*, No. 3, 423-439.

Seo, M., Bartunek, J. & Barrett, L. (2010). "The Role of Affective Experience in Work Motivation: Test of Conceptual Model", *Journal of Organizational Behaviour*, Vol. 31, No. *7*, 951-968.

Sheldon, K. & Elliot, A. (1999). "Goal Striving, Need Satisfaction, and Longitudinal Well Being: The Self Concordance Model", *Journal of Personality and Social Psychology*, Vol. *76*, 482-497.

Sheldon, K. & Kasser, T. (1995). "Coherence and Congruence: Two Aspects of Personality Integration", *Journal of Personality and Social Psychology*, Vol. *68*, 531-543.

Shu, S. & Gneezy, A. (2010). "Procrastination of Enjoyable Experiences", *Journal of Marketing Research*, Vol. *47*, No. 5, 933-944.

Soane, E., Shantz, A., Alfes, K., Truss, C., Rees, C. & Gatenby, M. (2013). "The Association of Meaningfulness, Well Being, and Engagement With Absenteeism: A Moderated Mediation Model", *Human Resource Management*, Vol. *52*, No. 3, 441-456.

Soery, B. & Corrigall, E. (2009). "Emotional Labour: Links To Work Attitudes and Emotional Exhaustion, *Journal of Managerial Psychology*, Vol. *24*, No. 8, 797-813.

Saks, A. (2011). "Workplace Spirituality and Employee Engagement", *Journal of Management*, Vol. *8*, No. 4, 317-340.

Stamov-Robnagel, C. & Biemann, T. (2012). "Aging and Work Motivation: A Task Level Perspective", *Journal of Managerial Psychology*, Vol. *27*, No. 5, 459-478.

Stazyk, E. (2013). "Crowding Out PSM: Comparing Theoretical Expectations With Empirical Findings on the Influence of Performance Related Pay", *Review of Public Personnel Administration*, Vol. *33*, No. 3, 252-274.

Steel, P. & Konig, C. (2006). "Integrating Theories of Motivation", *Academy of Management Review*, Vol. *31*, No. 4, 889-913.

Steel, P. (2007). "The Nature of Procrastination: A Meta-Analytic and Theoretical Review of Quintessential Self Regulatory Failure", *Psychological Bulletin*, Vol. *133*, No. 1, 65-94.

Steers, R., Mowday, R. & Shapiro, D. (2004). "The Future of Work Motivation Theory", *Academy of Management review*, Vol. *29*, No. 3, 379-387.

Tajfel, H. & Turner, J. (1985). "The Social Identity Theory of Intergroup Behaviour" In S. Worchel and W. Austin (eds.), *Psychology of Intergroup Relations*, 2nd Edition, pp. 7-24, Chicago: Bason-Hall.

Tanghe, J., Wisse, B. & Van der flier, H. (2010). "The Role of Group Member Affect in the Relationship Between Trust and Cooperation", *British Journal of Management*, Vol. *21*, No. 2, 359-374.

Tanghe, J., Wisse, B. & Van der Flier, H. (2010). "The Formation of Group Affect and Team Effectiveness: The Moderating Role of Identification", *British Journal of Management*, Vol. *21*, No. 2, 340-358.

Thau, S., Troster, C., Aquino, K., Pillutla, M. & Cremer, D. (2013). "Satisfying Individual Desires or Moral Standards? Preferential Treatment and Group Members' Self Worth, Affect, and Behaviour", *Journal of Business Ethics*, Vol. *113*, No. 1, 133-145.

Tomasello, M., Carpenter, M., Call, J., Behne, T. & Moll, H. (2005). "Understanding and Sharing Intentions: The Origin of Cultural Cognition", *Behavioural and Brain Sciences*, Vol. *28*, 675-735.

Tsai, W., Chen, H. & Cheng, J. (2009). "Employee Positive Moods as a Mediator Linking Transformational Leadership and Employee Work Outcomes", *International Journal of Human Resource Management*, Vol. *20*, No. 1, 206-219.

Tubbs, M. & Ekeberg, S. (1991). "The Role of Intentions in Work Motivation: Implications for Goal Setting Theory and Research", *Academy of Management Review*, Vol. *16*, 180-199.

Twenge, J., Campbell, S., Hoffman, B. & Lance, C. (2010). "Generational Differences in Work Values: Leisure and Extrinsic Values Increasing, Social and Intrinsic Values Decreasing", *Journal of Management*, Vol. *36*, No. 5, 1117-1142.

Van Beek, I., Hu, Q., Schaufeli, W., Taris, T. & Schreurs, B. (2012). "For Fun Love, or Money: What Drives Workaholic, Engaged and Burned Out Employees at Work?", *Applied Psychology: An International Review*, Vol. *61*, No. 1, 30-55.

Van Den Berg, P. (2011). "Characteristics of the Work Environment Related To Older Employees' Willingness To Continue Working: Intrinsic Motivation as a Mediator", *Psychological Reports*, Vol. *109*, No. 1, 174-186.

Van Dick, R., Stelimacher, J., Wagner, U., Lemmer, G. & Tissington, P. (2009). "Group Membership Salience and Task Performance", *Journal of Managerial Psychology*, Vol. *24*, No. 7, 609-626.

Van, R. & Ellemers, N. (2002). "Context Effects on the Application of Stereotype Content to Multiple Categorization Targets", *Personality and Social Psychology Bulletin*, Vol. *29*, 679-690.

Vandenabeele, W. (2007). "Toward a Public Administration Theory of Public Service Motivation", *Public Management Review*, Vol. *9*, No. 4, 545-556.

Vandenabeele, W. (2011). "Who wants to Deliver Public Service? Do Institutional Antecedents of PSM provide an Answer", *Review of Public Personnel Administration*, Vol. *31*, No. 1, 87-107.

Van Dick, R. & Wagner, U. (2002). "Social Identification Among School Teachers: Dimensions, Foci and Correlates", *European Journal of Work and Organizational Psychology*, Vol. *11*, No. 2, 129-149.

Van Knippenberg, D. (2000). "Work Motivation and Performance: A Social Identity Perspective", *Applied Psychology: An International Review*, Vol. *49*, No. 3, 357-371.

Van Knippenberg, D. & Van Schie, E. (2000). "Foci and Correlates of Organizational Identification", *Journal of Occupational and Organizational Psychology*, Vol. *73*, No. 2, 137-147.

Van Knippenberg, D., Kooij de Bode, H. & Van Ginkel, W. (2010). "The Interactive Effects of Mood and Trait Negative Affect in Group Decision Making", *Organization Science*, Vol. *21*, No. 3, 731-744.

Van Vianen, A., Dalhoeven, B. & Pater, I. (2011). "Aging and Training and Development Willingness: Employee and Supervisor Mindsets", *Journal of Organizational Behaviour*, Vol. *32*, No. 2, 226-247.

Von Bonsdorff, M. (2011). "Age Related Differences in Reward Preferences", *International Journal of Human Resource Management*, Vol. *22*, No. 6, 1262-1276.

Vroom, V. (1964). *Work and Motivation*, New York: Wiley.

Wang, H., He, J. & Mahoney, J. (2009). "Firm Specific Knowledge Resources and Competitive Advantage: The Roles of Economic and Relationship Based Employee Governance Mechanisms", *Strategic Management Journal*, Vol. *30*, 1265-1285.

Ward, K. (2014). "Cultivating PSM Through Americorps Service: A Longitudinal Study", *Public Administration Review*, Vol. *74*, No. 1, 114-125.

Wegge, J., Van Dick, R. & Von Bernstorff, C. (2010). "Emotional Dissonance in Call Centre Work", *Journal of Managerial Psychology*, Vol. *25*, No. 6, 596-619.

Wiese, B. & Freund, A. (2005). "Goal Progress Makes One Happy or Does It? Longitudinal Findings From the Work Domain", *Journal of Occupational and Organizational Psychology*, Vol. *78*, No. 2, 287-304.

Wright, B. (2007). "Public Service and Motivation: Does Mission Matter", *Public Administration Review*, Vol. *67*, No. 1, 54-64.

Wright, T. & Staw, B. (1999). "Affect and Favourable Work Outcomes: Two Longitudinal Tests of the Happy –Productive Worker Thesis", *Journal of Organizational Behaviour*, Vol. *20*, 1-23.

Wright, B. & Pandey, S. (2008). "Public Service Motivation and the Assumption of Person-Organization Fit Testing the Mediating Effect of Value Congruence", *Administration and Society*, Vol. *40*, No. 5, 502-521.

Zacher, H. & Frese, M. (2011). "Maintaining a Focus on Opportunities at Work: The Interplay Between Age, Job Complexity and the Use of Selection, Optimization and Compensation Strategies", *Journal of Organizational Behaviour*, Vol. *32*, No. 2, 291-318.

Zhang, Y. & Chiu, C. (2012). "Goal Attainment and Alignment of Personal Goals Predict Group identification Only When the Goals Are Shared", *Group Processes and Intergroup Relations*, Vol. *15*, No. 4, 425-437.

In: Advances in Business and Management
Editor: William D. Nelson

ISBN: 978-1-53612-615-0
© 2017 Nova Science Publishers, Inc.

Chapter 2

THE COST OF POOR SLEEP FOR EMPLOYEES AND THE WORKPLACE: A REVIEW AND CALL FOR INTERVENTION

Victoria A. Felix[*], Mercedes Gremillion and Walt Buboltz[†], PhD
Louisiana Tech University
Ruston, LA, US

ABSTRACT

According to the National Sleep Foundation's Sleep in America Poll (2008), 65% of a sample of 1,000 employed adults reported experiencing sleeping difficulties at least a few nights per week, while 44% report experiencing sleep difficulties every night or almost every night. When asked about the impact of sleepiness in the workplace, 29% reported that they have fallen asleep or became very sleepy while working, and 12% reported that they were late to work due to sleepiness. Poor sleep among employees in the workplace has been supported to negatively impact

---

[*] Email: vaf006@latech.edu.
[†] Email: buboltz@latech.edu.

employees' overall performance and well-being, while also impacting economic gains for the businesses (Burton, Chen, Schultz, & Xingquan, 2017). Poor sleep reported by employees is significantly associated with lowered cognitive performance, increased probability of accidents or injury in the workplace, increased risk for physical and/or mental health issues, and lowered productivity (Gaultney & Collins-McNeil, 2009). As for the businesses, it has been estimated that companies lose approximately $1,967 in productivity costs per employee annually due to poor sleep (Rosekind et al., 2010). Based on these research findings, it is recommended that employers promote and prioritize healthy sleep among their employees. Recommendations are made in keeping with this. Further, readers are provided with a comprehensive review of the literature which currently exists regarding sleep health and workplace productivity overall.

INTRODUCTION

By the numbers, a large majority of people around the world and in America, specifically, are plagued by problems related to both sleep quantity and sleep quality. In America alone, it is reported that adults are sleeping an average of only 6.8 hours on weekdays and 7.4 hours on weekends (National Sleep Foundation, 2005). It is further reported that 88% of people are experiencing at least one symptom of insomnia, and 94% are experiencing at least one symptom of a sleep disorder. Consider these numbers in combination with the fact that persons who rate their health or quality of life more highly also tend to report obtaining roughly 30 more minutes of sleep per night than persons reporting poor health (National Sleep Foundation, 2015). Further, persons with shorter sleep length and poorer sleep quality tend to report greater stress.

One of the variables that may play a key role in sleep health and stress among the adult population is involvement in the workforce. The National Sleep Foundation's Sleep in America Poll (2008) found that 65% of a sample of 1,000 employed adults reported experiencing sleeping difficulties at least a few nights per week, while 44% reported waking up without feeling refreshed for at least a few nights per week. When asked about the impact of sleepiness in the workplace, 29% of respondents reported that they have fallen asleep or become very sleepy while working, and an additional 12% reported that they were late to work due to sleepiness.

These statistics highlight the prevalence of sleep difficulties among adult samples, and provide insight into ways that sleep difficulties and employee workplace functioning are interrelated. One of the aims of this chapter is to review the theories and research demonstrating the relationships between sleep and cognitive performance and health in general. An additional aim of this chapter is to highlight ways this may be seen on the job, more specifically, and impact work. Recommendations are also made, in keeping with this, for workers and employers.

Sleep Deprivation and Cognitive Performance

When a person does not obtain an adequate amount of sleep to support their daytime alertness, they are said to be sleep deprived, or suffering from some form of sleep deprivation. (Kryger, Roth, & Dement, 2001). Sleep deprivation may be full or partial in nature. Full sleep deprivation is defined as the complete loss of sleep over an extended period of time, while partial sleep deprivation is defined as the partial reduction or loss of sleep over days or weeks. Both forms of sleep deprivation can be detrimental to a person's daily life (Lim & Dinges, 2010). Areas most affected include cognitive performance, as well as physical and mental health.

There are three theories that have been posed to explain the relationships between sleep deprivation and cognition, specifically. The first theory is known as the controlled attention hypothesis (Pilcher, Band, Odle-Dusseau, & Muth, 2007), which explains that "bottom-up" cognitive tasks, or tasks that are monotonous and require less cognitive energy, are more severely affected by sleep deprivation. "Top-down" tasks are less likely to be impacted by sleep deprivation because they encourage and require more attention and cognition comparatively.

The second theory, the neuropsychological hypothesis (Jones & Harrison, 2001), explains that sleep deprivation produces a reversible lesion in the prefrontal cortex of the brain, which significantly reduces one's performance on cognitive tasks for memory, fluency, and response inhibition. Numerous researcher teams have found research to support this theory, including Harrison, Horne, and Rothwell (2000). Specifically, Harrison et al., (2000) found when comparing the cognitive performance of young adults with and without sleep deprivation, that sleep deprived participants performed significantly worse on cognitive tests requiring prefrontal cortex activation than their research counterparts. The effects seen were found to be reversible.

The last theory is known as the vigilance hypothesis (Balkin, Rupp, Picchioni, & Wesensten, 2008; Durmer & Dinges, 2005). This theory asserts that vigilance and sustained attention are of fundamental importance for the performance of cognitive tasks. If a person is sleep deprived, then sustained attention is compromised, and this person will have greater difficulty performing cognitive tasks. Alhola and Polo-Kantola (2007) elaborate on this theory by explaining that total or full sleep deprivation is associated with deficits in attention, working memory, long-term memory, and decision-making. Meanwhile partial sleep deprivation is associated with deficits in attention, rather exclusively, including a person's level of vigilance.

Full Sleep Deprivation

Full sleep deprivation has a wide variety of possible causes and consequences (Boonstra, Stins, Daffertshofer, & Beek, 2007). Full sleep deprivation may be caused by sleep disorders, such as insomnia, or may be due to lifestyle choices, including working night shifts. Research supports that full sleep deprivation can have a negative effect on attention, mood, and cognition overall (Franzen, Siegle, & Buysse, 2008; Lim & Dinges, 2010).

Franzen et al., (2008) examined the relationship between one night of total sleep deprivation and the effects on mood and attention, specifically vigilance. Results indicated that the day following sleep deprivation, participants reported an increase in negative mood, higher levels of reactivity to emotional stimuli, and significantly slower reaction times on a test of psychomotor vigilance performance when compared to the non-sleep deprived participants.

Research has also supported that beyond attention, mood, and the like, working memory can also be compromised by sleep deprivation (Turner, Drummond, Salamat, & Brown, 2007). Turner et al., (2007) tested participants' verbal working memory performance and attention before and after 42 hours of sleep deprivation. They found statistically independent declines in working memory span and attention following the sleep deprivation period compared to pretest.

Further, Lim and Dinges (2010) conducted a meta-analysis of 70 articles and 147 data sets to investigate the relationship between full sleep deprivation and cognitive performance. They included research that assessed the speed and accuracy of cognitive performance across various memory domains, including simple attention, complex attention, working memory, processing speed, short-term memory, and reasoning. Results indicated that there were significant differences in performance across all of the cognitive domains for sleep-deprived participants. The largest effect size was found for simple attention tasks, followed by complex attention, processing speed, working memory, and short-term memory respectively. Reasoning skills did not yield a significant effect size. Lim and Dinges (2010) note that results indicate sleep deprivation has a more deleterious effect on variables requiring less cognitive functioning.

Partial Sleep Deprivation

Partial sleep deprivation has similar deleterious effects on a person's attention, performance, and cognition overall, as does total or full sleep deprivation.

Van Dongen, Maislin, Mullington, and Dinges (2003) investigated the performance on a sustained attention reaction-time task based on differing durations of chronic sleep deprivation. Sixty-six participants were randomly separated into groups in which they slept for three, five, seven, or nine hours for a seven day period, followed by a three day restoration period in which they slept for eight hours per night. Researchers note that results differed for each sleep group.

Among participants whom only slept for three hours, there was a significant decline in speed on the psychomotor vigilance task, and reaction times steadily declined over the seven day period. In the five and seven hour sleep groups, results show that speed declined initially, but then stabilized during the seven day period. There were no changes in performance for participants in the nine hour sleep group. During the three day recovery period, the performance for participants in the three hour sleep group recovered rapidly after the first night of recovery.

Philip et al., (2012) investigated the relationship between chronic sleep restriction and cognitive performance on a reaction time test. Eighteen participants were randomly assigned to an acute or chronic sleep deprivation group. Participants in the acute sleep deprivation group were instructed to stay awake for one night, while the participants in the chronic group were instructed to sleep for four hours per night for five consecutive nights. Following acute or chronic sleep deprivation, participants were asked to complete a simple reaction time tests.

Results indicated that the number of lapses during the reaction time test were significantly higher after the night of acute sleep deprivation and after the second night of chronic sleep deprivation. Additionally, the number of lapses that occurred in the acute and chronic sleep deprivation groups did not significantly differ from each other. These results provide evidence that acute and chronic sleep deprivation can have similar effects on cognition.

To further this point, consider the work of Lo et al., (2012). Lo et al., (2012) tested 36 participants, measuring the effects of partial and acute sleep deprivation on cognitive domains, including alertness, sustained attention, and executive functions including working memory. Results supported that subjective alertness and sustained attention were more significantly affected by acute and chronic sleep deprivation than working memory with a higher cognitive load. These results provide evidence that sleep deprivation significantly impacts tasks that are less cognitively demanding but may not have a similar effect on tasks that require higher

The Cost of Poor Sleep for Employees and the Workplace 65

levels of executive functioning. Such findings are in keeping with the conclusions drawn by researchers Lim and Dinges (2010) in their meta-analysis looking at the effects of full sleep deprivation.

Sleep Deprivation and Physical and Mental Health

In addition to affecting cognitive performance, sleep deprivation has also been found to significantly effect a person's physical and mental health. These effects are somewhat variable.

Physical health

Poor sleep quantity and quality have been found to be associated with weakened or comprised immune systems. There are many theories that explain ways that sleep and immune system are connected, with one theory summarizing that disruptions in the circadian rhythm impact immune cells specifically (T. Bollinger, A. Bollinger, Oster & Solbach, 2010).

Research supports that sleep disturbances are associated with increased risk for infectious disease. For example, poor sleep has been associated with an increased susceptibility to contract the common cold (Cohen, Doyle, Alper, Janicki-Deverts, & Turner, 2009). Cohen et al., (2009) found in their study that persons reporting less than seven hours of sleep were 2.94 times more likely to develop the rhinovirus than those reporting eight or more hours of sleep. Additionally, participants with less than 92% sleep efficiency were 5.50 times more likely to develop a cold. Cohen et al., (2009) controlled for virus-specific antibody titers, demographics, season, body mass, socioeconomic status, psychological health, and health practices in their study.

In keeping with this, Patel et al., (2012) note that short sleep duration, specifically, obtaining less than five hours of sleep per night, and prolonged sleep duration, obtaining more than nine hours of sleep per night, has been correlated with an increased risk of pneumonia.

Research has also supported that disturbances in sleep are associated with increased risk of cardiovascular disease, diabetes, and obesity (see

Benham, 2010 & Irwin, 2015 for a review). Individuals obtaining shorter amounts of sleep, that is, less than five hours, and longer amounts of sleep, more than nine hours, are at a significantly higher risk of experiencing coronary heart disease or stroke (Cappuccio, Cooper, Elia, Strazzullo, & Miller, 2011). Additionally, poor sleep quality is significantly associated with increased risk of high blood pressure (Mesas et al., 2014).

Knutson, Ryden, Mander, and Van Cauter (2006) found that both short sleep quantity and poor sleep quality also were predictive of a person's risk for type 2 diabetes. Shorter sleep duration was significantly associated with increased body mass index (BMI) among men, and poor sleep quality was significantly associated with higher BMI among women (Meyer, Wall, Larson, Laska, & Neumark-Sztainer, 2012). Notably, a higher BMI, in itself, has also been found to be linked with cardiovascular disease, diabetes, and other health ailments in and of itself.

Research supports that both sleep and psychological stress play a role in physical illness. Benham (2010) conducted a study based on McEwen's (2006) stress-health model. This model explains that psychological stress and poor sleep predict allostatic load, which then predicts illness. Allostatic load is defined as physiological strain from repeated adaption to stressors. Further, this model explains that physical illness also affects sleep and psychological stress. Benham's (2010) study hypothesized that self-reported illness would be positively associated with self-reported psychological stress and sleep. Additionally, they hypothesized that adding sleep as a predictor in the stress-health relationship would improve the predictive power of the model. Results of Benham's (2010) study were in keeping with the proposed hypotheses.

Specifically, Benham (2010) found that there was a significant relationship between higher stress and poor health, as was predicted. Additionally, poor sleep quality and greater daytime sleepiness were significantly associated with poor health, as predicted. Further, when sleep was added to the model, the stress-health model accounted for 56% of the variance in scores on the Cohen-Hoberman Inventory of Physical Symptoms (Cohen & Hoberman, 1983).

Beyond this, it has been reported that sleep plays a role not simply in physical health, but also in predicting a person's perceived physical health concerns. Steptoe, Peacey, and Wardle (2006) collected data from a sample of over 17,000 participants across 27 universities in 24 countries. Participants were asked to report sleep and self-rated health, and covariates in the analyses included age, sex, socioeconomic status, smoking, body mass index, physical activity, depression, alcohol consumption, country of origin, and recent use of health services. Results indicated that participants reporting a short sleep duration, less than six hours, were more likely to report poor self-rated health than participants reporting obtaining seven to eight hours of sleep. There were no significant relationships found among self-rated health and longer sleep duration.

Mental health

Research supports that sleep disturbances play a role in a person's mental health too. Specifically, sleep deprivation can cause an increased risk of or maintenance of a plethora of mental health symptoms (Riemann, Berger, & Voderholzer, 2001; Harvey, 2011).

Early research using polysomnographic procedures to analyze sleep architecture provided evidence that individuals experiencing depression have disturbances in sleep efficiency, reduced slow-wave sleep, and disruption of REM sleep latency (Kupfer, Harrow, & Detre, 1969).

Harvey (2011) reviews that individuals with a diagnosis of depression reporting sleep disturbances have an increased likelihood of experiencing a mood episode, or relapsing if mood is stable. Results of a meta-analysis including 143 studies indicated that mood is more impacted by sleep deprivation than cognitive and motor functioning (Pilcher & Huffcutt, 1996). Furthermore, among college students, Nyer et al., (2013) found that participants reporting depressive symptoms and sleep disturbances endorsed more intense and frequent symptoms of anxiety when compared to participants reporting depressive symptoms without sleep disturbance.

Research has also consistently supported the relationship between insomnia and depression. Staner (2010) reviews evidence supporting that there is a bidirectional relationship between insomnia and depression.

Research has supported that depression is a risk factor for developing insomnia (Ohayon, Caulet, & Lemoine, 1998), while research also supports that individuals with a diagnosis of insomnia are more likely than others to experience a depressive episode (Ford & Kamerow, 1989). Staner (2010) argues that when both disorders are present in a person, they may maintain or exacerbate symptoms associated with each. In keeping with this, it is recommended that treatment interventions focus on managing symptoms of both diagnoses.

Interestingly, research has been conducted to investigate underlying mechanisms that could theoretically explain the relationship between sleep disturbance and mental health. One line of research that may be particularly applicable in a workplace environment is the relationship between emotion regulation and sleep. Emotion regulation can be defined as the ability to notice, experience, and express emotions in a proper way (Gross, & Jazaieri, 2014).

Brain structures and neurochemicals that are involved in emotion regulation are also involved in sleep (Goldstein & Walker, 2014). Further neurological research has supported that there is greater amygdala activation in response to negative stimuli among sleep deprived persons when compared to persons not sleep deprived (Yoo, Gujar, Hu, Jolesz, & Walker, 2007). Yoo et al., (2007) note such results are indicative that sleep deprived individuals are more likely to respond at a greater intensity to negative emotions than participants with healthier sleep.

Palmer and Alfano (2017) report that sleep disturbances may negatively impact a person's ability to notice positive situations, modify situations by appropriately expressing emotions, regulate emotions internally when external situations are unable to be modified, and engage in cognitive reframing to change the way an emotional situation is perceived overall. Such facts have startling implications for social relationships, and have been linked to such.

In a three year longitudinal study among a sample of college students, Tavernier and Willoughby (2015) found that participants reporting better sleep quality also had more positive social relationships than persons with poor sleep quality. This relationship was mediated by emotion regulation, with person's having better sleep quality also having better regulation.

Similar results were previously obtained by Haack and Mullington (2005). Haack and Mullington (2005) examined the effect of partial sleep deprivation on physical well-being and mood. Participants were assigned to obtain either four hours of sleep or eight hours of sleep over a twelve day period. They were also asked to rate their affect (optimism-sociability), sleepiness (tiredness-fatigue), mood (anger-aggression), and bodily discomfort on a daily basis. Results indicated that the ratings of optimism-sociability significantly declined over the consecutive days of sleep restriction for the group sleeping four hours per night compared to those sleeping eight.

Another variable that plays a role in sleep health is psychological stress. Among a sample of two-year college students, Wallace, Boynton, and Lytle (2017) found that stress and depression were both significant predictors of sleep quality. Blaxton, Bergeman, Whitehead, Braun, and Payne (2017) conducted a study to investigate the relationships between sleep, stress, and the subsequent day's affect with age as a moderator. Results indicated that increases in sleep quality and decreases in stress interacted and significantly predicted higher positive affect and lower negative affect. Among older adults, better sleep quality enhanced positive affect during times of lower reported stress, while for younger adults the same was true during times of higher stress.

Sleep Deprivation and Cognitive Performance in the Workplace

Both full and partial sleep deprivation have been shown to have a significant impact on cognitive performance in life, in general, as well as in the workplace, more specifically. Areas of functioning or abilities most affected on the job seem to include attention, working memory, learning, and decision-making overall (see Gaultney & Collins-McNeil, 2009 for a review).

In their study assessing the effects of sleep deprivation on the cognitive performance of medical residents and interns, Kim et al., (2006) found that sleep deprivation had the potential to effect both attention and working memory. Notably, they found that sleep deprived persons in their study, more frequently complained of difficulties in learning and concentration. They also showed delayed reactions times when partaking in a visual task, and more commission errors when partaking in an auditory task. Kim et al., (2006) report that while sleep deprivation affected attention and motor performance in participants, verbal learning appeared to be unaffected.

Similar results specific to psychomotor performance were also found among nurses (Johnson, Brown, & Weaver, 2010) and person's deemed middle-aged (Philip et al., 2012). Johnson et al., (2010) found that sleep deprived nurses were significantly more likely to have lower performance in attention, concentration, processing speed, and quality of performance. Meanwhile, Philip et al., (2012) found persons of varying professions who were of middle-age had increased reactions times on tasks completed following a period of sleep restriction overall.

Lockley (2007) found that the amount of hours worked by a medical professional, such as a nurse or physician, has serious implications for both safety and performance. Specifically, Lockley (2007) reports that nurses working shifts greater than 12.5 hours were significantly more likely to experience decreased vigilance on the job, suffer from occupational injury, or make a medical error. Physicians-in-training, working increased amounts of hours on the job and variable shifts, were more likely to experience an occupational sharps injury or a motor vehicle crash on the drive home from work than their counterparts. They were also more likely to make a serious or even fatal medical error. On-call residents made twice as many attentional failures when working overnight and committed 36% more serious medical errors. They also reported 300% more fatigue-related medical errors that had the potential to leading to patient death.

Gold et al., (1992) found that nurses who worked shift work were twice as likely to nod off while driving to or from work and were also twice as likely to report accidents or errors related to sleepiness when compared with nurses who worked only consistently timed shifts. Similar results were found by Fido and Ghali (2008). They report that among employees with variable shift schedules and consistent shift schedules, it was found that participants with varying schedules were more likely to report persistent sleep disturbances, poor concentration, and poor work performance.

Weinger and Ancoli-Israel (2002) provide a review of the effects sleep deprivation can have on clinical performance among medical staff, including physicians. They report that the dangers of impaired cognitive performance can be extensive, and that patient safety is the ultimate concern. Impaired cognitive performance may lead to minor errors, but can also result in the loss of human life. Comparisons are made between a sleep deprived physician and a sleep deprived pilot. Today, restrictions specific to the number of hours worked in a given amount of time are commonplace for pilots, but remain rare for physicians, nurses, and other medical staff.

Professions of many occupations seem to also suffer from poor decision-making as a result of sleep deprivation. Killgore, Lipizzi, Kamimori, and Balkin (2007) report that when sleep deprived, individuals showed impaired performance on a task associated with risky decision-making. Specifically, people were more likely to make more disadvantageous high-risk when sleep deprived than when not. In addition to this, Killgore et al., (2007) discovered that, contrary to popular belief perhaps, caffeine did not help to improve decision-making during times of sleep deprivation. Killgore et al., (2007) hypothesize their findings are the product of a decreased ability to integrate emotion and cognition when sleep deprived. They caution this could be a serious problem for persons working as police officers, military personnel, or medical workers who must make fast decision that affect both their and others' safety and well-being.

In keeping with this, Scott, Arslanian-Engoren, and Engoren (2014) investigated the association between sleep and fatigue with decision regret among critical care nurses. Sampling a total of 605 nurses, they found that decision regret was reported by 157 of 546 nurses. Nurses with decision regret, they note, also reported more fatigue, more daytime sleepiness, less intershift recovery, and worse sleep quality than did nurses without decision regret. Scott et al., (2014) hypothesize that nurses who experience impairments due to fatigue, loss of sleep, and an inability to recover between shifts are more likely than their colleagues to report decision regret.

Going beyond cognitive performance specifically, it has also been found that sleep deprivation can impact general productivity of workers. A study comparing participants with insomnia to participants classified as good sleepers found that 40.6% of participants in the insomnia category reported experiencing reduced productivity at work when compared to 12.3% in the good sleeper's category (Daley et al., 2009). Increased occurrences of accidents, mood and anxiety disorders, chronic health problems, increased health-care utilization, and absenteeism were also reported for the insomnia group, but not for the good sleepers group comparatively.

Rosekind et al., (2010) report that among a sample of 4,188 employees working at four United States corporations, a large majority were suffering from partial sleep deprivation. Further, persons suffering from insomnia and insufficient sleep had significantly worse productivity, performance, and safety outcomes. Fatigue-related productivity losses were estimated to cost $1,967 per employee annually. Worse outcomes were seen among individuals working variable shift work. These same persons also reported less total sleep, more awakenings, and worse sleep quality ratings overall. They also were more likely to suffer from insomnia.

Rosekind et al., (2010) report that decreased productivity and sleep deprivation were associated with attention fatigue, poor decision-making, decreased memory, and decreased motivation to work. Persons suffering with sleep deficits and/or problems also were more likely to report unintentional sleep at work, injury at home due to being sleep or tired, nodding off while driving, and having a near miss or automobile accident due to sleepiness or tiredness.

Sleep Deprivation and Physical and Mental Health in the Workplace

Sleep deprivation has a large effect on physical and mental health both in general, and on the job specifically. This has serious implications both for employees and employers alike, and is highly likely to affect work. Effects are variable, though all lead to decreased earnings overall.

Physical health

As mentioned previously, is has been documented the sleep deprivation can have a major impact on a person's physical health (Benham, 2010; Cappuccio et al., 2011; Cohen et al., 2009; Irwin, 2015; Knutson et al., 2006; Mesas et al., 2014; Patel et al., 2012). Sleep deprivation can also lead to increased rates of absenteeism at work (Lallukka et al., 2009).

Lallukka et al., (2009) report, specifically, that sleep disturbances have been associated with sickness absence in the workplace. They examined the relationship between sleep disturbances, including early morning awakenings, insomnia-related symptoms, sleeping pills, variation in sleep duration, being more tired than others, and excessive daytime sleepiness, and sickness absence. Results indicated that for male participants, all of the sleep disturbance variables except excessive daytime sleepiness were significantly associated with sickness absence. For female participants, insomnia-related symptoms, early morning awakenings, being more tired than others, and sleeping pills were associated with sickness absences respectively.

Going being absenteeism, sleep disturbances have also been found to be associated with increased presenteeism at work (Burton, Chen, Schultz, & Xingquan, 2017; Guertler et al., 2015; Kessler et al., 2011). Presenteeism is defined simply as working while sick (Johns, 2010).

Burton et al., (2015) report finding a strong U-shaped relationship between health care costs, short-term disability, absenteeism, and presenteeism and the hours of sleep obtained by employees. The nadir of the "U" they note, occurs for seven to eight hours of sleep per night.

Guertler et al., (2015) report that sleep quality is also related to presenteeism. Specifically, individuals with poorer sleep quality in addition to suboptimal duration, and lower work sitting time, were more likely to have increased rates of presenteeism even when controlling for a multitude of variables including sex, age, marital status, income, occupation, health, and the like. Presenteeism, Johns (2010) reports has been found to cause productivity loss, poor health, exhaustion, and workplace epidemics, and is of a serious concern for companies. Johns (2010), like many others, notes that presenteeism may be worse for a company's status than absenteeism.

Kessler et al., (2011) further reports of the productivity and performance deficits caused by presenteeism, comparing this with absenteeism. They note that insomnia is significantly associated with lost work performance due to presenteeism, but not absenteeism, with an annualized individual-level association of insomnia with presenteeism equivalent to 11.3 days of lost work performance annually. At a population level, this generalizes to approximately 252 days and a record $63.2 billion lost annually. Such findings may only be described as startling.

Presenteeism has also been found to be linked with an increased amount of time spent not on task, a decrease in quality of work, an increase in mistakes and/or errors, and an increased occurrence of on the job injury for employees respectively (Schultz, Chen, & Edington, 2009).

Poor sleep quantity and sleep quality have been found to be associated with work injury of any and every type (Uehli et al., 2013). Specific injuries, however, do seem more common. The strongest association, Uehli et al., (2013) report was found for musculoskeletal injuries and falls with short sleep duration. In a follow-up study conducted to this, Uehli et al., (2014) report that workers with sleep problems had a 1.62 times higher risk of being injured comparatively.

Kling, McLeod, and Koehoom (2010) report in their investigation of Canadian workers, it was found that trouble sleeping was significantly associated with work injury in both men and women. Men in trades and transportation jobs, women in processing or manufacturing jobs, and who work rotating shifts were at the highest increased risk for work injury associated with trouble sleeping. Hirsch Allen et al., (2016) further report that individuals suffering with obstructive sleep apnea, specifically, were twice as likely to suffer at least one occupational injury compared with individuals without obstructive sleep apnea in their investigation of 1,235 patients enrolled at a hospital sleep laboratory. Hirsch Allen et al., (2016) also found that persons suffering from obstructive sleep apnea were almost three times more likely to suffer from an injury more likely related to reduced vigilance when compared with their research counterparts.

Mental health

Sleep deprivation can have a significant impact on mental health. This can in turn effect an employee's work or ability to work much like physical health can or may.

Rosen, Gimothy, Shea, and Bellini (2006) report there exists a clear association between sleep deprivation, mood, empathy, and burnout among workers. Specifically, the prevalence of depression and burnout was more common among persons suffering from chronic sleep deprivation than those who were not sleep deprived. Rosen et al., (2006) report that empathy appeared to be unaffected by sleep deprivation. Further, that being chronically sleep deprived and becoming depressed was significant over and above developing burnout comparatively.

Literature documents that compared to non-depressed individuals, those with depression have more unemployment, absences, and at-work performance deficits (Lerner & Henke, 2008). Work impact of depression seems to be related to symptom severity. Symptom relief appears to only partly reduce the adverse work outcomes of depression, indicating that prevention is key.

Simon et al., (2001) note, nevertheless, that treatment is beneficial both for employees and employers alike. They note that productivity gains following effective depression treatment are likely to far exceed direct treatment costs. Such assertions were made by reviewing published works in four specific categories. This included naturalistic cross-sectional studies that found greater self-reported work impairment among depressed worker, naturalistic longitudinal studies that found a synchrony of change between depression and work impairment, uncontrolled treatment studies that found reduced work impairment with successful treatment, and controlled trials that typically found greater reduction in work impairment among treated patients.

The direct and indirect costs of employee depression, anxiety, and emotional disorder is great. Johnson, Westerfield, Momin, Phillippi, and Naidoo (2009) report that for one large company alone, depression, anxiety, and emotional disorders were the fifth costliest of all disease categories. The average cost per case was $1,646, with 53% coming from indirect costs and 47% from direct costs. They note this figures are generalizable to most any large company.

Hilton, Staddon, Sheridan, and Whiteford (2009) examined the impact of mental health symptoms on heavy good drivers' performance. They found, interestingly, that depression, anxiety, and stress had little effect on driver absenteeism rates or self-rated driving performance. However, individuals suffering from severe and very severe depression had an increased odds ratio for being involved in an accident or near miss in the past 28 days. This odd ratio, they explain, is akin to driving with a blood alcohol content of 0.08% or driving while drunk.

Evans-Lacko and Knapp (2016) assessed the extent and cost of depression-related absenteeism and presenteeism in the workforce across eight countries. They report that mean depression-related presenteeism costs per person were highest in the United States and Brazil. These costs averaged $5,524 and $5,788 respectively. It is reported that costs associated with presenteeism tended to be five to ten times higher than those associated with absenteeism.

Anxiety alone can also have a significant impact on employment and work performance. Waghorn, Chant, White, and Whiteford (2005) reports that anxiety disorders are associated with reduced labor force participation, degraded employment trajectories, and impaired work performance compared to people without disability or long-term health concerns comparatively.

Anxiety can also lead to or exacerbate depression. Specifically, Tennant (2001) notes that acute work-related stressful experiences may contribute to depression. Further, they note that a variety of enduring structural occupational factors may also contribute to psychological issues.

In addition to depression and anxiety, Leger et al., (2006) report that sleep deprived persons are more likely to suffer from a lower work-related self-esteem, less satisfaction with their job, and less efficient functioning at work. Drake, Roehrs, Richardson, Walsh, and Roth (2004) report that sleep deprived persons, specifically shift workers with shift-work sleep disorder, also have a greater propensity for ulcers, accidents related to sleepiness, absences, depression, and missed social activities when compared with shift workers without sleep issues.

It is noted that missed social activities may be linked with a decreased propensity for emotion regulation, and thus an increased propensity for over-reaction or awkward interactions. Gaultney and Collins-McNeil (2009) note that sleepy people are more likely to report feeling stressed, sad, and angry, and to have a worse attitude in general. Anger might be displayed in a negative way such as road rage, threatening employees' health as well as that of the public, and possibly increasing employer liability. All outcomes are likely to push others away and may cause and/or reinforce the occurrence of self-isolation by those who are sleep deprived.

Additional studies report that emotion regulation is a variable which is significantly associated with resolving interpersonal conflict at work (Gilin Oore, Leiter, & LeBlanc, 2015). Gilin Oore et al., (2015) note that persons with emotion regulation problems have increased rates of interpersonal conflict at work and are less likely to experience resolve in their conflicts. Problems with emotion regulation and decreased quality of life, in general, are both associated with sleep deprivation and problems on the job specifically (Gaultney & Collins-McNeil, 2009).

Budnick and Barber (2015) report that employees experiencing sleep disturbances are more likely than those employees not experiencing sleep disturbances, to interpret their workplace in a negative way. This subsequently increases workplace stressors and can increase the strain on employee health. Such findings remain significant when it is considered that frequently being bothered or upset at work is associated with changes toward poorer sleep quality (Burgard & Ailshire, 2009). Burgard and Ailshire (2009) report that such an association, in their investigation of 3,617 people, was not better explained by stressful experiences at home.

RECOMMENDATIONS

Clearly, it would seem, change is needed to increase sleep quantity and quality among individuals. Such changes are of benefit both for the person making the changes, as well as their work. Recommendations are made in keeping with this for employees and employers alike.

Employees

Employees should consider ways in which to improve their sleep hygiene (National Sleep Foundation, 2003). The National Sleep Foundation (2003) notes that the most important sleep hygiene practice is maintaining a regular wake and sleep pattern seven days a week. Additionally, it is advised that individuals go to bed within an hour of the same time each night, and wake within an hour of the same time each day (National Sleep Foundation, 2013). Individuals are further encouraged to only spend the recommended amount of time in bed. For adults, ages 18-64, this is typically seven to nine hours (National Sleep Foundation, 2016a).

Other sleep hygiene practices recommended by the National Sleep Foundation (2003) include avoiding napping during the day. It is noted that adults do not need daytime naps, unless they are not getting the proper sleep quantity or quality at night (Sleep Health Foundation, 2011). Naps can be useful tools, however, for those who are not getting enough or good quality sleep. If a nap should occur, it should happen no later than mid-afternoon. Further, it is suggested that naps not last long then 15 to 20 minutes. Anything longer, it is reported may result in the experience of "sleep inertia." Sleep inertia is a grogginess upon waking that may be hard to "shake off."

Stimulants such as caffeine, nicotine, and alcohol should also be avoided, especially close to bedtime (National Sleep Foundation, 2003). Generally the recommendation is that these substances should not be imbibed within four to five hours of sleep, though some sources recommend longer periods of abstinence. Certain foods are also discouraged, including spicy dishes and chocolate, which is known to contain caffeine. Large portions are also not recommended, and it is noted that dietary changes have been linked to some sleep problems.

Exercise is touted as helping to promote good sleep (National Sleep Foundation, 2003). Recommendations include vigorous exercise in the morning or in the late afternoon. Though vigorous exercise is best, for those who this is not a possibility, light exercise is recommended (National Sleep Foundation, 2013). Light exercise, it is noted, is better than none at all. All cardio-based and strength-training exercises, similar to stimulants, should be avoided four to five hours before sleep. Relaxing exercise, like yoga or stretching can be done before bed, however, and may help initiate and maintain a restful night's sleep (National Sleep Foundation, 2003).

Additional sleep hygiene recommendations include ensuring adequate exposure to natural light in the day (National Sleep Foundation, 2003). A key factor in regulating sleep is exposure to light or darkness (National Sleep Foundation, 2016b). For this reason, it is recommended that individuals also avoid sleeping with lights on, as this may trigger the body to stay alert and avoid sleep. Regulating exposure to light is an effective way to keep circadian rhythms in balance.

The National Sleep Foundation (2003) recommends that individuals strive to establish a regular relaxing bedtime routine. This may include drinking warm milk or hot tea, engaging in yoga or stretching, or reading. It is advised that emotionally upsetting conversation or materials should be avoided immediately before bedtime because this can result in excess worry and stress. For individuals who tend to stress and worry, the

National Sleep Foundation (2013) recommends keeping a "worry book" next to their bed. Instead of letting worries fill the mind and disrupt sleep, it is suggested they be noted in the "worry book," to be handled upon waking.

The National Sleep Foundation (2013) reminds the public that the bed should only be used for sleep and sex. This will help strengthen the association in the mind between the bed and sleep. If need be, remove computers, televisions, and any school-related or work materials from the bedroom. Individuals should no watch television, listen to music, or read while in bed. This can confuse the mind as to whether it is supposed to be awake or resting, working or sleeping.

Additionally, it is recommended that the sleep environment be made to be a pleasant and relaxing place (National Sleep Foundation, 2003). The bed should be comfortable, the temperature of the room, not too hot or too cold, and again, lights should be minimal. If you are unable to fall asleep after 15-20 minutes of trying, it is recommended that you get up and go to another room (National Sleep Foundation, 2013). Engage in something relaxing that will help ease you into sleep. Even try something that is boring to put your mind at ease. Recommendations may include reading a phone book. This is not the time to engage in intense physical exercise, watch television, or begin or continue on a major school or work project.

Individuals who experience excessive daytime sleepiness, snoring, and/or those who "stop breathing" in their sleep should contact a health care professional for a sleep apnea screening or a general consultation (National Sleep Foundation, 2013). These specific behaviors are of great concern and should be addressed immediately. Help is available for these things.

Employers

Employers should also consider what they can do to improve the sleep quantity and sleep quality of individuals. Rosekind et al., (2010) recommend that employers adopt workplace flexibility, noting this can contribute to positive lifestyle behaviors, including those associated with improved sleep quantity and sleep quality. Flexibility in general is recommended, though specific recommendations are also made as it relates to scheduling.

Research shows that allowing for "unwinding" time between work and home improves sleep patterns (Rosekind et al., 2010). Adequate rest between work periods and workdays may help to increase unwinding and, in turn, sleep quality. Employers are also urged to set consistent shifts for their employees (Fido & Ghali, 2007; Gold et al., 1992; Lockley, 2007). Variable shift-work is not recommended and is in fact contraindicated based on the research available.

Employers are advised to consider whether the benefits outweigh the drawbacks of having employees work night shifts for their specific company. Johnson et al., (2010) report that persons working nights shifts are more likely to suffer from impaired attention, problems with concentration, as well as difficulties with processing speed, and decreased performance overall. Such troubles are often related to on the job accidents and fiscal losses (Rosekind et al., 2010).

Lockley (2007) as well as Weinger and Ancoli-Israel (2002) also advise that employers reframe from having employees work shifts lasting twelve or more hours. Additionally, having persons remain on-call for extended periods of time is not recommended and contraindicated.

Kessler et al., (2011) and Schultz et al., (2009) recommend that as a last consideration, with respect to scheduling, that employers consider allowing for a greater amount of sick leave overall. It is advised that such action could help lower the occurrence of presenteeism on the job.

Beyond this, Rosekind et al., (2010) recommend that employers partake in educating workers about the importance of sleep. They should also teach employees how to effectively and safely manage sleep loss/fatigue through a variety of strategies such as naps and exercise as discussed above. Kessler et al., (2011) note that when education is not enough, specific referrals may be necessary. They recommend the use of insomnia disease management programs for those suffering from chronic insomnia. Programs are also in place to help people with sleep apnea.

In addition to addressing sleep specifically, Bhui, Dinos, Stansfels, and White (2012) recommend that employers also address the stress their employees may be experiencing at work. Bhui et al., (2012) report that individual interventions like cognitive-behavioral therapy can improve individuals' mental health, while physical activity as an organizational intervention can reduces rates of absenteeism. Gilin Oore et al., (2015) further recommend other organizational interventions, including individual training, work group conflict training, and meditation, to aid in the occurrence and magnitude of workplace conflict. Conflict may be independent of or secondary to stress. Any intervention, however, is likely to be a win for the person and their job.

CONCLUSION

By the numbers, a large majority of people are plagued by problems related to both sleep quantity and quality (National Sleep Foundation, 2008). Problems related to sleep quantity and quality include issues with cognitive performance, as well as concerns related to both physical and mental health (Gaultney & Collins-McNeail, 2009). Specifically, concerns include problems with attention, working memory, learning, decision-making, and general performance. Additionally, problems may be seen as it relates to susceptibility for illness, general wellness or well-being, productivity, injury, mood, emotion regulation, sociability, and stress. These are concerns which may appear in a person's everyday life, but also spillover into a persons' work.

The effects of sleep on cognitive performance and physical and mental health can be significant for companies. Outcomes include decreased productivity of workers, increased absenteeism and presenteeism, lost revenue, and increased on-site accidents, injuries, and deaths.

It is recommended to combat the effects that sleep has on cognitive performance and physical and mental health generally, and in the workplace specifically, that employees and employers take action. Intervention should occur both in the form of defense and offense, as discussed above. Intervention is believed to result in better outcomes for all persons involved.

REFERENCES

Alhola, P., & Polo-Kantola, P. (2007). Sleep deprivation: Impact on cognitive performance. *Neuropsychiatric Disease and Treatment, 3*(5), 553-567. Retrieved from http://www.ncbi.nlm.nih.gov/pmc/articles/PMC2656292/.

Balkin, T. J., Rupp, T., Picchioni, D., & Wesensten, N. J. (2008). Sleep loss and sleepiness: Current issues. *Chest, 134*(3), 653–660. doi:10.1378/chest.08-1064.

Benham, G. (2010). Sleep: An important factor in stress-health models. *Stress & Health: Journal of the International Society for the Investigation of Stress, 26*(3), 204-214. Doi:10.1002/smi.1304.

Bhui, K. S., Dinos, S., Stansfeld, S. A., & White, P. D. (2012). A synthesis of the evidence for managing stress at work: A review of the reviews reporting on anxiety, depression, and absenteeism. *Journal of Environmental & Public Health, 2012*, 1-21. doi:10.1155/2012/515874.

Blaxton, J. M., Bergeman, C. S., Whitehead, B. R., Braun, M. E., & Payne, J. D. (2017). Relationships among nightly sleep quality, daily stress, and daily affect. *The Journals of Gerontology: Series B (Psychological Sciences and Social Sciences), 72*(3), 363-372. doi:10.1093/geronb/gbv060.

Bollinger, T., Bollinger, A., Oster, H., & Solbach, W. (2010). Sleep, immunity, and circadian clocks: A mechanistic model. *Gerontology: International Journal of Experimental, Clinical, Behavioural and Technological Gerontology, 56*(6), 574-580. doi:10.1159/000281827.

Boonstra, T. W., Stins, J. F., Daffertshofer, A. A., & Beek, P. J. (2007). Effects of sleep deprivation on neural functioning: An integrative review. *Cellular and Molecular Life Sciences, 64*(7-8), 934-946. doi:10.1007/s00018-007-6457-8.

Budnick, C. J., & Barber, L. K. (2015). Behind sleepy eyes: Implications of sleep loss for organizations and employees. *Translational Issues in Psychological Science, 1*(1), 89-96. doi:10.1037/tps0000014.

Burgard, S. A., & Ailshire, J. A. (2009). Putting work to bed: Stressful experiences on the job and sleep quality. *Journal of Health and Social Behavior, 50*(4), 476-492. doi:10.1177/002214650905000407.

Burton, W. N., Chen, C.-Y., Schultz, A. B., & Xingquan, L. (2017). Association between employee sleep with workplace health and economic outcomes. *Journal of Occupational & Environmental Medicine, 59*(2), 177-183. doi:10.1097/JOM.0000000000000934.

Cappuccio, F. P., Cooper, D., D'Elia, L., Strazzullo, P., & Miller, M. A. (2011). Sleep duration predicts cardiovascular outcomes: a systematic review and meta-analysis of prospective studies. *European Heart Journal, 32*(12), 1484-1492. doi:10.1093/eurheartj/ehr007.

Cohen, S., & Hoberman, H. M. (1983). Positive events and social supports as buffers of life change stress. *Journal of Applied Social Psychology, 13*(2), 99–125. doi:10.1111/j.1559-1816.1983.tb02325.x.

Cohen, S., Doyle, W., Alper, C., Janicki-Deverts, D., & Turner, R. (2009). Sleep habits and susceptibility to the common cold. *Archives of Internal Medicine, 169*(1), 62-67. doi:10.1001/archinternmed. 2008.505.

Daley, M., Morin, C. M., LeBlanc, M., Grégoire, J. P., Savard, J., & Baillargeon, L. (2009). Insomnia and its relationship to health-care utilization, work absenteeism, productivity and accidents. *Sleep Medicine, 10*(4), 427-438. doi:10.1016/j.sleep.2008.04.005.

Drake, C. L., Roehrs, T., Richardson, G., Walsh, J. K., & Roth, T. (2004). Shift work sleep disorder: Prevalence and consequences beyond that of symptomatic day workers. *SLEEP, 27*(8), 1453-1462. doi:10.1093/ sleep/27.8.1453.

Durmer, J. S., & Dinges, D. F. (2005). Neurocognitive consequences of sleep deprivation. *Seminars in Neurology, 25*(1), 117–129. doi:10.1055/s-0029-1237117.

Evans-Lacko, S., & Knapp, M. (2016). Global patterns of workplace productivity for people with depression: Absenteeism and presenteeism costs across eight diverse countries. *Social Psychiatry and Psychiatric Epidemiology*, *51*(11), 1525-1537. doi:10.1007/s00127-016-1278-4.

Fido, A., & Ghali, A. (2008). Detrimental effects of variable work shifts on quality of sleep, general health and work performance. *Medical Principles & Practice*, *17*(6), 453-457. doi:10.1159/000151566.

Ford, D. E., & Kamerow, D. B. (1989). Epidemiologic study of sleep disturbances and psychiatric disorders. An opportunity for prevention? *JAMA: The Journal of the American Medical Association*, *262*(11), 1479-1484. doi:10.1001/jama.1989. 03430110069030.

Franzen, P. L., Siegle, G. J., & Buysse, D. J. (2008). Relationships between affect, vigilance, and sleepiness following sleep deprivation. *Journal of Sleep Research*, *17*(1), 34-41. doi:10.1111/j.1365-2869.2008.00635.x.

Gaultney, J. F., & Collins-McNeil, J. (2009). Lack of Sleep in the Workplace: What the psychologist-manager should know about sleep. *The Psychologist-Manager Journal*, *12*(2), 132-148. doi:10.1080/10887150902905454.

Gilin Oore, D., Leiter, M. P., & LeBlanc, D. E. (2015). Individual and organizational factors promoting successful responses to workplace conflict. *Canadian Psychology/Psychologie Canadienne*, *56*(3), 301-310. doi:10.1037/cap0000032.

Gold, D. R., Rogacz, S., Bock, N., Tosteson, T. D., Baum, T. M., Speizer, F. E., & Czeisler, C. A. (1992). Rotating shift work, sleep, and accidents related to sleepiness in hospital nurses. *American Journal of Public Health*, *82*(7), 1011-1014. doi:10.2105/AJPH.82.7.1011.

Goldstein, A. N., & Walker, M. P. (2014). The role of sleep in emotional brain function. *The Annual Review of Clinical Psychology*, *10*(1), 679-708. doi:10.1146/annurev-clinpsy-032813-153716.

Gross, J. J., & Jazaieri, H. (2014). Emotion, emotion regulation, and psychopathology: An affective science perspective. *Clinical Psychological Science*, *2*(4), 387-401. doi:10.1177/21677026 14536164.

Guertler, D., Vandelanotte, C., Short, C., Alley, S., Schoeppe, S., & Duncan, M. J. (2015). The association between physical activity, sitting time, sleep duration, and sleep quality as correlates of presenteeism. *Journal of Occupational and Environmental Medicine, 57*(3), 321-328. doi:10.1097/JOM.0000000000000355.

Haack, M., & Mullington, J. M. (2005). Sustained sleep restriction reduces emotional and physical well-being. *Pain, 119*(1-3), 56-64. doi:10.1016/j.pain.2005.09.011.

Harrison, Y., Horne, J. A., & Rothwell, A. (2000). Prefrontal neuropsychological effects of sleep deprivation in young adults- A model for healthy aging? *SLEEP, 23*(8), 1067–1073. doi:10.1093/sleep/23.8.1f.

Harvey, A. G. (2011). Sleep and circadian functioning: Critical mechanisms in the mood disorders? *The Annual Review of Clinical Psychology, 7,* 297-319. doi:10.1146/annurev-clinpsy-032210-104550.

Hilton, M. F., Staddon, Z., Sheridan, J., & Whiteford, H. A. (2009). The impact of mental health symptoms on heavy goods vehicle drivers' performance. *Accident Analysis & Prevention, 41*(3), 453-461. doi:10.1016/j.aap.2009.01.012.

Hirsch Allen, A. J., Park, J. E., Daniele, P. R., Fleetham, J., Frank Ryan, C., & Ayas, N. T. (2016). Obstructive sleep apnea and frequency of occupational injury. *Thorax, 71*(7), 664-666. doi:10.1136/thoraxjnl-2015-207994.

Irwin, M. R. (2015). Why sleep is important for health: A psychoneuroimmunology perspective. *The Annual Review of Psychology, 66,* 143-172. doi:10.1146/annurev-psych-010213-115205.

Johns, G. (2010). Presenteeism in the workplace: A review and research agenda. *Journal of Organizational Behavior, 31*(4), 519-542. doi:10.1002/job.630.

Johnson, A., Brown, K., & Weaver, M. (2010). Sleep deprivation and psychomotor performance among night-shift nurses. *AAOHN Journal: Official Journal of the American Association of Occupational Health Nurses, 58*(4), 147-154. doi:10.3928/08910162-20100316-02.

Johnson, K., Westerfield, W., Momin, S., Phillippi, R., & Naidoo, A. (2009). The direct and indirect costs of employee depression, anxiety, and emotional disorders- An employer case study. *Journal of*

Occupational & Environmental Medicine, 51(5), 564-577. doi:10.1097/JOM.0b013e3181a1fc8.

Jones, K., & Harrison, Y. (2001). Frontal lobe function, sleep loss and fragmented sleep. *Sleep Medicine Reviews, 5*(6), 463–475. doi:10.1053/smrv.2001.0203.

Kessler, R. C., Berglund, P. A., Coulouvrat, C., Hajak, G., Roth, T., Shahly, V., Walsh, J. K. (2011). Insomnia and the performance of US workers: Results from the America insomnia survey. *SLEEP, 34*(9), 1161-1171. doi:10.5665/SLEEP.1230.

Killgore, W. D. S., Lipizzi, E. L., Kamimori, G. H., & Balkin, T. J. (2007). Caffeine effects on risky decision making after 75 hours of sleep deprivation. *Aviation, Space, and Environmental Medicine, 78*(10), 957-962. doi:10.3357/ASEM.2106.2007.

Kim, H. J., Lee, J. H., Choi, K.-G., Park, K.-D., Chung, E. J., Kim, E. J., & Lee, H. W. (2006). Effects of sleep deprivation on attention and working memory in medical residents and interns. *Journal of Sleep Medicine, 3*(2), 85-92. doi:10.13078/jksrs.06015.

Kling, R. N., McLeod, C. B., & Koehoom, M. (2010). Sleep problems and workplace injuries in Canada. *SLEEP, 33*(5), 611-618. doi:10.1093/sleep/33.5.611.

Knutson, K. L., Ryden, A. M., Mander, B. A., & Van Cauter, E. (2006). Role of sleep duration and quality in the risk and severity of type 2 diabetes mellitus. *Archives of Internal Medicine, 166*(16), 1768-1774. doi:10.1001/archinte.166.16.1768.

Kryger, M. H., Roth, T., & Dement, W. C. (2001). Principles and practice of sleep medicine. *Depression and Anxiety, 13*(3), 157. doi:10.1002/da.1030.

Kupfer, D., Harrow, M., & Detre, T. (1969). Sleep patterns and psychopathology. *Acta Psychiatrica Scandinavica, 45*(1), 75–89. doi:10.1111/j.1600-0447.1969.tb06203.x.

Lallukka, T., Kaikkonen, R., Härkänen, T., Kronholm, E., Partonen, T., Rahkonen, O., & Koskinen, S. (2014). Sleep and sickness absence: A nationally representative register-based follow-up study. *SLEEP, 37*(9), 1413-1430. doi:10.5665/sleep.3986.

Leger, D., Massuel, M. A., Metlaine, A., SISYPHE Study Group. (2006). Professional correlates of insomnia. *SLEEP, 29*(2), 171-178. Retrieved from http://www.journalsleep.org/Articles/290207.pdf.

Lerner, D., & Henke, R. M. (2008). What does research tell us about depression, job performance, and work productivity? *Journal of Occupational & Environmental Medicine, 50*(4), 401-410. doi:10.10697/JOM.0b013e31816bae50.

Lim, J., & Dinges, D. F. (2010). A meta-analysis of the impact of short-term sleep deprivation on cognitive variables. *Psychological Bulletin, 136*(3), 375-389. doi:10.1037/a0018883.

Lo, J. C., Groeger, J. A., Santhi, N., Arbon, E. L., Lazar, A. S., Hasan, S., & Shin, Y. (2012). Effects of partial and acute total sleep deprivation on performance across cognitive domains, individuals and circadian phase. *PloS One, 7*(9), 1-16. doi:10.1371/journal.pone.0045987.

Lockley, S. W. (2007). Effects of health care provider work hours and sleep deprivation on safety and performance. *The Joint Commission Journal on Quality and Patient Safety, 33*(11), 7-18. doi:10.1016/S1553-7250(07)33109-7.

McEwen, B. S. (2006). Sleep deprivation as a neurobiologic and physiologic stressor: Allostasis and allostatic load. *Metabolism, 55*(Suppl 2), S20-S23. doi:10.1016/j.metabol.2006.07.008.

Mesas, A. E., Guallar-Castillón, P., López-García, E., León-Muñoz, L. M., Graciani, A., Banegas, J. R., & Rodríguez-Artalejo, F. (2014). Sleep quality and the metabolic syndrome: the role of sleep duration and lifestyle. *Diabetes/Metabolism Research & Reviews, 30*(3), 222-231. doi:10.1002/dmrr.2480.

Meyer, K. A., Wall, M. M., Larson, N. I., Laska, M. N., & Neumark-Sztainer, D. (2012). Sleep duration and BMI in a sample of young adults. *Obesity, 20*(6), 1279-1287. doi:10.1038/oby.2011.381.

National Sleep Foundation. (2003). Sleep hygiene. Retrieved from https://sleepfoundation.org/ask-the-expert/sleep-hygiene.

National Sleep Foundation. (2005). 2005 Adult sleep habits and styles. Retrieved from http://www.sleepfoundation.org/article/sleep-america-polls/2005-adult-sleep-habits-and-styles.

National Sleep Foundation. (2008). 2008 Sleep in America poll. Retrieved from https://sleepfoundation.org/sites/default/files/2008%20POLL%20SOF.PDF.

National Sleep Foundation. (2013). International bedroom poll first to explore sleep differences among six countries. Retrieved from http://sleepfoundation.org/media-center/press-release/national-sleep-foundation-2013-international-bedroom-poll.

National Sleep Foundation. (2015). Sleep and pain. Retrieved from https://sleepfoundation.org/sleep-polls-data/sleep-in-america-poll/2015-sleep-and-pain.

National Sleep Foundation. (2016a). How much sleep do we really need? Retrieved from https://sleepfoundation.org/how-sleep-works/how-much-sleep-do-we-really-need.

National Sleep Foundation. (2016b). Lights out for a good night's sleep. Retrieved from https://sleepfoundation.org/sleep-news/lights-out-good-nights-sleep.

Nyer, M., Farabaugh, A., Fehling, K., Soskin, D., Holt, D., Papakostas, G. I., Mischoulon, D. (2013). Relationship between sleep disturbance and depression, anxiety, and functioning in college students. *Depression and Anxiety*, *30*(9), 873-880. doi:10.1002/da.22064.

Ohayon, M. M., Caulet, M., & Lemoine, P. (1998). Comorbidity of mental and insomnia disorders in the general population. *Comprehensive Psychiatry*, *39*(4), 185-197. doi:10.1016/S0010-440X(98)90059-1.

Palmer, C. A., & Alfano, C. A. (2017). Sleep and emotion regulation: An organizing, integrative review. *Sleep Medicine Reviews*, *31,* 6-16. doi:10.1016/j.smrv.2015.12.006.

Patel, S. R., Malhotra, A., Gao, X., Hu, F. B., Neuman, M. I., & Fawzi, W. W. (2012). A prospective study of sleep duration and pneumonia risk in women. *SLEEP*, *35*(1), 97-101. doi:10.5665/sleep.1594.

Philip, P., Sagaspe, P., Prague, M., Tassi, P., Capelli, A., Bioulac, B., Taillard, J. (2012). Acute versus chronic partial sleep deprivation in middle-aged people: Differential effect on performance and sleepiness. *SLEEP,* *35*(7), 997-1002. doi:10.5665/sleep.1968.

Pilcher, J., Band, D., Odle-Dusseau, H., & Muth, E. (2007). Human performance under sustained operations and acute sleep deprivation conditions: toward a model of controlled attention. *Aviation, Space, and Environmental Medicine, 78*(5 Suppl), B15-B24. Retrieved from https://www.ncbi.nlm.nih.gov/pubmed/17547301.

Pilcher, J. J., & Huffcutt, A. J. (1996). Effects of sleep deprivation on performance: A meta-analysis. *SLEEP, 19*(4), 318-326. doi:10.1093/sleep/19.4.318.

Riemann, D., Berger, M., & Voderholzer, U. (2001). Sleep and depression-Results from psychobiological studies: An overview. *Biological Psychology, 57*(1-3), 67-103. doi:10.1016/S0301-0511(01)00090-4.

Rosekind, M. R., Gregory, K. B., Mallis, M. M., Brandt, S. L., Seal, B., & Lerner, D. (2010). The cost of poor sleep: Workplace productivity loss and associated costs. *Journal of Occupational and Environmental Medicine, 52*(1), 91-98. doi:10.1097/JOM.0b013e3181c78c30.

Rosen, I. M., Gimothy, P. A., Shea, J. A., & Bellini, L. (2006). Evolution of sleep quantity, sleep deprivation, mood disturbances, empathy, and burnout among interns. *Academic Medicine, 81*(1), 82-85. doi: 10.1097/00001888-200601000-00020.

Schultz, A. B., Chen, C.-Y., & Edington, D. W. (2009). The cost and impact of health conditions on presenteeism to employers: A review of the literature. *PharmacoEconomics, 27*(5), 365-378. doi: 10.2165/00019053-200927050-00002.

Scott, L. D., Arslanian-Engoren, C., & Engoren, M. C. (2014). Association of sleep and fatigue with decision regret among critical care nurses. *American Journal of Critical Care, 23*(1), 13-23. doi: 10.4037/ajcc2014191.

Simon, G. E., Barber, C., Birnbaum, H. G., Frank, R. G., Greenberg, P. E., Rose, R. M., Kessler, R. C. (2001). Depression and work productivity: The comparative cost of treatment versus nontreatment. *Journal of Occupational & Environmental Medicine, 43*(1), 2-9. doi:10.1097/00043764-200101000-00002.

Sleep Health Foundation. (2011). Common myths about sleep. Retrieved from http://sleephealthfoundation.org.au/files/pdfs/Sleep-Myths.pdf.

Staner, L. (2010). Comorbidity of insomnia and depression. *Sleep Medicine Reviews, 14*(1), 35-46. doi:10.1016/j.smrv.2009.09.003.

Steptoe, A., Peacey, V., & Wardle, J. (2006). Sleep duration and health in young adults. *Archives of Internal Medicine, 166*(16), 1689-1692. doi:10.1001/archinte.166.16.1689.

Tavernier, R., & Willoughby, T. (2015). A longitudinal examination of the bidirectional association between sleep problems and social ties at university: The mediating role of emotion regulation. *Journal of Youth and Adolescence, 44*(2), 317-330. doi:10.1007/s10964-014-0107-x.

Tennant, C. (2001). Work-related stress and depressive disorders. *Journal of Psychosomatic Research, 51*(5), 697-704. doi:10.1016/S0022-3999(01)00255-0.

Turner, T. H., Drummond, S. A., Salamat, J. S., & Brown, G. (2007). Effects of 42 hr of total sleep deprivation on component processes of verbal working memory. *Neuropsychology, 21*(6), 787-795. doi:10.1037/0894-4105.21.6.787.

Uehli, K., Mehta, A., Miedinger, D., Hug, K., Scindler, C., Holsboer-Trachsler, E., Künzli, N. (2013). Sleep problems and work injuries: A systematic review and meta-analysis. *Sleep Medicine Reviews, 18*(1), 61-73. doi:10.1016/j.smrv.2013.01.004.

Uehli, K., Miedinger, D., Bingisser, R., Dürr, S., Holsboer-Trachsler, E., Maier, S., Leuppi, J. D. (2014). Sleep problems and work injury types: A study of 180 patients in a Swiss emergency department. *Swiss Medical Weekly, 143.* doi:10.4414/smw.2013.13902.

Van Dongen, H., Maislin, G., Mullington, J., & Dinges, D. (2003). The cumulative cost of additional wakefulness: dose-response effects on neurobehavioral functions and sleep physiology from chronic sleep restriction and total sleep deprivation. *SLEEP, 26*(2), 117-126. doi:10.1093/sleep.26.2.117.

Waghorn, H., Chant, D., White, P., & Whiteford, H. (2005). Disability, employment, and work performance among people with ICD-10 anxiety disorders. *Australian and New Zealand Journal of Psychiatry, 39*(1-2), 55-66. doi:10.1111/j.1440-1614.2005.01510.x.

Wallace, D. D., Boynton, M. H., & Lytle, L. A. (2017). Multilevel analysis exploring the links between stress, depression, and sleep problems among two-year college students. *Journal of American College Health*, *65*(3), 187-196. doi:10.1080/07448481.2016.1269111.

Weinger, M. B., & Ancoli-Israel, S. (2002). Sleep deprivation and clinical performance. *JAMA, 287*(8), 955-957. doi:10.1001/jama.287.8.955.

Yoo, S. S., Gujar, N., Hu, P., Jolesz, F. A., & Walker, M. P. (2007). The human emotional brain without sleep- A prefrontal amygdala disconnect. *Current Biology, 17*(20), R877–R878. doi:10.1016/j.cub.2007.08.007.

In: Advances in Business and Management ISBN: 978-1-53612-615-0
Editor: William D. Nelson © 2017 Nova Science Publishers, Inc.

Chapter 3

THE RESILIENCE OF THE INFORMAL SECTOR IN THE CONTEXT OF MAJOR WIDESPREAD CRISES IN DEVELOPING COUNTRIES: EVIDENCE FROM AN AFRICAN COUNTRY'S INFORMAL SECTOR

Alidou Ouedraogo, PhD
Department of Business,
University of Moncton, Moncton, NB, Canada

ABSTRACT

Very small companies including informal sector, are confronted with recurrent crises, sometimes-brutal ones such as floods that menace their survival, growth, and development thereby necessitating the capacity to be resilient. In fact, without unemployment benefits, insurance, or even family or institutional support, certain entrepreneurs disappear while others rebound from disasters and become even stronger. Such a reality leads to our research question: "What are the factors that determine the ability of the informal sector to endure large scale crises?" This is the core of our research, which, by using a qualitative methodology, we seek to understand the factors that define business resilience in the face of large-scale crises. The main results are considered as follows: (i) business resilience depends in part upon the level of resources prior to the crisis, (ii) the dynamism of the entrepreneur, (iii) the vitality of the activity sector, (iv) the importance of the resources allocated after the crisis, and (v) the solidarity of family and friends when it comes to moral support.

Keywords: informal sector, major crisis, resilience, developing country

1. Introduction

Understandably, the ability to rebound after a major crisis is a strong sign of performance. Companies used to confront increasingly with crises that affect their performance, competitiveness, and even their survival. Natural disasters that are often the cause of very small business failures are increasing in frequency and intensity. Their catastrophic effects create even greater uncertainty. The only certainty is that we live in an uncertain world.

Between 1901 and 1910, 82 catastrophes numbered worldwide; between 2003 and 2012, they climbed to over 4,000 disasters, 50 times that of the 20th century (Report on sustainable development, 2014). For us, a catastrophe a sudden event that causes very great trouble or destruction.

The consequences of natural disasters are extreme devastation. "Worldwide phenomena such as climatic changes and numerous economic disruptions due to food shortages and energy quagmires show that the progress made in the reduction of poverty and human development can be rapidly wiped out or annulled by an economic shock, a natural disaster, or a political conflict[1]." The superscript one should appear after the quotation mark.

According to the "Centre européen de pévention du risque d'inondation" (CEPRI), "… the potential loss of economic activity varies from 40% to 60% of the total dollar value caused by flooding." (CEPRI, 2012, page 9).

---

[1] UN Secretary General report on reviewing and reinforcing social development in the contemporary world presented during the 53rd session of the Committee for Social Development held in New York from February 4-13 2015, page 19.

If this percentage of economic loss appears high, the loss is much worse at the small local business level where a single catastrophe can wipe out a large part of a small company's assets or even result in a total write-off. Such a loss can in turn affect larger companies that rely on local suppliers or locally produced goods thus causing a cascading effect upon the worldwide supply chain, one consequence of global markets that underscores the vulnerability of companies throughout the chain. A study conducted in 2011 by *Basic Capabilities Index (BCI)* in 62 countries showed that 85% of companies affected by at least one interruption in their supply chain. They caused mainly by natural (climatic) disasters (51%) and by earthquakes (20%) in Japan and New Zealand.

Africa hasn't been spared such crises with continuing conflicts, terrorist attacks, Ebola virus outbreaks, natural disasters, and humanitarian disasters that strike individuals, communities, and companies largely controlled by the informal sector. According to Mr. Torres of OIT,[2] the formal sector accounts for only 5% of worldwide employment opportunities. These crises place a new burden on the continent and hamper its social and economic development despite the preventive measures and crisis management programs implemented by governments.

Helen Clark, administrator for the United Nations Development Program, states unequivocally that: *"Regardless of the effectiveness of the inherent risk reduction measures, crises will continue to be felt with potentially destructive consequences. It is therefore vital to reinforce the ability to be properly prepared for disasters and the means to overcome their impact in order to help the communities affected to better manage and cope with the inevitable shock."*[3] Such a perspective called, appropriately, "resilience." The same report (p. 5) continues: *"any means or program to ensure the continuation of human development must be based on resilience. The essential goal of resilience is to ensure that the State, its communities, and world institutions work towards a means of automatically protecting people."* Hence, resilience is now at the very core

---

[2] Report dated February 6, 2015 by the Commission for Social Development during its 53rd session.
[3] Report on human development 2014.

of policy and strategy planning for socio-economic development or simply for human development, thus providing further thought for researchers. Resilience represents the third of four priority actions of the new 2016-2030.

The collapse of the companies in the informal sector, already marginalized, could result in serious socio-economic crises among the populations in developing countries; whereas, if they are resilient, they could improve the well-being of the populations they serve and contribute to the sustainable development of their country.

Previous studies on resilience, conducted notably by Weick (1993), Ouedraogo & Boyer (2012), Chaabouni (2014), Duquenois (2011), Bellache (2010), Bernard (2016), Bullough (2013) and Bullough (2014) concentrated on specific aspects of individual, entrepreneurial, and organizational themes. When they examined companies, generally they chose large corporate entities, along with some small and medium-sized businesses (SMB). Rarely did they examine micro-companies and never specifically in this sector. These companies because of a lack of sufficient resources and no risk protection insurance are seriously affected. Therefore, the relevancy of our research question is clear: "What are the factors that determine the ability of informal sector companies to be resilient when faced with a major crisis?"

Our research objective is to understand the means or the tools needed to help companies rebound after a major crisis. As such, we seek to determine and explain the factors of resilience. A factor is an element that contributes to a certain result uniquely tied to resilience in our current context.

Factors of resilience known, mastered and diffused will be of considerable interest for not only a company's owners and managers, but also useful in reducing the thousands of workers migrating from countries in crisis to developed countries. These workers seek to establish roots and sometimes even risk their lives to begin anew. Our research project will offer some practical applications to economic partners on how to manage very small companies (VSC), notably those that comprise the informal sector. Specifically, on how to assist governments in formulating socio-economic development policies, on how to help technical and financial partners (TFP) wishing to lend their advice to the informal sector, in short, on how to help owners learn how to survive a crisis. Our research will contribute to understanding the factors of resilience.

To accomplish these aims, we must first define the key concepts and the theoretical framework. We shall then present our methodology, our principle results, followed by a discussion, the contributions and limits of our research, and concluding observations.

2. REVIEW OF THE SECONDARY LITERATURE

We begin our review of the secondary literature with the definition of the following concepts: informal sector, crisis, major widespread crises, and resilience.

2.1. Definitions

2.1.1. Informal Sector

After almost half a century after its formulation, the informal sector is a dynamic reality but a very elusive concept.

While conducting research in Ghana in the 1970s for the International Labour Office (ILO), the anthropologist Keit Hart identified for the first time a new socio-economic work environment, which he referred to as an "informal sector," in other words, a non-regulated sector that is defined according to the following 7 criteria:

1. Ease of start-up;
2. Non-regulated competitive markets;
3. A family owned business;
4. Operations on a small scale;
5. Use of local resources;

6. Adapted work methods that are labour intensive; and
7. Training acquired outside the school system.

Since the initial adoption of the informal sector concept, its application has evolved considerably. By 1989, Williard (1989) counted 27 different terminologies used in various studies to identify such an entrepreneurship: unofficial economy, unregistered, undeclared, marginal, invisible, *et cetera*. Five years later, De Soto, H. (1994) used the term "popular economy." Since 2002, the International Labour Office (ILO) retained the concept of an informal economy (ILO, 2014). In any case, insofar as our research is concerned, we shall use the definition of the "Institut National de la Statistique et de la Démographie" (INSD) which defines it as follows: "the total number of production units (PU) devoid of any administrative registration or formal written accounting."[4]

Meanwhile, it noted that the supporters of the dual theory (who saw it more as an epiphenomenon destined to disappear with modern evolution) became aware that an inverse effect was true. The informal sector had, spread in fact, throughout the world.

Moreover, looking at developing countries classified according to the ILO, and according to the latest estimates, non-agricultural employment in the informal sector represents the following: 82% of the total employment in South Asia; 66% in Sub-Saharan Africa; 65% in Eastern Asia and South-East Asia (excluding China); 51% in Latin America; and 10% in Eastern Europe and Central Asia (ILO, 2014).

One should note that the informal economy exists throughout the developed world with the estimates for 2013 as follows: 18.4% of GDP in the European Union (EU-27),[5] and 8.6% in Australia and Canada, Japan and New Zealand according to (ILO, 2014, p 9).

---

[4] A production unit is either a brick and mortar establishment in which the economic activity is conducted (boutique, store, shop, etc.) or an itinerant establishment in an appropriate local that shifts location (public works, home business, *et cetera*).
[5] "UE-27" designates the 27 member European Union.

2.2. Definition of a Major Crisis

Before proceeding to define a major crisis, we shall first define the noun *crisis* and its many qualitative descriptions. The adjective *major* includes more severe types that informal sector owners must face.

2.2.1. Crisis

The using of the concept of crisis depends on the context, the inherent disciplines, and by various authors. Divergent points of view even surface between researchers in the fields of Sciences and Management. For some, a crisis is an abnormal event that is unforeseen and destabilizing for the organisation. For Pearson and Clair (1988) and Weick (1988), an unexpected event threatens the existence of the organisation.

According to certain researchers, a crisis is not spontaneous but rather follows a path that eventually leads towards a breakdown in activities. Thus, Lagadec (1999) and Rosenthal (2003) talk of a rupture, not as an "unforeseen" crisis but rather an "unexpected" one. Reilly (1993), for whom crises are more likely dangerous and may produce toxic ruptures that threaten the survival of the organization, also shares this vision. Pauchant (1988) defines a crisis as an accumulation of probable events at the level of a department or of an entire organization that could halt present and future operations.

Finally, other researchers concentrate on the particular difficulties caused by a crisis and the urgency that it creates. Volpi (2003) defines a crisis as a difficult period where economic, political, and ideological aspects all come into play and felt as a paroxysmal onslaught during which time one must resolve numerous contradictions. It is characterize by an emergency, a resulting destabilisation, and a direct consequence on vital interests. However, what defines precisely a major crisis?

2.2.2. Major Crisis

According to Dautun (2007), a major crisis occurs when there is a disturbance of a land mass, territory vulnerable to some event be it accidental, or imposed three conditions must be meet:

- A geographic territory, with organizations at risk and vulnerable to a catastrophe;
- One or a series of events that initiated the crisis was caused by a natural disaster, an industrial accident, or by an act of terrorism;
- Aggravating circumstances whether they be technical, human, or managerial.

Analysed under these circumstances, both crises and catastrophes fall under the same terminology in that a crisis is not necessarily a catastrophe and vice versa. In our research framework, we retain the concept of major crisis as best described by the literature we shall now examine resilience.

2.3. Emergence of the Concept of Resilience and Its Etymology

Before delving into the definitions of resilience, it is useful to research its origins and historical development, a difficult task even for seasoned experts' familiar with *a fortiori*. According to Theis (2006), if the scientific study of resilience began recently in the 1970s, the concept has existed for a long time according to Vannistendael (1994) who places its origins "as old as humanity." This same theory is shared by the historian Gianfransco (1999), who, after examining mythology, concludes that "if resilience is recent, reality is, nevertheless, quite old."

The American Emmy Werner, who held a doctorate in child psychology from the University of Nebraska, altered modern research on the concept of resilience. She first used the term "resilience" (1989-1992) while she was analysing the data of a longitudinal research project that initially had nothing to do with resilience. In order to evaluate the consequences of long-term stress during prenatal and perinatal periods, she selected a focus group from 1955 and followed it for more than 30 years. In total, she followed her sample group of 698 children belonging to various ethnic groups from mainly disadvantaged areas on the Island of Kauai in the Hawaiian Islands. From this population sample, 201 children were "vulnerable but invincible" because of numerous risk factors. The team was surprised to learn that one-third (⅓) of the children at risk never underwent any particular problem during their childhood. They evolved normally without any therapeutic action and became happy competent adults. At the same time, numerous high-risk children who did undergo problems during their childhood were capable of rebounding during adolescence or by adulthood. Werner used the word "resilience" for the first time to qualify this group of children. Emmy Werner, known as the "mother" of resilience,[6] remarked that the children had a least one attentive teacher that listened to them, encouraged their participation, and described to what extent the children had turned their school into a "second home."

2.3.1. Resilience - Multidimensional and Multidisciplinary

Resilience entered mainstream terminology in fields such as sociology, anthropology, psychology, ecology, physics, and management sciences. It also appeared in numerous world publications such as research articles and theses treating diverse subjects. We can now provide a few examples, certainly not exhaustive, that illustrate the definition of resilience.

Organizational resilience is the ability of an organization to face adversity (Liu, 2012). In management terms, resilience is the ability of a company to overcome the impact of a cessation of activities and the ability to concentrate its efforts on continuing to supply the required services Kadige (2009).[7]

These definitions show the importance of the concept and especially its heterogeneity but they do not take into account the specificity of our informal companies. Therefore, we propose the following definition for resilience of a company in the informal sector: *the ability of a company in the informal sector to survive, even thrive, following a major upheaval or a crisis resulting in partial or total losses of one or more key (material, human, financial ...) resources.*" This definition considers the context of the crises and defines resilience not only as a return to normality. It also considers different situations the company faces post-crisis such as

---

[6] www.akadem.org consulted on 15 January 2016 à 17h30 which bibliographical style are you using?
[7] www.lecercledusavoir.fr/cariboost2. Your citation method is inconsistent – in font as well.

collapse, survival, a return to pre-crisis conditions, and an increase or expansion of the state of affairs either through the continuity of its activities or by the dissolution of the existing organization as it moves to new activities.

2.3.2. Literature Review -- Resilience

"Resilience is a multidimensional characteristic that varies with the context, time, age, gender, cultural origin, and as well as with the same individual faced with different circumstances in life" Connors and Davison (2003) as quoted by Risquez (2013, p 46).

According to Weick (1993), four sources of resilience have identified, namely: i) maintaining a virtual role if the organization collapses; ii) adopting an attitude of calm whereby the organization maintains a reasonable distance from some experience, beliefs, and its present. Then, iii) maintaining the interaction between members of the organization; iv) and creating the improvisation that is essential to finding a solution to the crisis.

Our research is part of the published scientific works based on crisis management and thematic methodology conducted by the following researchers. Begin (2010) examined organizational resilience using a case study based on a family business. Coutu (2002) studied the dimensions of organizational resilience. William (2009) entitled his work "Organizational resilience: Concepts and training activities." Chaabouni and Very (2014) presented work on resilience of companies during periods of long-term crisis. Finally, Teneau (2011), who studied the effects of compassion on organizational resilience. All of these researchers employed important points of view but they did not specifically look at the resilience of companies in the informal sector following a major catastrophe.

Authors have suggested many approaches. Altintas and Royer (2008) identified four sources of resilience by studying the Mann Gulch fire that resulted in the deaths of most of the firefighters Weick (1993). These are:

1. Maintaining an automatic virtual command center in case the existing organizational structure collapses, hence an essential need for leadership.
2. Maintaining a wise course of action by keeping "a reasonable distance from one's beliefs, experience, and history to avoid errors in interpretation.
3. Interaction between members to maintain a collective cognitive structure.
4. Improvisation that is necessary to find a solution that will lead to the resolution of the event.

Our research framework includes the theoretical approach to resilience based on a family enterprise founded in 1826 (Begin, 2010) and the resilience of Tunisian entrepreneurs after long-term crises (Chaabouni, 2014). In this domain, resilience relies on three overlapping and interconnected dimensions, namely:

1. An ability to absorb the unexpected or endure a catastrophe by allowing the company to continue functioning and by mobilising internal and external resources. In the case of family companies, moral support still considered a "toxic handler"[8] where the financial support of family members represents a potential legal dilemma during turbulent periods.
2. An ability for renewal by which the company can re-invent itself in the future and find new solutions whether for new activities, modifying the organization, or re-thinking its business model. This ability for renewal is a proactive ability by relying on the willingness of management to seize the opportunities. In terms of resilience, this means emerging even stronger after the crisis.
3. An ability to acquire knowledge granting the opportunity to become stronger by adding to his personal experiences (Weick and

---

[8] The toxic handler is a concept used by Gilles TENEAU in his thesis on "Compassion in organizational resilience - the contribution of the toxic handler," location?, publisher? May 2008.

Sutcliffe, 2007) and to learn from these lessons and experiences to better anticipate or react to future crises. However, many researchers recognize that this ability is difficult to observe. Nevertheless, our research on crisis management in uncertainties situations has allowed us to note that this method offers considerable weight when the crisis is of external origin such as the floods of September 1, 2009 in Ouagadougou (Burkina Faso), notably with personnel on the institutional level.

According to Madni, (2009), there are four axes of organizational resilience:

1. Avoid disruptions -- this axis results in a proactive style that aims to anticipate uncertainty.
2. Resist disruptions -- this axis channels the robust business system to absorb the shock without modifying balance or equilibrium.
3. Adaptation -- this axis takes the flexibility of the system to reconfigure itself vis-à-vis the function of the pressure exerted.
4. Recovery - the ability of the system to find, as best as possible, an equilibrium close to that which existed before the crisis.

3. METHODOLOGY

The resilience of companies in developing countries, especially in the informal sector, is very recent and the pertinent literature is rare. We had decided to use extensively the existing literature and to consult with experts, partners, and other people in the field. Instead, we decided to choose owner-managers whose companies existed at the time of the 2009 of September 1 crisis. Despite the relatively long interval of 7 years, the victims seriously affected by the crisis hold all of these memories with a certain exactitude in their minds and are able to relate verbally the events as they happened with no ambiguity whatsoever. Considering the qualitative nature of the research, the sample size is not necessarily important; according to Mongeau (2009) p. 94, the sample size is determined by the saturation point. In other words, "... when additional interviews no longer enrich the chosen model ... in practice, 7 to 12 interviews generally allows us to reach this saturation."

In consideration of the above, we chose a field sample composed of two very distinct groups:

1. The first group is comprised of experts having a deep knowledge of very small informal sector companies and a deep understanding of the crises and obstacles that they must overcome.
2. The second group represents four entrepreneurs whose companies either rebounded or disappeared because of the flooding of 2009 of September 1.

3.1. Data Collection

An interview guide have been elaborated for each group to standardize the interviews and it was pre-tested before being administered to those responsible in the informal sector, namely, the administrators, the technical and financial partners, the support system personnel, and the company owners themselves.

3.2. Data Collection Method

Data collected using two methods: Direct observation and face- to-face interviews using our standardized guide. We obtained the means and the permission to contact them and to schedule a meeting according to their availability. The interviews took place from June 21 to June 27, 2016 at the office, business locale, or home, and at flexible times whether day or night to meet their needs. These meetings lasted on average one hour with numerous local interruptions. The information obtained was voice recorded with permission to ensure accuracy.

Data Collection, Treatment and Qualitative Analysis Using the Software QSR NVIVO 9.

The collected data then transferred to a word processor, Word 2013, before sent as input data to the QSR NVivo 9 IT software, an appropriate choice for analysing qualitative data. After the data crunching, we reviewed the output to be certain that it was exhaustive before creating the parent and child nodes.

We then encoded the answers to the existing nodes. The primary question encoded under the parent node, the secondary questions encoded under the child nodes, and all the answers transferred to their respective places. We then exported the node contents to Word, which allowed us to synthesize the answers by considering the node hierarchy.

4. Results

In terms of results, we can state that there is a strong desire of informal sector entrepreneurs' to participate of the survey following the different factors of resilience:

4.1. Analysis of the Resilience Factors of Informal Sector Companies

A number of factors contribute to the demise of companies, most notably natural disasters. Therefore, it is very important to understand the factors that favour their rebound following a crisis. The following factors been identified as resilience factors in the informal sector.

4.1.1. Resilience Factor Linked to Strategy

Most persons interviewed believe that entrepreneurs in the informal sector have strategies that can allow them to survive catastrophes and even thrive. According to Lautier (1994), p 59, strategy "... is based on a long term project that requires taking into account a conflicting environment."

Consequently, their strategy relies on *"... directing their energies to compete in a new marketplace, diversifying, and diversifying their point of sales. Imagination is essential to anticipate the future"* [emphasis added?]. To survive and to compete, «They must create new partnerships, and change their sector of activity, all of which requires diversification.

However, a minority of people believe that most informal sector companies do not have a crisis strategy. These people believe that companies in the informal sector have no official structures, therefore, no strategy to even develop a durable resilience policy. If a strategy does exist, it is one purely for survival, and not a true company strategy since they operate day to day."

Due to the specificity of these companies characterized, in part, by the absence of a structure yet satisfactorily meeting the immediate and local needs of their clients, each individual company develops its own initiatives to quickly manage crises where in a purely techno-scientific sense, the word "strategy" may not apply.

4.1.2. Resilience Factors Due to the Knowledge of the Risk and Known Methods to Avoid It

All of the onsite workers interviewed were unanimous in recognizing that the knowledge of the risks allowed the informal sector company to be resilient thereby *helping to reduce the risks and favour the development of the activities of the company.* "... the better we understand the risks, the better we can prevent them, possibly even overcoming them." How do you cite properly interview material?

> "If you work in a particular field, you must know that there are certain risks since you yourself may one day disappear or fall sick or a disaster may arrive with all its problems. If you know the risks, you can study the opportunities in other sites or in other fields of work. You diversify your activities in other fields or place of work."

4.1.3. Resilience Factors Due to the Entrepreneur or the Owner

According to all persons interviewed, the resilience of an informal sector company depends on the entrepreneur himself. He makes the decisions and takes all the risks. *"The more dynamic and entrepreneurial he is, the greater are the possibilities that he will rebound since he knows how to nurture relationships."*

"The activity that I manage is one which feeds my family. This is my life's work; that is why I must take it seriously and follow through, and not be foolhardy." "Even if you did not go to school, you must admit that if your colleague has formal education, and he has a house and a vehicle, you must have them as well and your food, lodging, and transportation all stem from your work. This is no laughing matter because you must anticipate in order succeeding."

4.1.4. Resilience Factors Related to Resources Owned Before the Crisis

Almost all those interviewed agreed that the resources available before the catastrophe counted as a resilience factor. As justification, they stated:

"If the company has a high credit rating or standing, then all that is needed is to reassign or infuse new resources to kick-start the company's activities …."
"With large-scale activities, the company can survive; if the resources are too low, owners must find someone who has the means to help them overcome the current dilemma. That person must provide the owner with available credit. If the State intervenes to help everyone, it will surely be in default of payment. Other institutions such as FASI and FAARF exist for such reasons."

A smaller group believes that the existing resources before the catastrophe are insufficient because, though one can have the resources; one may not know how to use them to rebound. For this group, it's the vision and the resources after the catastrophe that allows a company to rebound. *"Money is important but it's mainly the vision that allows the owner to develop the manpower and the resources. Therefore, money by itself is not exclusive but it may facilitate resilience."*

4.1.5. Resilience Factor Related to the Type of Activity

All our field experts agreed unanimously that the resilience of a company is a function of the activity domain insofar as whether there are highly perishable activities. *"For example, an entrepreneur who sells cement or flour is ruined financially (bankruptcy) in case of a flood because of his economic mix compared to someone who sells construction material or parts."*

> "For example, a telephone salesman who returns home with his merchandise is less vulnerable that car a salesman who must keep his stock exposed in a flood zone."

4.1.6. Resilience factors related to the environment

When examining the environment in a broad sense (physical, socio-economic, political, institutional, legal framework), the field players are unanimous in agreeing that it represents a resilience factor that needs to be studied. *"The environment can represent many opportunities to rebound. It may offer support, a reduction in tax rates, an extension of a deadline, or a chance to obtain other loans that allows you to quickly re-establish your business."*

"It may assist disaster-stricken companies in obtaining aid from politicians and organizations, along with advice on how to best jumpstart your activities."

Nevertheless, a key player observes that everything is connected. *"In order to promote a favourable and economical environmental development with incentives to rebound after a disaster, we must take into account the political context, difficulties with legal texts, the environment, landscaping, and any other factors present at the time."*

4.1.7. Resilience Factors Related to Legal Formalization

Most our sample group interviewed agree that the legal formalization of a company is a resilience factor since it is structuring with a certain visibility and a guarantee that grants access to public markets. The owner has something to show to financial institutions with which he can more easily obtain the funds to rebound after a catastrophe. "If the company is formalized, it can access public markets where friendship s paramount to securing contracts. It is not that beneficiaries work harder than others do but more a network of contacts, something the informal sector must do to hire sub-contractors in order to earn a living:

> "If we know the existence of a particular company, we can better follow it throughout its evolution. Like a doctor overseeing a patient, a well-known and highly valuable company has a better chance at survival."

However, a minority of our experts believe that formalization would not guarantee resilience. They state that formalization only results in obtaining the necessary documentation to prove you own a business. All depends on the abilities of the business owner. "Formalization only means having administrative documents; and, if we do not have a sound business model, it will lead to losses. You need to have business acumen. There is a time delay between managing the business and actually placing an order. We must have modern management tools." Another participant also adds; *"We may have certain advantages but taxes are merciless."*

4.1.8. The Most Determinant Factor for Resilience

There are several views regarding which factor is the most determinant when considering resilience. "If the owner is not intelligent, if a disaster strikes, he will not be able to rebound quickly and he will not be the type to seek formalization."

> "Everything revolves around him. If he is not inclined to do something, even if resources are placed at his disposal, it will be in vain."

A minority believes that it is the available resources owned before the crisis, that is the most important. In their view, if considerable resources are available before the crisis than the company will rebound more easily.

However, for another minority, it is the resources available after the catastrophe that matters. In the informal sector, some owners hoard their finances at home or at their workplace; consequently, I can lose all our resources during the catastrophe, a habit that would hinder any rebuilding effort.

This exploratory analysis, realized by using the software NVIVO, allows us to state that we have handled rich and varied qualitative data,

The Resilience of the Informal Sector in the Context ...   111

both before and after a crisis, to understand better the resilience factors of very small companies when they undergo major crises. Thus, we can state that Burkina does not yet have a unified definition of the informal sector. There exists an institutional framework but no specific policy for the informal sector. There are numerous determinant factors for the collapse of informal companies, but the statements that we collected from field manager/owners corroborate, in part or in whole, our analysis. Company resilience in the informal sector depends on strategy, the field of activity, the environment, on the owner or manager, formalization, the understanding of the risks and measures to avoid them, and the existing resources before the crisis.

4.1.9. From Theory to Practice: Four Case Studies on Firm Resilience

4.1.9.1. Resilience of an Informal Sector Firm: Survival of the Fittest

The interviews with the company owners in the informal sector held at their place of work or any other location chosen by them at their convenience. They interrupted by customer sales and coloured by strong emotions. The mere recollection of the events that transpired was quite vivid and clear as if it had happened yesterday. The memories of such traumatic events, even 7 years later, produced strong emotions and elicited empathy and compassion from all of us. A transcript of the four interviews follows.

4.1.9.2. Summary of Case Study, Resilient Company N°1

History: My name is Mrs. Z C, 53 years old, married, mother of four children. After 7 years of training on the Ivory Coast, I opened my own beauty salon at Ouagadougou in 1987. My business registered with the government commerce department and I had a dozen employees and others in training. I paid myself a salary of 200,000 of local CFA currency per month with a total profit of approx. 1,000,000 of local CFA currency ($ 2500) per year. After 3 years of training, I would give those apprentices in training their "accreditation" and equipment to start their own business. I trained many whom then start working for themselves and earning an honourable life. It was during this time that the flood of 1 September 2009 occurred.

Consequences: In the salon, more than 30 complete sets of garments and other losses recorded. In the yard, two homes destroyed resulting in material and financial losses of more than 2,000,000 million of local CFA currency ($ 5000) of tontine annuity. It was really a deplorable situation. Unfortunately, I received no benefits or help from anyone.

Resilience strategy: Re-starting activity made possible by a credit of 1,800,000 of CFA currency ($ 4500) from Ecobank by virtue of a lien on a title of land and the progressive reimbursement of the rest owed due to economic gains.

Post-crisis situation and perspectives: After the floods, the salon stayed closed for 3 days after which I re-opened to resume my work. Two years later, I forced to convert my salon into a restaurant. Presently I have 7 to 10 employees with a daily turnaround of 100,000 of CFA currency ($ 250) to 140,000 of CFA currency ($350). My long-term project is to begin serving a buffet every weekend for persons with a modest revenue and install air-conditioning in my restaurant.

4.1.9.3. Summary of Case Study, Resilient Company N°2

History: My name is Mr. N. A., 45 years old, married, father of five children, who cannot read or write and left school (CM2). My enterprise (boutique) created in 2004, is not registered, and no written accounting. I memorize all my accounts. I was the victim of the 2005 flood where I lost 1.5 million francs, and then in 2009 on September 1, I lost everything in the flood, including even the banco location.

Indescribable consequences: The locale in banco and everything that it contained, such as money and material, all swept away in the floodwaters with merchandise of approx. 4 million of local CFA currency. The water then filled up in the locale I used for my home right up to the roof. I managed to escape with nothing in my hands in order to save my life. I lost everything in no time and… I did not know what to do … I placed myself in God's Hands. Thanks to the precious advice I received from my parents, I found the courage to start over again.

The Resilience of the Informal Sector in the Context ...

Resilience strategy: Even if all my resources were gone, I can say that the company survived since it rebuilt in a different zone less prone to flooding. I obtained financial aid from my brothers for 500,000 of local CFA currency to restart my own company and return to work in order to take charge of my disenfranchised family. It is because of the financial assistance from my brothers that became the key factor of the resilience of my company.

Current situation and perspective: The Company has worked out well and I have purchased many of my goods on credit but since I cannot read or write, I am not in a position to conduct an overall evaluation at this moment to state my sales revenue. When I have a bit more funds, I will open a new boutique in another point of sale.

4.1.9.4. Summary of Case Study, Resilient Company N°3

History: My name is Mr. Z. J., 34 years old, married, father of two children, who left school CM2 (pre-secondary). My company is n't registered with the government and I have no written accounting. After 12 years of service working for a large company in town, I set up my workshop in 2006 right at the end of the Boulmiougou Bridge where all was well until the flood of September 1, 2009.

Consequences: On September 1, 2009, I went to my work place and everything I owned was lost in the floodwaters. I could only cry for there was nothing left. My bed, material, and furniture valued at 115,000 of local CFA currency ($225) and my tools and even my local, which I was renting at 5,000 of local CFA currency ($10) per month, were all gone. I was very discouraged but when we have nothing left, we must surrender to God's will.

Resilience strategy: After the flood, I offered my services to other shop-owners looking for contracts. I earned between 1500 and 2000 of local CFA currency ($ 2 and $ 3) per day that allowed me to feed my small family and to pay for gas for my cycle. The children did not eat as they would have liked to, but they survived. I then received material and financial support from my parents and friends, enough to open a new workshop located in a non-flood zone. Since I was very serious about my work, I obtained many orders, so much so that I shared contracts with other labourers in order to meet deadlines and my company is now more profitable than before. Thus, I managed to rebound after the catastrophe.

Current situation and perspectives: I still owe about 30,000 of local CFA currency ($ 50) to the owners of the furniture that was lost in the flood. They never claimed a cent, however I feel it is a moral obligation to reimburse them. Looking forward, I purchased a lot in Boassa where I have already laid a foundation with 5 tons of cement bricks to build two rooms and build shop from mud and thatch.

4.1.9.5. Summary of a Case Study, Non-Resilient Owner N°4

History: My name is Mr. Y. M, married, father of 3 children, 47 years old, never went to school but I can read and write in French. My company (food) created in 2003 and registered with the government. I also have an IFU identification. I do my own accounting on an income-expense. My store was at first located near a large passage where I was the frequent target of thieves. Eventually I moved near National Route 1 next to the market "Nab Pug Yaar" where all was well and prosperous. I had five employees. It was here that I faced the flood on September 1, 2009.

Consequences: The store was heavily damaged by the flood, included the stock of food (rice, biscuits, etc.) and other food products were underwater. Close to 6 million of local CFA currency. My home wasn't spared and the main building worth more than 1 million francs was lost, forcing me to rent a home with the few financial resources left over from my company. These funds were sufficient for only a few months. Before, my sales amounted to about 9 million per year.

It was and still is a very difficult situation since my two children had to quit school. I had to let go my employees since I could no longer pay their salaries and to look for a new locale. Married life, which before was enviable, had now become unliveable. Apart from those people who helped me on the day of the flood recover some belongings, I received no help whatsoever although I was twice part of the government census.

Resilience strategy: I asked for a loan of 3 million from the credit union but they offered only 500,000 of local CFA currency in return for a lien of a lot in Koudougou. At first, I refused but then I accepted, overall, but it was necessary for me to sell the rest of my inventory to cover the loan in order to recover the PUH of my lot that I could sell for 7 million to kick-start my business. I tried to import salt as a commodity but that too failed. It was the lack of resources after the flood that was the main reason for my failure at starting over.

Table 1. Factors of resilience according to our sample group

Resilience Factors	Key Components as per Resource group	Key Components as per Owner/Sample Group
Strategy	- Ability to face a new marketplace;	Financial loans from credit union, with teamwork - case study n° 1 resilient, not so for case study 4, non- resilient. Solidarity/Teamwork among family and friends case studies n°2 & 3.
	- Diversify work sites and products;	
	- Work towards new partnerships;	
	- Change activity sector;	
Understanding Risks	- Understand the risks associated with one's activity	
Owner/Manager	-Being dynamic and creative;	
	-open to cultivating new relationships;	
	-fix ambitious goals and discipline yourself in managing your objectives;	
	-Be proactive & anticipate;	
Resources available before crisis	- Have sufficient solvency before crisis;	
Field of Activity	-Choose products not vulnerable to flooding;	
Environment	-Study the environment;	
	- Choose locale that is accessible and outside flood zones;	
	-Develop a secure economic zone by seeking incentives such as easier access to credit and longer payback periods;	
	-Seek a fund to offset losses after a crisis;	
	- Solidarity and moral support;	
Management	-Have a sound business model;	
	-Use modern management techniques;	

Post-crisis situation and perspectives: My Company was a write-off and I live from day to day playing cards. However, I have a lot to sell, and with the proceeds, I will go Dakar, which I had previously visited to study the market to start-up a new activity.

The analysis of the three resilient companies detailed above shows that resilience factors were indeed related to: the domain of activity, the strategy used, the dynamism of the owner, the existing resources before the crisis (but especially those available after the catastrophe), and the environment and management abilities. See Table 1 above.

5. DISCUSSION

We chose a sample group comprised of pertinent and diversified companies for our case studies of informal sector companies, including those businesses that rebounded and those who failed in order to gain the most knowledge on the resilience of these companies.

Case No 1 is a service company (hair stylist). After the shock, the material, the employees, and the clients were always available which, combined with the loan credit obtained, certainly helped the company to rebound even if the owner believes that the recovery was due to his strategy (credit). Nonetheless, the analysis shows that we must take into account his energetic response, the resources previously available, and the field of activity that is the least vulnerable to catastrophes.

As for case No 2, also a service company (retailing), all the resources swept away by the floodwaters. Left to his own resources, he would not have survived elsewhere. However, because his family closed ranks, they provided him with the financial resources that allowed him to rebound. According to the owner, the resilience of his company was due to solidarity and moral comfort. The analysis shows that we should also take into account his energetic response and his perseverance.

Company No 3 is also a service company (workshop) that, like the previous case, was also totally lost in the flood. Against all odds, his dynamic effort coupled with the solidarity of family and friends allowed him to rebound, even if solidarity seems to be the only factor of resilience.

Case study n°4 represents a commerce in food retail. Despite his dynamic attempts to save his business, including obtaining the necessary financing after the crisis, his company only lasted a few months due to insufficient resources. The availability of previous resources (employees, merchandise) and even financial credit were not enough to guarantee resilience. The weakness of the resources mobilized after the crisis and the nature of the activity (food store that was highly vulnerable to water damage) were the factors that doomed his commerce.

For the record, the resilience factors of the companies identified by our experts differ from those chosen from the victims in the field. In fact, companies 2 and 3 could rebound because of solidarity by friends and family after they had lost everything.

The resources that the companies had available before the crisis were difficult to determine since they do not have specific accounting to this effect. The company resources belong to the owner who uses them as he wishes without having to report to anyone. If a crisis arises, he can use all the available resources at his disposal whether they belong officially to him or to the company, considering that the objective is to survive and rebound afterwards. As we have shown, two companies could rebound without any resources after the flood since they had lost everything to the floodwaters.

As well, the resources available before the crisis, specifically the urban housing permits, were used as a guarantee to obtain loans from local financial institutions, and they helped Case Study No 1 rebound but not Case Study No 4. Consequently, we will point of some of previous results: (i) the ability to group automatically them as new (Chaabouni, 2014); (ii) in the study «resilience and capacity range of companies in the lengthy crisis period in Tunisia" (Chaabouni, 2014). Also (iii), the work of Duquesnois (2011) on the "Strategy of small companies in industries that are in a period of crisis that seek their identity in specialized strategies and differentiation rather than in low cost strategies and finally, (IV) "Resilience that places greater importance on the availability of resources before the crisis" as a factor of resilience (Kendra, 2003).

Moreover, the analysis shows that an illiterate entrepreneur who is not up to the task … can be a factor in the demise of a company while someone else who is dynamic and innovative can be a factor in the resilience of the company. This conclusion corroborates with the results of the thesis by Khalil (2014) where the manager/owner is the organizational resource, the nexus that supplies other resources and delivers a decisive factor in the success or failure of the company Ayala (2011, pg. 60), and who is the link between the resilient entrepreneur and the resilient company.

The majority of our resource team considered the formalization or the degree of formalization as a factor of resilience. From the four cases studies, two officially registered with the Commerce Department and two had no such registration. Among the two that were registered, one survived and the other disappeared. The remaining two who had no official status rebounded, which now requires us to put into perspective whether official status is indeed a factor of resilience.

The results also do not corroborate the studies written by Gily (2013, p 553) who concludes that "The nature of the knowledge acquired by an organization, referred to as cognitive capital, and the specificity of the type of management, namely, nature and quality, together form the basis of organizational resilience."

6. Conclusion: Contributions and Limitations

The research on the resilience of companies in the informal sector during times of major crisis such as the September 1st, 2009 flood has allowed us the opportunity to underscore the tremendous resilience these organizations have when faced with the unknown. Although we thought that many owner/managers perished in the first few hours of this unprecedented catastrophe in the history of Burkina Faso, they survived and rebounded.

The other owner/managers who did not rebound left the area for other regions or other countries looking for a better life. Those who have stayed continue the struggle with all the means at their disposal to improve their way of life as our Case Study No 4 stated so well.

Rebounding from the crisis with their company renewed was also an important way of renewing their familial, social, and professional relationships, and important by reaffirming themselves and by regaining their dignity as responsible people in business here to stay. Therefore, they shouldn't be considered as second-class citizens or unreliable entrepreneurs, for the informal sector deserves the respect and the support of all stakeholders in society. Their contribution in socio-economic development is considerable even if their individual budgets, assets or income tax payment remain weak.

From a scientific viewpoint, research on the resilience of informal sector companies is practically non-existent. The results we obtained on the resilience of organizations in this sector may lay the foundation or enrich our knowledge base in this area of study. It represents a small step, not a giant leap, toward understanding the factors of resilience by these companies in crisis mode.

On the managerial side, the owners demonstrate incredible imagination in finding solutions to their problems and in adopting strategies sometimes recommended by large family companies such as diversification, and the careful management of resources to ensure the sustainability of their livelihood. We see here that intelligent illiterate people can govern their affairs according to their intuition and experience. Improving their training and their abilities in risk management adapted to their situations will only improve their performance.

On the operational side, the results will assist business associates by providing them with greater knowledge on the mechanisms of resilience in this sector in order to better accompany them on the path ahead. It will allow entrepreneurs themselves to engage in a reflection upon their usual practices and the consequences that their actions have on resilience in order to be better prepared to face future crises.

The results also provide a basis for reflection from which the State and the territorial authority can learn in order to improve their risk management policies and from which the families and communities can be better prepared to play their vital roles in case of a crisis.

Despite these appreciable contributions, our research contains limitations that should mentioned. The limitations are due to the qualitative nature of the research that does not lend itself to a generalization of the results for analysing larger samples.

Moreover, the interviews reflect only the perceptions of the managers present. There are no written documents to reinforce their views and the employees themselves have not provided us with any information regarding resilience. Triangulation of the results is difficult, if not impossible.

We now conclude by answering our own research question: "What are the factors that determine the capacity of resiliency in informal sector companies faced with a major crisis?"

Regarding the resilience of these informal companies, our results stipulate that they do not depend on previously available resources before the crisis. They depend on many factors among which are the energy of the entrepreneur, the field of activity, the resources mobilized after the crisis, and the solidarity shown by family and friends, not to mention the moral support. Our work done, we now look forward to future research to continue this field of study.

As well, considering the small size of our sample, we hope that future researchers will strive to adopt a quantitative method in order to test our results on a larger sample.

REFERENCES

Aissa, H. B. (2001). *Quelle méthodologie de recherche appropriée pour une construction de la recherche en gestion? [What research methodology is appropriate for a construction of management research]*. Laval: Presse université Laval.

Altintas, G., Royer, I. (2008). Gestion des crises externes: de la résilience à l'apprentissage. [External Crisis Management: From Resilience to Learning.] *AIMS*.

Anaut, M. (2003). La résilience. Surmonter les traumatismes. [Resilience. Overcoming trauma] *Nathan Université collection* 128, 38.

Avenier, M. J. & Gavard-Perret, M. L. (2012). *Inscrire son projet de recherche dans un cadre épistémologique. [Register your research project in an epistemological framework]* France: Pearson.

Avenier, M. J. (2012). À quoi sert l'épistémologie dans la recherche en sciences de gestion? [What is the use of epistemology in management science research?] *AEGIS le Libellio*, volume 8, n°4, 14-25.

Ayala, J. P. (2011). La résilience de l'entrepreneur. Influence sur le succès des affaires. Une analyse longitudinale. [The resilience of the entrepreneur. Influence on the success of the business. Longitudinal analysis]. *International Journal of Production Research*, vol. 49 8-19 septembre, 5375-5393.

Basly, S. (2006). L'internationalisation de la PME familiale: apprentissage organisationnel et développement de la connaissance. [The internationalization of the family SME: organizational learning and development of knowledge.] *XVème conférence de l'Association Internationale de Management Stratégique*. Annecy.

Begin, L. (2010). La résilience organisations Le cas d'une entreprise familial. [The Resilience Organizations The Case of a Family Business]. *Revue française de gestion* N°200/2010, 127-142.

Bellache, Y. (2010). *L'économie informelle en Algérie, une enquête auprès des ménages: le cas de Bejaia. [The informal economy in Algeria, a household survey: the case of Bejaia]* Université de Paris-Est.

Bentalet, E. (2008). Très petites, petites et moyennes entreprises: entre tradition et innovation. Une récession des travaux du Céreq (1985-2007). [Very small, small and medium enterprises: between tradition and innovation. A recession of Céreq's work (1985-2007)] *Centre d'études et de recherches sur les qualifications*, 72.

Bernard, S. (2016). Résilience et entrepreneuriat: une approche dynamique et biographique de l'acte d'entreprendre. *Mangement*, 89-123.

Bit, (1991). Le dilemme du secteur non structuré. [The dilemma of the informal sector.] Bureau international du travail. Genève.

Bit, (2014). La transition de l'économie informelle vers l'économie formelle. [The transition from the informal economy to the formal economy] *Conférence international du travail 103ème session*. Genève.

Boist M., M. (2010). Integrating Modernist and postmodernist Perspectives on Organisations: A complexity science Bridge. *Academy of Management Review*, vol. 35 n°3, 415-433.

Bullough, A. (2013). Entrepreneurial resilience during challenging times. *Business Horizons*, 343-350.

Bullough, A. R. (2014). Danger Zone entrepreneurs: the importance of resilience and self-efficacy for entrepreneurial intentions, Entrepreneurship Theory and practice. *Business Horizons*, 473-499.

Bureau, B., Fendt, J., (2010). L'entreprenariat au sein de l'économie informelles dans les pays développés: Une réalité oubliée? [Entrepreneurship in the informal economy in developed countries: A forgotten reality?] *AIMS*, 24.

Chaabouni, J. (2014, mai). Éventail de capacités et résilience des entreprises en période de crise de longue durée. [Range of Capabilities and Business Resilience in Times of Long-Term Crisis]. *XXIII conférence internationale de management stratégique*.

Chaabouni, J., & Very, P. (2014). *Éventail de capacités et résilience des entreprises en période de crise de longue durée*. [Range of Capabilities and Business Resilience in Times of Long-Term Crisis] Rennes.

Clark G. Kaidige, d. d. (2009, Septembre). Intelligence, Entrepreneuriat et résilience d'entreprise. [Intelligence, Entrepreneurship and Enterprise Resilience] *Revue Proche-Orient - Études en management*.

Clusel, S. (2012). *Définition d'une démarche de réduction des vulnérabilités des TPE/PME fondée sur le cycle de vie.* [Definition of an approach to reduce vulnerabilities of VSE / SMEs based on the life cycle] Paris: HAL.

Coutu, L. (2002). How resilience works. *Harvard Business Review*, vol. 80, N°5, 46-55.

Creswell, J. W., & Plano Clark, V. L. (2006). *Designing and Conducting Mixed Methods Research*. Thousand Oaks, CA: Sage.

Dautun, C. (2007). *Contribution à l'étude des crises de grande ampleur: connaissance et aide à la décision pour la sécurité civile.* [Contribution to the study of large-scale crises: knowledge and decision support for civil security]

De Soto, H. (1994). L'autre sentier: la révolution informelle dans le Tiers-Monde. [The other path: the informal revolution in the Third World] *La Découverte*, 369.

Denis, J.-P. (juin 2007). La recherche académique française en PME: les thèses, les revues, les réseaux. [French academic research in SMEs: theses, journals, networks] *Regards sur les PME*, n° 14, 128. DOI: 10.1177/1049731508318695

Duquenois, F. (2011, décembre). *Les stratégies des petites entreprises dans les industries en crise: Une étude des caves particulières de la région viticole du Languedoc-Roussillon.* [Small business strategies in industries in crisis: A study of the particular cellars of the Languedoc-Roussillon wine region.]

Duquesnois, F. (2011). Les stratégies des petites entreprises dans les industries en crise: une étude des caves particulières de la région vitivinicole du Languedoc-Roussillon. [Strategies of small businesses in industries in crisis: a study of the particular cellars of the wine-producing region of Languedoc-Roussillon.]

Gianfransco, A. (1999). La résilience: du mythe à la réalité. Essai d'interprétation historique. Souffrir mais se reconstruire. ERRES, 82.

Gily, J. P. (2013). Résilience des organisations et des territoires: rôle des sociétés pivots. [Resilience of organizations and territories: role of pivotal societies].

Hart, K. (1973). Informal Income opportunities and Urban Employment in Ghana. *Journal of Modern African Studies*, N°2, 61-89.

Khalil, E. K. (2014). *Le Management des PME dans un Contexte de crise. le cas du Liban.* [SME management in a crisis context. the case of Lebanon.]

L'Autier, B. (2006). Économie informelle [Informal Economy], in J- L Laville A. D Cattani, *dictionnaire de l'autre économie*, Folio actuel, Gallimard. 210-219.

Lautier, B. (1994). *L'économie informelle dans le tiers monde.* [The informal economy in the third world] Paris: La Découverte.

Liu, R. Z. (2012). Organizational resilience perspective: facilitating organizational adaptation analysis. *IPEDR* Vol 28 (2012) C (2012) LACSIT Press, Singapore.

Madni, A. M. (2009). Towards a conceptual framework for resilience engineering. *IEEE System Journal* Vol. 3 N°2, 181-191.

Martin Bapelo, F. (2009). Introduction: le secteur informel et pauvreté en Afrique - instruments de mesures, analyses et politiques économiques. [Introduction: The informal sector and poverty in Africa - measurement tools, analysis and economic policies.] *Journal statistique africain*, N°9, 24-42.

Mongeau, P. (2009). *Réaliser son mémoire ou sa these* [Realize your dissertation or thesis] Coté Jeans & Coté Tenue de soirée. Québec : Presse de l'université du Québec.

Noiseux, Y. (2000). *Le secteur informel au Mexique*. [The informal sector in Mexico] Montréal.

Ouedraogo. A et Boyer. M, (2012). Firm governance and organizational resilience in a crisis context: A case study of a small research-based venture Enterprise. *International Business research*; vol 5, n°12.

PNUD (2014), Rapport sur le développement durable. [Sustainability Report] Washington DC. USA: communication development incorporated.

Provost, A. (1999). Apport de la théorie des conventions dans la coexistence de diverses formes 'organisation" [Contribution of the theory of conventions in the coexistence of various forms 'organization'] *séminaire de recherche de l'IAG*. Université catholique de Louvain, Belgique.

Risquez, F. (2013). Le rôle du Dirigeant résilient dans l'engagement organisationnel des employés et la performance organisationnelle à la suite d'une période critique. [The role of the Resilient Officer in the organizational commitment of employees and organizational performance after a critical period] *HEC Montréal*.

Risquez, F. (2013). *Le rôle du dirigeant résilient dans l'engagement organisationnel des employés et performance organisationnelle à la suite d'une période critique.* [The role of the executive resilient in the organizational commitment of the employees and organizational performance after a critical period] HEC Montréal.

Rutter, M. (1985). Resilience in face of adversity. Protective factors and resistance to psychiatric disorder. *British journal of Psychiatry*, vol. 147, 598-611.

Teneau, G. (2011). La compassion dans la résilience organisationnelle. [Compassion in Organizational Resilience] *Apport du toxic Handler*. Paris.

Theis, A. (2006). Thèse: Approche psychodynamique de la résilience. [Thesis: Psychodynamic approach to resilience] Université de Nancy 2.

Thietart, R. A. et al. (2014). *Méthodes de recherche en management, 4eme édition*. [Management Research Methods, 4th Edition.] Paris: DUNOD.

UNSDR, 2015. Bilan mondial 2015- version de poche rendre le développement durable. [Global Review 2015- pocket version make sustainable development.] Belley: Imprimerie Gonnet, Belley, France.

Vanistendael, S. (1994). "L'enfance dans le monde. Famille et résilience." ["Childhood in the world. Family and resilience. "]. *BICE*, vol 21, n°1, 4.

Weick, K. (1993). The collapse of sense making in organisations: The Mann Gulch Disaster. *"Administrative Science"* Quarterly, vol. 38, pp. 628-653.

William, P. (2009). La résilience Organisationnelle: Concept et activités de formation. [Organizational Resilience: Concept and training activities.] Montréal.

Williard, J. C. (1989). L'économie souterraine dans les comptes nationaux. Économie et statistique. [The underground economy in the national accounts. Economics and statistics] *INSSE*

In: Advances in Business and Management
Editor: William D. Nelson

ISBN: 978-1-53612-615-0
© 2017 Nova Science Publishers, Inc.

Chapter 4

OPEN INNOVATION: A VIRTUOUS PROCESS OF INBOUND AND OUTBOUND KNOWLEDGE FLOWS

Diego Matricano

Department of Management,
Università degli Studi della Campania "Luigi Vanvitelli"

ABSTRACT

Open innovation processes – OIPs are very common practices on which worldwide companies are leveraging in order to innovate (Chesbrough & Crowther 2006). When dealing with OIPs, managers, practitioners, and scholars mainly pay attention to inbound knowledge flows, i.e., the processes through which companies get innovative ideas and insights from the crowd. Very scarce attention, instead, is paid on outbound knowledge flows, i.e., intellectual property rights and brand out-licensing or new products and services offered onto markets (Gassmann et al. 2010; Schroll & Mild 2011). The choice to focus mainly on inbound knowledge flows, to the detriment of outbound knowledge flows, cannot be meant only as a practical choice made by managers and practitioners according to their interests and then followed by scholars. The above choice, in fact, implies something more.

By caring less about outbound knowledge flows, in fact, it seems that managers, practitioners, and scholars risk missing half of the process through which innovation can nurture and favour itself and be fostered. If they do not consider the whole OIP, then it is not possible to assess what happens to innovative ideas and insights collected by companies, how they are embodied in intellectual property rights, brand out-licensed or transformed into new products/services, how they are offered to final markets and – above all – how they move forward the frontiers of innovation both in practical terms (as a new technological standards) and in consumers' mind. According to the above, the present chapter aims to propose a whole process of open innovation.

In order to achieve the just-cited aim, the chapter is structured as it follows. After defining the main aspects of inbound and outbound knowledge flows, attention is focused on the whole process through which innovation nurtures and favours itself. Theoretically, the whole process can be divided into eight stages: 1) launch of open innovation processes; 2) proposal of insights and ideas by the crowd; 3) collection and selection of proposed insights/ideas; 4) internalization of the most fitting insights/ideas in intellectual property rights/brand out-licensing or in new products/services; 5) their offer to the market; 6) purchase by other companies or by the crowd; 7) collection of feedback; 8) moving of frontiers of innovation both in practical terms (as a new technological standards) and in consumers' mind.

According to the theoretical speculation, only if OIPs are considered as a whole, then companies can aspire to move forward the frontiers of innovation.

INTRODUCTION

Even if nearly fifteen years have passed since Chesbrough (2003) remarked the passage from a closed to an open approach to innovation, some aspects related to open innovation processes – OIPs have not been properly disclosed yet.

From a theoretical perspective, it is clear what companies are expected to do, i.e., they are expected to combine internal and external ideas, knowledge, capabilities and intangible resources in order to foster innovation (Chesbrough 2003). From a pragmatic perspective, however, it is not clear how to define and implement them in order to maximize expected returns (Laursen & Salter 2006; Enkel et al. 2009; Dahlander &

Gann 2010; Gassman et al. 2010; Mazzola et al. 2012; Podmetina & Smirnova 2013), especially in terms of new technological standards to propose. This is rather evident from the review of dedicated literature.

Some management scholars have investigated the genesis of OIPs (Enkel et al. 2009; Loren 2011), their dissemination (Chesbrough & Crowther 2006), their typologies (Phillips 2011), their relationship with implemented strategies (Chesbrough & Appleyard 2007; Kelley 2011), or with business models (Frankenberger et al. 2014). A conspicuous strand of research has been focused on the execution of OIPs (Chesbrough 2004; Felin & Zenger 2014) – in particular attention has been paid to applications to be used (Rayna & Striukova 2015), soft skills to be developed (Martino & Bartolone 2011), leadership to exert (Heim 2011), and crowd motivations (Carpenter 2011). Still other scholar, then, have investigated the most common mistakes to be avoided (Gaule 2011) and the probable developments of OIPs (Gassmann et al. 2010; Shapiro 2011; Chesbrough 2012). Of course, it is not possible to ignore all the contributions that have investigated the OIPs in reference to specific industries (Chesbrough & Crowther 2006; Laursen & Salter 2006; West & Gallagher 2006; Bughin et al. 2008; Sarkar & Costa 2008; Enkel et al. 2009; Chiaroni et al. 2010; Di Minin et al. 2010, 2016; Enkel & Gassman 2010; Sieg et al. 2010; Bianchi et al. 2011; De Massis et al. 2012; Karlsson & Sköld 2013; King & Lakhani 2013; Lazzarotti et al. 2013) from which very intriguing results derive.

As a matter of fact, the already cited management scholars have investigated the above aspects mainly in reference to inbound knowledge flows. This is confirmed by West & Bogers (2014). From a review of 165 articles about open innovation, the scholars find that 118 articles are about inbound OIPs, 50 about outbound OIPs, and 70 consider coupled OIPs (Enkel et al. 2009), that is both inbound and outbound OIPs. Clearly, management scholars have investigated inbound OIPs more than outbound and coupled OIPs. In reference to this last topic, it seems appropriate to cite another contribution, authored by Grönlund et al. (2010), in which the scholars rebuild a whole OIP by splitting it into four stages. Over the first stage, managers evaluate if the OIP that is going to be launched is in line with the business model (i.e., the way companies create and capture value) and to what extent the process can leverage on core capabilities hold by companies. Over the second stage, managers evaluate if the business model and core capabilities should be redefined in order to maximize the output generated by the OIP. It might happen, in fact, that companies are not ready to create and capture value. If companies are not, then the third stage of the process takes place. Over this stage, managers redefine their core capabilities and business model in order to make them able to create and capture value. Only after the previous three stages, managers can decide to start the fourth and final stage. During this stage, managers can decide if and what knowledge or technology can be internalized according to the core capabilities and to the business model previously developed or improved. At the same time, managers can also think about the possible ways through which internally developed knowledge and technology can be externalized. As it can be noted from the above, also Grönlund et al. (2010) – who rebuild a coupled OIP – are mainly focused on what companies need to put into practice in order to acquire externally originated knowledge (inbound) rather than on what companies need to put into practice in order to externalize internally originated knowledge (outbound).

The fact that managers, practitioners, and scholars are mainly interested in inbound OIPs represents a relevant gap in the dedicated literature. In order to support and share the idea that both inbound and outbound knowledge flows need to be considered when dealing with OIPs, the chapter is structured as it follows. In the following lines, attention is focused only on the process through which companies can acquire insights and ideas proposed by the crowd. The aim of the paragraph is to emphasize what managers, practitioners, and scholars agree on when dealing with inbound OIPs. After that, attention moves towards outbound OIPs – i.e., the processes through which companies can externalize internally generated knowledge and innovation. By reflecting on inbound and outbound OIPs, it is possible to speculate on the state-of-the-art of OIPs. It seems that managers, practitioners, and scholars consider inbound and outbound OIPs as two different phenomena that are not correlated and –

this is the most critical aspect – do not nurture each other. On the contrary, managers, practitioners and scholars should know that inbound and outbound OIPs need to be considered together if companies really aim to affirm their knowledge and innovation on the market (as a new technological standard). In this vein, an eight-stage model is proposed in the last part of the chapter. Hopefully, this model can shape a virtuous process of open innovation that can drive companies to move forward the frontiers of innovation.

INBOUND KNOWLEDGE FLOWS

As already said, management scholars – who mainly refer to inbound knowledge flows when dealing with OIPs (Chesbrough 2004; Chesbrough & Crowther 2006; Laursen & Salter 2006; Henkel et al. 2014) – share and support the idea that "*many industrial companies now acquire technology from external sources in order to strengthen and speed up their internal innovation process*" (Lichtenthaler et al. 2011, p. 45). In particular, companies aim to acquire external inputs and contributions – like insights and ideas – by research organizations (such as universities), suppliers and customers and even by competitors (Podmetina & Smirnova 2013). This represents an evolution of what happened in innovation networks (Matricano & Sorrentino 2015). Starting from the above, the main scope of this paragraph is to fix some aspects of inbound OIPs on which there is a general agreement between managers, practitioners and scholars.

First of all, companies aiming to launch OIPs need to define the scope of these processes (Danneels 2002; Faems et al. 2010; Gassman et al. 2010; Du et al. 2014). Very often, in fact, OIPs are launched in order to acquire insights and ideas referred to R&D activities (Ili et al. 2010; Carpenter 2011; Lichtenthaler et al. 2011). However, it can also happen that companies launch OIPs in order to get some insights and ideas about the market they are in. In this last case, OIPs can be considered as marketing activities (Kelley 2011). A very interesting contribution concerning the above difference has been proposed by Du et al. (2014)

who classify the inbound OIPs according to involved partners and thus they support the idea that companies can start *science-based* or *market-based partnerships*. In some industries, where R&D expenditures are increasing more and more, *science-based partnerships* are the best way through which companies can get specialized knowledge at a low price and risk. Companies just internalize specialized knowledge they need and so they can easily try to maximize the returns of OIPs. *Market-based relationships*, instead, are the best way to get specific knowledge from customers who can give precious insights and ideas about products/services to be offered onto markets.

The above difference, between *science-based* and *market-based* OIPs, is very important in reference to the management of OIPs and in particular with the selection of the target to be involved. As noted by Grönlund et al. (2010), in fact, inbound OIPs can involve innovation intermediaries, research institutions, suppliers, competitors or firms in other industries. In this vein, Felin and Zenger (2014) seem to match the aim of OIPs with the target to hit. The scholars suggest that inbound OIPs can be managed through markets and contracts (if external partners possess solution elements) or through partnerships, alliances and corporate venture capital if problems to be solved are of intermediate complexity (these cases take place in reference to *science-based* OIPs). Otherwise, OIPs can be managed through contests, tournaments and innovation platforms. This happens if partners can manage relevant knowledge and offer complete solutions and can be referred to both *science-based* and *market-based* OIPs. Eventually, OIPs can be managed through the involvement of users and user communities. Both users and user communities do not aim to solve the companies' problems but they can be useful to explore uncertain situation and offer possible solutions (also in this case there is a reference to both *science-based* and *market-based* OIPs).

At this stage, according to the scope to pursue and to the target to hit, companies need to take some decisions concerning the involvement of the crowd and the involvement and readiness of the company. In reference to the involvement of the crowd, companies need to define: whether they ask for the proposal or the judgement of ideas to the crowd (Hopkins 2011);

the characteristics and size of the target (Hopkins 2011; Phillips 2011); the questions to be asked (Phillips 2001); the users' motivation to leverage on (Carpenter 2001); and the incentives to be offered (Hopkins 2011).

At the same time, companies need to define their own involvement and readiness. Before launching OIPs, in fact, companies need to wonder if they can internalize new insights and ideas coming from the outside. In this vein, as proposed by Grönlund et al. (2010), it is appropriate to recall the concept of *core capabilities* (Hayes 1985; Rumelt 1987) that can be labelled as such "*if they differentiate a company strategically*" (Leonard-Barton 1992, p. 111). Companies work on them in order to achieve superior performances. However, this result can be achieved or not. It can be achieved if companies are able to modify, improve, redefine their *core capabilities*, by leveraging on the so-called *dynamic capabilities* (Prahalad & Hamel 1990; Teece et al. 1997). In other words, companies can modify their *core capabilities* and adapt them to different scenarios and situations. On the contrary, superior performances cannot be achieved if companies are not able to modify their *core capabilities*. In this case, *core capabilities* turn into *core rigidities* – it is argued that "*core rigidities are the flip side of core capabilities*" (Leonard-Barton 1992, p. 118) – and *dynamic capabilities* are not useful to achieve the expected aim. Among the reasons that can prevent companies from modifying their *core capabilities* in a successful way, it is possible to include *path-dependence* (David 1985, 1997, 2000; Arthur 1988; Arrow 1994). According to this theory, previous choices can limit the future alternatives to choose between (Liebowitz & Margolis 1995) and so – in the specific case – core capabilities cannot be modified, improved, or redefined.

At this stage, it is appropriate to clarify which are the *core capabilities* that companies need to modify in order to be involved in and ready for OIPs (Lichtenthaler & Lichtenthaler 2009). Absorptive capacity (Cohen & Levinthal 1990) is one of the *core capabilities* to be modified. Through inbound OIPs companies can get insights and ideas – both *science-based* and *market-based* – to be internalized. This means that they need to develop the capacity to gain insights and ideas proposed by the crowd and then to exploit them (Andersén & Kask 2012). This is the *absorptive capacity*, i.e., "*the ability of a firm to recognize the value of new external information, assimilate it and apply it to commercial ends*" (Cohen & Levinthal 1990, p. 128). Some scholars (Zahra & George 2002) split the absorptive capacity into potential and realized absorptive capacity. By potential absorptive capacity they refer to the acquisition and to the assimilation of external knowledge. Instead, by realized absorptive capacity they refer to the transformation and the exploitation of absorbed knowledge. The fact that this capacity can be homogeneously (Andersén & Kask 2012) or heterogeneously deployed in the company (Camisón & Forés 2010) does not drive to question its relevance. What matters herein is that companies can try to overcome the employees' "*not-invented-here*" syndrome – according to which they cannot or they do not want to develop knowledge coming from the outside – since it can prevent inbound OIPs (Lichtenthaler et al. 2011).

Another capability that companies need to modify in order to be involved in and ready for OIPs deals with their business model and its adaptation to unexpected situations and scenarios (Grönlund et al. 2010). Companies launching OIPs need to be ready to modify their business model making it novelty-centred, efficiency-centred or half-away between novelty- and efficiency-centred (Zott & Amit 2007) according to the results of the OIPs. According to Zott & Amit, "*novelty-centred business model design is the conceptualization and adoption of new ways of conducting economic exchanges, which can be achieved, for example, by connecting previously unconnected parties, by linking transaction participants in new ways, or by designing new transaction mechanisms*" (*ibidem*, p. 184) while "*efficiency-centred design refers to the measures that firms may take to achieve transaction efficiency through their business models*" (*ibidem*, p. 185).

From the above review it is possible to disclose what managers, practitioners, and scholars agree on when dealing with inbound OIPs. Companies implementing inbound OIPs need to define the scope they want to achieve, the target to hit, the main aspects referred to the involvement of the crowd, the absorptive capacity to be developed and the business model to be implemented/modified. Only if companies focus on the above aspects

Open Innovation 135

and implement them in a proper way, then they can really aspire to spin-in new intriguing insights and ideas by the outside (Grönlund et al. 2010).

OUTBOUND KNOWLEDGE FLOWS

Differently from inbound OIPs, outbound OIPs take place when companies externalize (through commercialization) knowledge and innovation that – totally or partly – derive from the outside and are internally modified (Gassmann 2006; Lichtenthaler & Ernst 2007; Lichtenthaler 2009, 2011; Chiaroni et al. 2010; Grönlund et al. 2010; West & Bogers 2014) and are unused or under-utilized (Chesbrough & Bogers 2014). This topic seems to be less felt by managers, practitioners and scholars (West & Bogers 2014). Thus, as argued by the above-cited scholars (*ibidem*), the topics of value creation and capture still need to be explored.

From the review of dedicated literature, it seems that three main aspects emerge in reference to outbound OIPs. The first deals with the "*not-sold-here*" syndrome. The second deals with the target to involve. The third deals with the amount of new knowledge to disclose.

The "*not-sold-here*" syndrome (Lichtenthaler et al. 2011) reveals itself when companies do not want to externalize new knowledge and innovation that have not been fully generated from the inside. In their view, the fact that new knowledge and innovation derive from insights and ideas proposed by the crowd can be detrimental to their image. As a matter of fact, the "*not-sold-here*" syndrome can be detrimental to the innovation process as a whole. Companies affected by this syndrome, in fact, can decide not to launch inbound OIPs or to launch them without exploiting the insights and ideas proposed by the crowd. In this last case, the crowd is useful only to address the internal innovation processes. Companies not affected by this syndrome, instead, can decide to start and manage outbound OIPs and so they have to face other problems dealing with the target to involve and the amount of knowledge to be disclosed.

In reference to the target to be involved, companies need to determine if they want to share their new knowledge with other companies – by managing intellectual property rights or brand out-licensing (Chesbrough & Crowther 2006) – or with customers – by offering new products/services onto market. Of course, the choice does not seem to depend on the company but on the nature of knowledge to be shared (Moghaddam & Tarokh 2012).

What companies need to decide – and this is the third problem to be solved – is the amount of knowledge and innovation to be disclosed. In reference to this, see Bogers (2011) who proposes a very interesting contribution. By rebuilding all the possible alternatives, it can be argued that the amount of knowledge to be disclosed moves along a *continuum*. At one extreme it is possible to find secrecy, intellectual property rights or brand out-licensing (Chesbrough & Crowther 2006). In this case, companies tend not to disclose knowledge and innovations they hold (they try to keep it secret) or they tend to disclose them only if they know there is no risk for value capture. At the other extreme it is possible to find free revealing (Harhoff et al. 2003; Hertel et al. 2003; Henkel 2006; von Hippel & von Krogh 2006). Put simply, by free revealing companies tend to disclose all their knowledge and innovation. For this reason, this approach has been defined as an *"altruistic and intrinsically motivated information sharing"* (Henkel et al. 2014, p. 880). As noted by Henkel (2006), there are some antecedents that drive companies to practice free revealing. These are: a further community-based development of knowledge and innovation (von Hippel 2001), the satisfaction of not homogeneous needs (Franke & von Hippel 2003), the modular technology at the basis of shared knowledge and innovation (Baldwin & Clark 2003). Of course – and this is a very important point that cannot be ignored – only if one (or even all) of the above antecedents are verified then companies can practice free revealing and maximize their profits (Henkel 2006).

In the middle of the above-cited *continuum* (ranging from secrecy to free revealing), it is possible to arrange selective revealing according to which companies *"do not reveal out of principle but rather as a result of weighing the commercial pros and cons"* (Henkel et al. 2014, p. 880). In this case, in fact, companies aim to disclose only a part of their knowledge and innovation. Of course, both in reference to market and technical aspects companies are expected to get positive results by selective revealing (Henkel et al. 2014). According to the scholars, in reference to market, selective revealing can have a positive effect on companies' reputation; a word-of-mouth advertising can be started; eventually, the market demand can be increased because of reduced prices and increased customizability. In reference to technical aspects, instead, the scholars highlight that selective revealing can have a positive effect for companies, especially in reference to production costs (by reducing them), to reliability, to the use of standard components and to access to new markets.

By considering the above advantages linked to selective revealing, all the companies should be interested in realizing it. As a matter of fact, companies are prevented from putting into practice selective revealing because of connected risks. Imitation and loss of competitive advantage, reduced compatibility, reliability, safety and security and an increase in maintenance cost are the main risks associated with selective revealing (Henkel et al. 2014). The decision about practicing or not selective revealing, then, cannot be generalized but depends on each specific case (*ibidem*). Only if companies can minimize competitive losses then selective revealing is put into practice (Henkel 2006).

The above literature review can partly explain why managers and practitioners, and by consequence scholars, are not deeply interested in outbound OIPs even if they should. Through them, in fact, companies could affect and modify competitive dynamics. They could differentiate their offering from competitors or they could share new knowledge and innovation on the market – this is clearly evident from selective revealing through which companies can involve other subjects in order to co-create value and propose a new technological standard in the industry they are in (Chesbrough & Appleyard 2007; Henkel et al. 2014). The major problem related to outbound OIPs seems to be linked to the fact that companies cannot easily compare commercial pros and cons (Hertel et al. 2003) and this can prevent managers and practitioners, and by consequence scholars, from interesting in outbound OIPs.

THE STATE-OF-THE-ART OF OPEN INNOVATION PROCESSES

After reviewing both inbound and outbound knowledge flows, it seems possible to speculate on the state-of-the-art of OIPs.

For a start, it seems appropriate to recall two very important contributions, authored by Lichtenthaler et al. (2011) and by Podmetina & Smirnova (2013).

Lichtenthaler et al. (2011), aiming to classify a sample of 211 companies according to their level of openness, have considered two variables in order to proceed with the classification: the "*not-invented-here*" (which has previously been referred to inbound OIPs) and the "*not-sold-here*" syndromes (which has previously been referred to outbound OIPs). Both these syndromes have been classified as limited or high. The scholars have identified four groups of companies. The first one, that Lichtenthaler et al. (2011) name as "technology isolationists", show a high level of "*not-invented-here*" and "*not-sold-here*" syndromes. These companies are still based on closed innovation and – not surprisingly – they represent 36% of the sample. The second group, named "technology fountains", is characterized by high "*not-invented-here*" syndrome. They do not absorb external knowledge (there is no reference to inbound OIPs). They only transfer their knowledge to external partners (by managing intellectual property rights and brand out-licensing). 26.6% of the sample belongs to this group. On the contrary, the third group – named "technology sponges" – is characterized by high "*not-sold-here*" syndrome. Companies included in this group, in fact, absorb external knowledge (they practice inbound open innovation) but they do not transfer their knowledge to external partners. Companies belonging to this group are 21.3% of the sample. Eventually, there is a small group of companies (16.1% of the sample) that Lichtenthaler et al. (2011) define "technology brokers". These companies put into practice both inbound and outbound open innovation. They show a limited level of "*not-invented-here*" and "*not-sold-here*" syndromes.

From the above contribution, very interesting results seem to emerge. First of all, more than one third of the sample practices neither inbound nor outbound OIPs (36%). The fact that these companies suffer of "*not-invented-here*" and "*not-sold-here*" syndromes let us realize that many companies do not practice OIPs yet. This seems to be confirmed by Henkel et al. (2014, p. 879) who argue: "*for firms steeped in the paradigm of closed innovation, the transition to open innovation is challenging*". Another interesting result concerns inbound and outbound knowledge flows. According to the above contribution (*ibidem*) nearly half of the sample (47.9% out of the total) practices inbound or outbound OIPs. However, it clearly emerges that companies – classifies as "technology fountains" or "technology sponges" – keep them clearly separate. As a result, it seems that companies consider inbound and outbound knowledge flows as two different phenomena. The third and last result emerging from the above contribution is the low percentage of companies acting like "technology brokers", i.e., practicing both inbound and outbound OIPs. Despite the percentages emerging from the above contribution (*ibidem*), the nomenclature used by the above scholars gives a clearer idea of the state-of-the-art of OIPs. "Technology fountains" only externalize their knowledge and innovation, while "technology sponges" only internalize insights and ideas. Only few companies manage both inbound and outbound OIPs and act as "technology brokers".

A similar result comes out from another study conducted by Podmetina & Smirnova (2013) about 206 companies. Out of the whole sample, 49% of companies in the sample practice closed innovation; 31.1% implement inbound OIPs, 13.1% implement outbound OIPs and only 6.8 practice both inbound and outbound OIPs.

From a practical point of view, the choice to focus on one or both the processes can be easily understood: companies just exploit their competences by doing what they are able to do. From a strategic point of view, instead, this choice needs to be questioned and properly evaluated. For this reason, two well-known models are going to be recalled in the next lines. The first is the SECI model (Nonaka 1991), while the second is the exploration and exploitation model (March 1991).

The SECI model (Nonaka 1991) and its further developments (Nonaka 1994; Nonaka & Takeuchi 1995; Nonaka et al. 1996, 2000, 2014; Nonaka & Konno 1998; Nonaka & Nishiguchi 2001; Nonaka & Toyama 2003) remind us that companies need to pass through four phases in order to create and disseminate new knowledge. These four phases are labelled as: 1) socialization; 2) externalization; 3) combination; and 4) internalization (SECI). During the socialization phase, tacit knowledge is exchanged (Argote & Ingram 2000). During the externalization phase, tacit knowledge created through the act of socialization is transformed into explicit knowledge. Over the combination phase, explicit knowledge is systemized and then turned into new explicit knowledge (Nonaka & Takeuchi 1995). Eventually, during the internalization phase explicit knowledge is turned into tacit one (Nonaka 1991). At this stage, new knowledge has been created and disseminated.

The exploration and exploitation model (March 1991) – originally proposed in reference to organizational learning – drives attention toward a delicate trade-off (*ibidem*, p. 85) that has been largely investigated by management scholars (Benner & Tushman 2003; Brady & Davies 2004; Gupta et al. 2006; Andriopoulos & Lewis 2009; Raisch et al. 2009; Eriksson 2013) and has been renamed as ambidexterity (Tushman & O'Reilly 1996; O'Reilly & Tushman 2004, 2011). On the one hand, companies aim to exploit their competencies, knowledge and technologies in order to try to get to positive results. On the other hand, companies aim to explore new alternatives despite the risky results. Over a process of mutual learning, companies need to be aware that if they aim to improve reliability of performance they need to leverage on exploration of unknown alternatives rather – or earlier – than on exploitation of known alternatives. This seems to be an effective way to enhance long-term innovation and to compete on turbulent markets (Eriksson 2013).

By reflecting on the SECI model and on the exploration/exploitation model – on the one hand – and on the implementation and management of OIPs – on the other hand, a very intriguing speculation seems to be possible. Inbound OIPs (i.e., internalization of ideas and insights) seem to be referable to the phases of combination and internalization of the SECI model and to exploration of new alternatives. When implementing inbound OIPs, in fact, companies get new insights and ideas from the outside. They try to enrich the basis of knowledge they hold by internalizing external knowledge and by combing it with the one they already have. By doing it, they also try to explore new alternatives that strictly depend on the external knowledge that is acquired. Outbound OIPs (i.e., externalization of knowledge and innovation), instead, seem to be referable to the phases of socialization and externalization of the SECI model and to exploitation of known alternatives. By managing outbound OIPs, in fact, companies aim to offer to external parties new knowledge and innovation they have previously achieved. They try to externalize them or, in other words, they try to exploit them on the market.

The reference to both the SECI model and exploration/exploitation model seems very promising and meaningful. By reading and thinking of both of them, in fact, it seems that knowledge processes always need to be considered bi-directionally: both inside-out and outside-in. Relational capital (Matricano 2016) becomes crucial. Knowledge, in fact, needs to be internalized by companies, mixed and combined, and then externalized in order to achieve a sustainable competitive advantage. The fact the neither the SECI model nor the exploration/exploitation model ignore the knowledge development cycle (Bhatt 2000) – moving from knowledge capturing and storing, passing through its use and application and getting to knowledge transferring and sharing – is an important signal that cannot be underestimated. Accordingly, if companies put into practice only inbound or outbound OIPs, then the process through which new knowledge is created and disseminated is not complete. Thus, companies need to put into practice whole (inside-out and outside-in) processes, i.e., coupled OIPs.

A VIRTUOUS PROCESS OF OPEN INNOVATION

In order to clarify the relevance of coupled OIPs in order to create and disseminate new knowledge and to move forward the frontiers of innovation (Gassmann & Enkel 2004; Enkel et al. 2009; Faems et al. 2010; Lin et al. 2012; Mazzola et al. 2012; Podmetina & Smirnova 2013; Chesbrough & Bogers 2014; West & Bogers 2014), a virtuous process of open innovation is proposed herein. It is defined this way since it recalls the main stages of inbound and outbound OIPs and considers them as a process that continuously goes outside-in and inside-out. Over this process, ideas and insights are turned into new knowledge and innovation – this is what generally happens when companies involve external partners in innovation processes that are divided into the idea-generation phase, the idea-development phase and the commercialization phase (Moghaddam & Tarokh 2012). If new knowledge and innovation are launched onto markets, appreciated and shared then they determine a successful OIP and move forward the frontiers of innovation.

The eight stages in which a whole process of open innovation should be articulated in order to be virtuous are:

1. launch of open innovation processes;
2. proposal of insights and ideas by the crowd;
3. collection of proposed insights/ideas;
4. embodiment of the most fitting insights/ideas in intellectual property rights/brand out-licensing or in new products/services;
5. their offer to the market;
6. purchase by other companies or by the crowd;
7. collection of feedback;
8. moving of frontiers of innovation both in practical terms (with other companies) and in the consumer's mind.

As noted in reference to inbound OIPs, companies need to define the aim they want to achieve, the target to hit, the main aspects referred to the involvement of the crowd, the absorptive capacity to be developed and the business model to be implemented/modified. Once clarified all the above aspects, companies can launch a call to spin-in new insights and ideas by external partners (Grönlund et al. 2010), such as research organizations, universities, suppliers, customers, and even by competitors. This is the first phase of the process. The crowd, then, evaluates the possibility to join the call and propose insights and ideas that can be *science-based* or *market-based* (this is the second phase). Of course, *science-based* and *market-based* OIPs have different prerequisites. *Science-based* OIPs require specific capabilities and skills that external partners can have or not. *Market-based* OIPs, instead, do not. Of course, this has some implications also in reference to the amount of partners who can join a call. Insights and ideas are then collected and selected by the company (third phase). Of course, among the several collected insights and ideas, companies aim to select the ones that most fit with their *core capabilities*. This match is instrumental to the internalization of the most fitting insights/ideas in intellectual property rights/brand out-licensing or in new products/services (fourth phase). This creates new knowledge and innovation.

By carrying out these four stages, the inbound OIPs generally end – Piller & West (2014), in fact, propose a similar model of collaboration process that ends at this stage. Outbound OIPs, instead, start from here.

Generally, outbound OIPs start with the offering of knowledge and innovation – embodied in intellectual property rights/brand out-licensing or in new products/services – to the market (fifth phase). Other companies or the crowd can purchase them and so the process of externalization is carried out as well (sixth phase).

If the proposed process should stop here, it might be not virtuous. The six stages recalled above, in fact, just seem to describe what happens over inbound and outbound OIPs. Even if they are brought closer, they do not add anything to inbound and outbound OIPs as standing alone phenomena. In order to start and manage a virtuous process of open innovation, companies should be able to manage two more stages. One deals with collection of feedback (seventh phase). By offering intellectual property rights/brand out-licensing or new products/services to the market, companies can get information that need to be internalized – this is the "interaction mechanisms" (West & Boger 2013) that marks the starting of a new process and so of coupled OIPs – in order to realize if the previous stages of the OIP have been successful or not. If they have been so, companies can start the last stage of the process, they can move forward the frontiers of innovation both in practical terms and in the consumer's mind (eight phase). If the previous stages of the OIP have not been successful, companies can rebuild the process in order to understand where they went wrong and learn from that (Shepherd et al. 2013).

CONCLUSION

The theoretical analysis presented in this contribution has tried to underline the limitations that emerge when managers, practitioners, and scholars consider inbound and outbound OIPs as standing alone phenomena. By focusing attention only on the processes through which companies can get insights and ideas from the outside or alternatively only on the processes through which companies share their new knowledge and innovation with external partners, it seems that OIPs are implemented and investigated with a short-sighted approach that does not drive to move forward the frontiers of innovation. By recalling the SECI model (Nonaka 1991) and the exploration/exploitation model (March 1991), it derives that companies defining and implementing inbound OIPs just combine and internalize external insights and ideas and explore new alternatives. Instead, companies defining and implementing only outbound OIPs just socialize and externalize knowledge and innovation and exploit known alternatives. In both the cases, companies carry out only a half of an OIP and something is missing. For this reason, companies should put into practice coupled OIPs.

By implementing and managing both inbound and outbound knowledge flows, in fact, knowledge held by companies is enriched with insights and ideas coming from the outside, innovation is achieved and then it is offered onto markets. This seems to be the only way through which OIPs can become virtuous processes able to move forward the frontiers of innovation.

REFERENCES

Andersén, J. & Kask, J. (2012). Asymmetrically realized absorptive capacity and relationship durability. *Management Decision, 50* (1), 43-57.

Andriopoulos, C. & Lewis, M. W. (2009). Exploitation-exploration tensions and organizational ambidexterity: Managing paradoxes of innovation. *Organization Science, 20* (4), 696-717.

Argote, L. & Ingram, P. (2000). Knowledge transfer: A basis for competitive advantage in firms. *Organizational Behavior and Human Decision Processes, 82* (1), 150-169.

Arrow, K. J. (1994). Methodological Individualism and Social Knowledge. *American Economic Review, 84* (2), 1-9.

Arthur, W. B. (1988). Self-Reinforcing Mechanisms in Economics. In Anderson, P. W., Arrow K. J. and Pines, D. (eds.), *The Economy as an Evolving Complex System*. Readings (MA): Addison-Wesley.

Baldwin, C. Y. & Clark, K. B. (2003). Managing in an age of modularity. In Garud, R., Kumaraswamy, A. and Langlois, R. (eds.), *Managing in the Modular Age: Architectures, Networks, and Organizations*. Malden (MA): Blackwell Publishers, 84-93.

Benner, M. J. & Tushman, M. L. (2003). Exploitation, exploration, and process management: The productivity dilemma revisited. *Academy of Management Review, 28* (2), 238-256.

Bhatt, G. D. (2000). Organizing knowledge in the knowledge development cycle. *Journal of Knowledge Management, 4* (1), 15-26.

Bianchi, M., Cavaliere, A., Chiaroni, D., Frattini, F. & Chiesa, V. (2011). Organisational modes for open innovation in the bio-pharmaceutical industry: an exploratory analysis. *Technovation, 31* (1), 22-33.

Bogers, M. (2011). The open innovation paradox: knowledge sharing and protection in R&D collaborations. *European Journal of Innovation Management, 14* (1), 93-117.

Brady, T. & Davies, A. (2004). Building project capabilities: from exploratory to exploitative learning. *Organization Studies, 25* (9), 1601-1621.

Bughin, J., Chui, M. & Johnson, B. (2008). The next step in open innovation. *McKinsey Quarterly*, *4* (6), 1-8.

Camisón, C. & Forés, B. (2010). Knowledge absorptive capacity: New insights for its conceptualization and measurement. *Journal of Business Research*, *63* (7), 707-715.

Carpenter, H. (2011). Motivating the crowd to participate in your innovation initiative. In: Sloane, P. (ed.), *A Guide to Open Innovation and Crowd-sourcing. Expert Tips and Advice*. London: Kogan Page Publisher, 76-84.

Chesbrough, H. (2003). *Open Innovation: The New Imperative for Creating and Profiting from Technology*. Boston (MA): Harvard Business School Press.

Chesbrough, H. (2004). Managing open innovation. *Research-Technology Management*, *47* (1), 23-26.

Chesbrough, H. (2012). Open innovation: Where we've been and where we're going. *Research-Technology Management*, *55* (4), 20-27.

Chesbrough, H. & Appleyard, M. (2007). Open innovation and strategy. *California Management Review*, *50* (1), 57-76.

Chesbrough, H. & Bogers, M. (2014). Explicating open innovation: clarifying an emerging paradigm for understanding innovation. In Chesbrough, H., Vanhaverbeke, W. and West, J. (eds.), *New Frontiers in Open Innovation*. Oxford: Oxford University Press, 3-28.

Chesbrough, H. & Crowther, A. K. (2006). Beyond high tech: early adopters of open innovation in other industries. *R&D Management*, *36* (3), 229-236.

Chiaroni, D., Chiesa, V. & Frattini, F. (2010). Unravelling the process from closed to open innovation: evidence from mature, asset-intensive industries. *R&D Management*, *40* (3), 222-245.

Cohen, W. M. & Levinthal, D. A. (1990). Absorptive capacity: A new perspective on learning and innovation. *Administrative Science Quarterly*, *35* (1), 128-152.

Dahlander, L. & Gann, D. M. (2010). How open is innovation? *Research Policy*, *39* (6), 699-709.

Danneels, E. (2002). The dynamics of product innovation and firm competences. *Strategic Management Journal, 23* (12), 1095-1121.

David, P. A. (1985). Clio and the economics of qwerty. *The American Economic Review, 75* (2), 332-337.

David, P. A. (1997). *Path dependence and the quest for historical economics: one more chorus of the ballad of QWERTY*, University of Oxford Discussion Papers in Economic and Social History, n. 20.

David, P. A. (2000). Path-dependence, its critics and the quest for "Historical Economics". In Garrouste, P. and Ioannides, S. (eds.), *Evolution and Path Dependence in Economic Ideas: Past and Present.* Cheltenham (UK): Edward Elgar Publishing.

De Massis, A., Lazzarotti, V., Pizzurno, E. & Salzillo, E. (2012). Open innovation in the automotive industry: a multiple case-study, *Management of Technological Innovation in Developing and Developed Countries*, March, 217-236.

Di Minin, A., De Marco, C. E., Marullo, C., Piccaluga, A., Casprini, E., Mahdad, M. & Paraboschi, A. (2016). *Case Studies on Open Innovation in ICT* (No. JRC100823). Institute for Prospective Technological Studies, Joint Research Centre.

Di Minin, A., Frattini, F. & Piccaluga, A. (2010). Fiat: open innovation in a downturn (1993–2003). *California Management Review, 52* (3), 132-159.

Du, J., Leten, B. & Vanhaverbeke, W. (2014). Managing open innovation projects with science-based and market-based partners. *Research Policy, 43* (5), 828-840.

Enkel, E. & Gassman, O. (2010). Creative imitation: exploring the case of cross-industry innovation. *R&D Management, 40* (3), 256-270.

Enkel, E., Gassmann, O. & Chesbrough, H. (2009). Open R&D and open innovation: exploring the phenomenon. *R&D Management, 39* (4), 311-316.

Eriksson, P. E. (2013). Exploration and exploitation in project-based organizations: Development and diffusion of knowledge at different organizational levels in construction companies. *International Journal of Project Management, 31* (3), 333-341.

Faems, D., De Visser, M., Andries, P. & Van Looy, B. (2010). Technology alliance portfolios and financial performance: value-enhancing and cost-increasing effects of open innovation. *Journal of Product Innovation Management, 27* (6), 785-796.

Felin, T. & Zenger, T. R. (2014). Closed or open innovation? Problem solving and the governance choice. *Research Policy, 43* (5), 914-925.

Franke, N. & Von Hippel, E. (2003). Satisfying heterogeneous user needs via innovation toolkits: the case of Apache security software. *Research Policy, 32* (7), 1199-1215.

Frankenberger, K., Weiblen, T. & Gassman, O. (2014). The antecedents of open business models: an exploratory study of incumbent firms. *R&D Management, 44* (2), 173-188.

Gassmann, O. (2006). Opening up the innovation process: towards an agenda. *R&D Management, 36* (3), 223-228.

Gassmann, O. & Enkel, E. (2004). Towards a theory of open innovation: three core process archetypes. *R&D Management Conference (RADMA)*, Lisbon, Portugal.

Gassmann, O., Enkel, E. & Chesbrough, H. (2010). The future of open innovation. *R&D Management, 40* (3), 213-221.

Gaule, A. (2011). Common mistakes and stress points. In: Sloane, P. (ed.), *A Guide to Open Innovation and Crowd-sourcing. Expert Tips and Advice*. London: Kogan Page Publisher, 170-177.

Grönlund, J., Sjödin, D. R. & Frishammar, J. (2010). Open innovation and the stage-gate process: A revised model for new product development. *California Management Review, 52* (3), 106-131.

Gupta, A. K., Smith, K. G. & Shalley, C. E. (2006). The interplay between exploration and exploitation. *Academy of Management Journal, 49* (4), 693-706.

Harhoff, D., Henkel, J. & Von Hippel, E. (2003). Profiting from voluntary information spillovers: how users benefit by freely revealing their innovations. *Research Policy, 32* (10), 1753-1769.

Hayes, R. H. (1985). Strategic planning-forward in reverse. *Harvard Business Review, 63* (6), 111-119.

Heim, M. (2011). Leadership issues and challenges in the OI world. In: Sloane, P. (ed.), *A Guide to Open Innovation and Crowd-sourcing. Expert Tips and Advice*. London: Kogan Page Publisher, 65-75.

Henkel, J. (2006). Selective revealing in open innovation processes: The case of embedded Linux. *Research Policy*, *35* (7), 953-969.

Henkel, J., Schöberl, S. & Alexy, O. (2014). The emergence of openness: How and why firms adopt selective revealing in open innovation. *Research Policy*, *43* (5), 879-890.

Hertel, G., Niedner, S. & Herrmann, S. (2003). Motivation of software developers in open source projects: An Internet-based survey of contributors to the Linux kernel. *Research Policy*, *32* (7), 1159-1177.

Hopkins, R. (2011). What is crowd-sourcing? In: Sloane, P. (ed.), *A Guide to Open Innovation and Crowd-sourcing. Expert Tips and Advice*. London: Kogan Page Publisher, 15-21.

Ili, S., Albers, A. & Miller, S. (2010). Open innovation in the automotive industry. *R&D Management*, *40* (3), 246-255.

Karlsson, C. & Sköld, M. (2013). Forms of innovation openness in global automotive groups. *International Journal of Automotive Technology and Management*, *13* (1), 1-17.

Kelley, B. (2011). The importance of a strategic approach to open innovation. In: Sloane, P. (ed.), *A Guide to Open Innovation and Crowd-sourcing. Expert Tips and Advice*. London: Kogan Page Publisher, 37-42.

King, A. & Lakhani, K. R. (2013). Using open innovation to identify the best ideas. *MIT Sloan Management Review*, *55* (1), 41-48.

Laursen, K. & Salter, A. (2006). Open for innovation: the role of openness in explaining innovation performance among UK manufacturing firms. *Strategic Management Journal*, *27* (2), 131-150.

Lazzarotti, V., Manzini, R., Pellegrini, L. & Pizzurno, E. (2013). Open innovation in the automotive industry: why and how? Evidence from a multiple case study. *International Journal of Technology Intelligence and Planning*, *9* (1), 37-56.

Leonard-Barton, D. (1992). Core capabilities and core rigidities: A paradox in managing new product development. *Strategic Management Journal, 13* (S1), 111-125.

Lichtenthaler, U. (2009). Outbound open innovation and its effect on firm performance: examining environmental influences. *R&D Management, 39* (4), 317-330.

Lichtenthaler, U. (2011). Implementation steps for successful out-licensing. *Research-Technology Management, 54* (5), 47-53.

Lichtenthaler, U. & Ernst, H. (2007). External technology commercialization in large firms: results of a quantitative benchmarking study. *R&D Management, 37* (5), 383-397.

Lichtenthaler, U. & Lichtenthaler, E. (2009). A capability-based framework for open innovation: Complementing absorptive capacity. *Journal of Management Studies, 46* (8), 1315-1338.

Lichtenthaler, U., Hoegl, M. & Muethel, M. (2011). Is your company ready for open innovation? *MIT Sloan Management Review, 53* (1), 45-50.

Liebowitz, S. J. & Margolis, S. E. (1995). Path dependence, lock-in, and history. *Journal of Law, Economics and Organization, 11* (1), 205-226.

Lin, C., Wu, Y. J., Chang, C., Wang, W. & Lee, C. Y. (2012). The alliance innovation performance of R&D alliances - the absorptive capacity perspective. *Technovation, 32* (5), 282-292.

Loren, J. K. (2011). What is open innovation? In: Sloane, P. (ed.), *A Guide to Open Innovation and Crowd-sourcing. Expert Tips and Advice*. London: Kogan Page Publisher, 5-14.

March, J. G. (1991). Exploration and exploitation in organizational learning. *Organization Science, 2* (1), 71-87.

Martino, G. & Bartolone, J. (2011). Soft skills for open innovation success. In: Sloane, P. (ed.), *A Guide to Open Innovation and Crowd-sourcing. Expert Tips and Advice*. London: Kogan Page Publisher, 98-105.

Matricano, D. (2016). The impact of intellectual capital on start-up expectations. *Journal of Intellectual Capital, 17* (4), 654-674.

Matricano, D. & Sorrentino, M. (2015). Implementation of regional innovation networks: a case study of the biotech industry in Campania. *Sinergie – Italian Journal of Management*, *33* (97), 105-126.

Mazzola, E., Bruccoleri, M. & Perrone, G. (2012). The effect of inbound, outbound and coupled innovation on performance. *International Journal of Innovation Management*, *16* (6), 1-27.

Moghaddam, P. & Tarokh, M. J. (2012). Customer involvement in innovation process based on open innovation concepts. *International Journal of Research in Industrial Engineering*, *1* (2), 1-9.

Nonaka, I. (1991). The knowledge creating company. *Harvard Business Review*, November–December, 162-171.

Nonaka, I. (1994). A dynamic theory of organizational knowledge creation. *Organization Science*, *5* (1), 14-37.

Nonaka, I. & Konno, N. (1998). The concept of ba: Building a foundation for knowledge creation. *California Management Review*, *40* (3), 40-54.

Nonaka, I. & Nishiguchi, T. (2001). *Knowledge Emergence: Social, Technical, and Revolutionary Dimensions of Knowledge Creation*, Oxford University Press, New York.

Nonaka, I. & Takeuchi, H. (1995). *The Knowledge-Creating Company: How Japanese Companies Create the Dynamics of Innovation*, Oxford University Press, New York.

Nonaka, I. & Toyama, R. (2003). The knowledge-creating theory revisited: knowledge creation as a synthesizing process. *Knowledge Management Research & Practice*, *1* (1), 2-10.

Nonaka, I., Kodama, M., Hirose, A. & Kohlbacher, F. (2014). Dynamic fractal organizations for promoting knowledge-based transformation – A new paradigm for organizational theory. *European Management Journal*, *32* (1), 137-146.

Nonaka, I., Toyama, R. & Konno, N. (2000). SECI, Ba and leadership: a unified model of dynamic knowledge creation. *Long Range Planning*, *33* (1), 5-34.

Nonaka, L., Takeuchi, H. & Umemoto, K. (1996). A theory of organizational knowledge creation. *International Journal of Technology Management*, *11* (7-8), 833-845.

O'Reilly, C. A. & Tushman, M. L. (2004). The ambidextrous organization. *Harvard Business Review*, *82* (4), 74-81.

O'Reilly, C. A. & Tushman, M. L. (2011). Organizational ambidexterity in action: How managers explore and exploit. *California Management Review*, *53* (4), 5-22.

Phillips, J. (2011). Open innovation typology. In: Sloane, P. (ed.), *A Guide to Open Innovation and Crowd-sourcing. Expert Tips and Advice*. London: Kogan Page Publisher, 22-36.

Piller, F. & West, J. (2014). Firms, users, and innovation. An Interactive Model of Coupled Open Innovation. In Chesbrough, H., Vanhaverbeke, W. and West, J. (eds.), *New Frontiers in Open Innovation*. Oxford University Press, 29-49.

Podmetina, D. & Smirnova, M. (2013). R&D cooperation with external partners and implementing Open Innovation. *Journal of Innovation Management*, *1* (2), 103-124.

Prahalad, C. K. & Hamel, G. (1990). The core competence of the corporation. *Harvard Business Review*, May-June, 235-256.

Raisch, S., Birkinshaw, J., Probst, G. & Tushman, M. L. (2009). Organizational ambidexterity: Balancing exploitation and exploration for sustained performance. *Organization Science*, *20* (4), 685-695.

Rayna, T. & Striukova, L. (2015). Open innovation 2.0: is co-creation the ultimate challenge? *International Journal of Technology Management*, *69* (1), 38-53.

Rumelt, R. P. (1987). Theory, strategy, and entrepreneurship. In Teece, D. J. (Ed.), *The Competitive Challenge: Strategies for Industrial Innovation and Renewal*. Cambridge (MA): Ballinger, 137-158.

Sarkar, S. & Costa, A. I. A. (2008). Dynamics of open innovation in the food industry. *Trends in Food Science & Technology*, *19* (11), 574-580.

Schroll, A. & Mild, A. (2011). Open innovation modes and the role of internal R&D: An empirical study on open innovation adoption in Europe. *European Journal of Innovation Management*, *14* (4), 475-495.

Shapiro, S. (2011). Envisioning the future of innovation. In: Sloane, P. (ed.), *A Guide to Open Innovation and Crowd-sourcing. Expert Tips and Advice*. London: Kogan Page Publisher, 202-207.

Shepherd, D. A., Haynie, J. M. & Patzelt, H. (2013). Project failures arising from corporate entrepreneurship: Impact of multiple project failures on employees' accumulated emotions, learning, and motivation. *Journal of Product Innovation Management, 30* (5), 880-895.

Sieg, J. H., Wallin, M. W. & Von Krogh, G. (2010). Managerial challenges in open innovation: a study of innovation intermediation in the chemical industry. *R&D Management, 40* (3), 281-291.

Teece, D. J., Pisano, G. & Shuen, A. (1997). Dynamic capabilities of the firm: an introduction. *Strategic Management Journal, 18* (7), 509-533.

Tushman, M. L. & O'Reilly III, C. A. (1996). Ambidextrous organizations: Managing evolutionary and revolutionary change. *California Management Review, 38* (4), 8-29.

Von Hippel, E. (2001). Innovation by user communities: Learning from open-source software. *MIT Sloan Management Review, 42* (4), 82-86.

Von Hippel, E. & Von Krogh, G. (2006). Free revealing and the private-collective model for innovation incentives. *R&D Management, 36* (3), 295-306.

West, J. & Bogers, M. (2014). Leveraging external sources of innovation: a review of research on open innovation. *Journal of Product Innovation Management, 31* (4), 814-831.

West, J. & Gallagher, S. (2006). Challenges of open innovation: the paradox of firm investment in open-source software. *R&D Management, 36* (3), 319-331.

Zahra, S. A. & George, G. (2002). Absorptive capacity: a review, reconceptualization, and extension. *Academy of Management Review, 27* (2), 185-203.

Zott, C. & Amit, R. (2007). Business model design and the performance of entrepreneurial firms. *Organization Science, 18* (2), 181-199.

In: Advances in Business and Management
Editor: William D. Nelson

ISBN: 978-1-53612-615-0
© 2017 Nova Science Publishers, Inc.

Chapter 5

OCCUPATIONAL INJURIES FROM A FINNISH PERSPECTIVE

Simo Salminen

Department of Social Psychology, University of Helsinki, Finland

ABSTRACT

The aim of this review is to look at occupational injuries, their risk factors, risk groups and consequences from Finnish perspective. I examined risk factors like age, experience, stress, sleeping problems, haste and handedness. Some working conditions like fixed-term contracts and subcontracting increased the risk of occupational injury. Then different occupations with high risk of occupational injury (agriculture, construction, fire fighters) were examined. In every chapter I first presented Finnish studies on the topic and then compared them on studies from other countries. Finally, some conclusions about the situation and perspectives of Finnish study on occupational safety will be given.

1. INTRODUCTION

There were 117,908 occupational injuries for wage earners in Finland in 2015. Of these 97,431 occurred at workplaces and 20,477 during commuting (TVK, 2017). Their annual costs were estimated to be over EUR 2 billion (Rissanen & Kaseva, 2014). The construction industry had the highest number of fatalities, followed by the mechanical, wood, metal, machinery, and pulp and paper industries (Yrjänheikki & Savolainen, 2000).

2. SAFETY MANAGEMENT

Management of safety should be a part of general management (Salminen & Saari, 1995). Management's active participation in safety activities decreased injury rates according to the Finnish safety personnel (Uusitalo & Mattla, 1989). However, many of the Finnish managers approached safety from the traditional viewpoint as the reactive measurement of injuries and their costs (Nenonen et al., 2015). Hierarchical position at a Finnish nucler power plant influenced perceptions of values: technicians had lower means than foremen and managers (Reiman & Oedewald, 2004). Small and middle-sized companies in the United Kingdom had a written health and safety policy statement and participation of senior management in safety and health management than the Spanish small and middle-sized companies (Vassie et al., 2000). The owners of small companies in Quebec did not see specific problems in occupational health and safety management (Champoux & Brun, 2003). Safety management is a meaningful in injury prevention.

3. PERSONAL FACTORS

In this chapter I will concern individual factors that related to the occupational injuries. These are age, experience, stress, sleep problems, haste, and handedness.

3.1. Younger Workers

The injury frequency of young workers under 25 years of age is higher than that of middle-aged and older employees (Rissa & Sysi-Aho, 2012). According to two Finnish data sets, the injury frequency of young workers was higher than that of older workers. The young injury victims hurt themselves more often when feeding or cleaning machines (Salminen, 1996). A review of 63 non-fatal studies indicated that majority of them showed a higher injury among young workers (Salminen, 2004). The number of occupational injuries is increasing among young women (Salminen & Räsänen, 2003). These Finnish studies showed that both young men and young women had an elevated risk of occupational injury. This conclusion is confirmed by an American review (Runyan & Zakocs, 2000).

3.2. Older Workers

The employees over 63 years of age had a 36% higher injury frequency than the employees aged between 50 and 55 according to the official Finnish occupational injury statistics (Salminen et al., 2016). The analysis of 99 serious occupational injuries in Southern Finland showed that getting run over by moving vehicle was a specific risk for older employees (Salminen, 1993). A review of 45 studies of fatal occupational injuries showed that the older workers had a higher fatality rate than the younger workers (Salminen, 2004). In the earlier review of 22 studies Laflamme and Menckel (1995) concluded that injury frequency tended to decrease with age, whereas age-related injury severity increased with age. Later Schwatka and her co-workers (2012) reviewed 22 other studies and concluded that the older employees in construction industry had a lower injury rate than the younger employees, but their injury costs were higher.

3.3. Experience

The young workers are often also inexperienced workers, but not all inexperienced employees are young ones. The analysis of 99 serious occupational accidents in Southern Finland showed that the injury risk was highest for workers who had been less than one year in the service of their employers. Their proportion of the injury victims (31%) was almost twice that in the working population (Salminen, 1994). An analysis of 58,271 Italian workers with 10,260 occupational injuries showed that the injury rate decreased with job experience. The workers with job tenure of less than 6 months had 46% higher injury rate than those over 2 years of tenure (Bena et al., 2013). Among French railway workers (n = 164,814), injury rate decreased steadily with the increasing length of service (Chau et al., 2010). In the U. S. mining industry injuries to 10,345 employees from 2003 to 2007 were analyzed and the total mining experience increased the number of days away from work following an injury also increased (Margolis, 2010). The analysis of 549,829 injury reports in Ontario, Canada, from 1999 to 2008 showed the highest injury risk among employees working their first month in the company (Morassaei et al., 2013). However, the effect of strong tenure disappeared after controlling demographic/individual and other work factors among adult Canadians 25-70 years old beginning a new job (Breslin et al., 2008). My conclusion is that the new employees had the highest risk of injury especially during their first year in the service of the company.

3.4. Stress

Among 5,111 Finnish hospital workers, psychological distress was not associated with the occupational injuries. However, low decision latitude, low skill discretion and highly monotonous work were related to the ccupational injuries (Salminen et al., 2003). In a study of 1,209 Korean manufacturing workers, high job strain and high job demands increased the risk of occupational injury among men, whereas among women low job

Occupational Injuries from a Finnish Perspective 159

control was also a risk factor (Kim et al., 2009). High job strain was also the most important risk factor for the occupational injury (odds ratio = 2.4, 95% CI 1.7-3.3) among 874 German nurses (Nolting et al., 2002). Stress was strongly associated with the agricultural injuries in two studies made in Iowa country side (n = 989 families and 3270 farmers) (Thu et al., 1997). A meta-analysis of 45 studies with 60,240 subjects showed that hindrance stressors had a significant positive correlation with the occupational injuries (p = .14), whereas challenge stressors were unrelated to the occupational injuries (p = .00) (Clarke, 2012). The connections between the stress factors and the occupational injuries seem to depend on the types of stress measures.

3.5. Sleep Problems

The insomnia-problems have increased among Finnish working population. The sleep duration has decreased 5.5 minutes (about 4%) per each 10 years from 1972 to 2005. Sleeping problems have increased among middle-aged working population (Kronholm et al., 2008). A large study of Finnish public sector employees (n = 48 598) showed that men with the sleeping disturbances had 38% higher risk of occupational injury (OR = 1.38, 95% CI 1.02-1.87) than men without sleeping disturbances. Women with the difficulties initiating sleep had also an elevated risk of occupational injury (OR = 1.69, 95% 1.26-2.26) compared to women without the sleeping problems (Salminen et al., 2010). These results are confirmed by an American study with 4,991 employees, because those with the insomnia had 90% more workplace injuries than those without the insomnia (Kessler et al., 2012). The persistent insomnia among Swedish women (n = 4320) were related to occupational injury (Hägg et al., 2015). Based on the 27 observational studies with 268,332 employees, Uehli and her co-workers (2013) concluded in their systematic review and meta-analysis that the sleep problems increased the risk of work injury by 62% (RR = 1.62, 95% CI 1.43-1.84). About 13% of work injuries could be attributed to sleep problems. I can conclude that the sleep problems almost double the risk of occupational injury.

3.6. Haste

People today experienced haste or excessive speed at work. A Finnish study with 12,926 employed people showed that the employees in haste rather or very often (25%) were involved in occupational injuries significantly more often than those working in haste less often (8%, $p < 0.001$) (Salminen et al., 2017). Haste was a more significant factor in work-related traffic than leisure-time traffic according to Finnish sales and marketing staff, and construction workers (Salminen & Lähdeniemi, 2002). High work pressure increased the risk of occupational injury among 967 Finnish civil servants (Hinkka et al., 2013). In the other countries haste was studied especially among the professional drivers. A questionnaire study among 223 male Turkish professional drivers showed that time pressure correlated significantly with violations and errors in traffic (Öz et al., 2013). Hurrying was the most reported cause of work-related eye injuries in a study of 816 Turkish workers (Serinken et al., 2013). Difficulties to keep deadlines increased the risk of on-duty road accidents over three times (OR = 3.4) among 148 French drivers who had been in work-related road accidents (Fort et al., 2013). However, the time pressure was not associated with the number of reported injuries among French drivers (n = 171) (Coeugnet et al., 2013). On the other hand, a recent Danish study showed that time pressure increased the risk of occupational injury by 60% (Österlund et al., 2017). Haste seems to increase the risk of occupational injury, although this topic is rather new in the research.

3.7. Laterality

No significant difference was found between the left- and right-handers in injury involvement in a study of Finnish subjects (n = 8,568), who were born in 1966 in Northern Finland and were at age of 30 at the moment of the study. On the other hand, the ambidextrous men had an increased risk of traffic and home injuries, whereas the ambidextrous women had an elevated risk of work injuries compared to right-handers (Pekkarinen et al., 2003). Among 329 Welsh patients injured at work, the right-handers injured more often than the left-handers (Beaton et al., 1994). In the Philadelphia Hand Center most of patients (n = 125) were injured by the saw. A digital amputation was 4.9 times more likely for the left-handers than for the right handers (Taras et al., 1995). The left-handers were more often involved in injuries among Indian train drivers (n = 80) (Bhushan & Khan, 2006). Based on these results, it was not possible to make a logical conclusion (Salminen, 2012).

4. WORK CONDITIONS

In Finland, the effect of some working conditions on injury frequency was studied. These are reporting of near accidents, working as self-employed or in fixed-term contract.

4.1. Near Accidents

The so called ice berg model says that near accidents and more serious accidents caused from same reasons. Thus investigating near accidents give information about causes of serious accidents. However, a Finnish study of 99 serious accidents showed that fatalities and other serious accidents were due to different reasons (Salminen et al., 1992). In an experiment at a Finnish steel factory voluntary reporting of near accidents and accidents exposed especially serious injury risks. There occurred at least four times more near accidents than injury accidents (Laitinen, 1982). Later he (Laitinen, 1984) analyzed 233 accidents and 75 near-accidents from the same steel factory. In over half of the near-accidents were a possibility of death or a very serious permanent disability, whereas only 10% of the accidents were potentially so severe. A near-accident reporting period in Sweden had no effect on the accident occurrence (Carter & Menckel, 1985). Using the near-miss reporting system decreased the expected rate of OSHA recordable injuries annually by 16% in the American electrical power distribution production factory with approximately 600 workers (Lander et al., 2010). These results showed that the near-accident reporting system has no consistent effects on occupational injury rate.

4.2. Self-Employed

About 2.9% of workforce are self-employed persons in Finland in 2010 (EVA, 2017). Their risk of occupational injury was 40% higher than that of the average salaried employee (Pukkila, 1998). The Census of Fatal Occupational Injuries in 1993 counted 1,191 fatalities among the self-employed persons in U. S. They share a larger part of all fatal work injuries than their share of total employment. The self-employed had a higher risk especially on farms and in retailing (Personick & Windau, 1995). Based on the North Carolina Office of the Chief Medical Examiner's database from 1978 to 1994, 395 fatal injuries to self-employed (14.4%) and 1,654 fatalities to privately employed were found. The age-adjusted death rate for self-employed (7.0 per 100.000 workers-years) was higher than that of private employed (4.4). The occupational death rate was highest among the self-employed in retail and transportation industries (Mirabelli et al., 2003). Based on the information from the BLS Census of Fatal Occupational Injuries from 2001, Pegula (2004) calculated that the fatality rate of self-employed workers (11.2 per 100.000 workers) was 2.7 times higher than that of the wage and salary workers (3.9). Especially mining, agriculture and transportation had high fatality rate for self-employed workers. Thus these studies consistently showed that the self-employed workers had a higher risk of injury than wage and salary workers.

4.3. Fixed-Term Work

In Finland 34% of employees had a fixed-term work contract in 1998 (Jolkkonen & Koistinen, 2001) and they were mostly females working in public sector. Based on the three large Finnish data sets, Saloniemi and Salminen (2010) had indicated that the fixed-term employees did not have a higher occupational injury rate than the permanent employees. Hintikka (2011) showed that there was an increased risk of injury in the temporary agency work in Finland. In the Indian fertilizer producing industry (n = 726) temporary workers had 1.2-3.5 times more injuries than permanent workers (Saha et al., 2004). Later they (Saha et al., 2005) calculated that relative risk of injury frequency for temporary workers was 6.7 (95% CI 5.6-8.0) compared to permanent workers. A study based on three large Finnish data sets showed that there was no increased risk of violence among the fixed-term workers (Salminen & Saloniemi, 2010). In the other Finnish study, the fixed-term blue-collar employees (n = 1,127) had two times higher risk of physical strain of work: monotonous movements, difficult working positions, and heavy lifting during the daily work (Saloniemi et al., 2004). The Finnish review of 13 separate studies concluded that seven studies reported a higher risk of occupational injury among the temporary employees (Virtanen et al., 2005).

4.4. Immigrants

The comparison of 176 Finnish and 130 immigrant bus drivers showed that there was no significant difference in the occupational injuries by self-reporting and by company-records. It was indicated that under same working conditions, the immigrants can work as safely as the native employees (Salminen et al., 2009). The injury rate of Indian employees in Malaysia was three times higher (21.1) than that of Malay employees (6.8) (Abas et al., 2011). The migrant employees had 73% higher occupational injury rate than the Korean employees in 2007 (Cha & Cho, 2014). However, a review of 31 studies showed that immigrants had on average

2.13 times higher injury rate than native employees (Salminen, 2011). One explanation for the higher injury rate of immigrant employees is that they are working in more hazardous jobs. However, there was no empirical confirmation for this thesis from Canada (Tiagi, 2015).

5. INDUSTRY

The focus of occupational injury study has been of course to the most dangerous industries. Based on the representaive sample of Finnish working population, it was shown that agriculture and construction had the highest injury frequencies (Mattila & Salminen, 2013).

5.1. Agriculture

A large study based on the representative sample of Finnish employees showed that agriculture had the highest injury frequency (Mattila & Salminen, 2013). The relatively most dangerous types of operation in Finnish agriculture were the crop production and the milk production (Sinisalo, 2012). A total of 5,507 compensated injuries occurred in the Finnish farms in 2002 and 21% of them caused over 30 sickness days. Older age, male gender, higher income level, greater field size, residing on the farm, speaking Finnish language (vs. Swedish), occupational health service membership and animal production were the risk factors for serious farm-related injury (Rautiainen et al., 2009). The analysis of 78,679 Finnish farmers and their 24,424 occupational injuries from 2000 to 2004 showed that cattle-intensive geographic regions, occupational health service membership, large farm size, and farming alone were the risk factors for occupational injury. In addition, male gender, higher number of insurance years, and residing on the farm were the risk factors for injury (Karttunen & Rautiainen, 2013a). Cattle was the most important cause for injury among Finnish dairy farmers. Long work history, small-scale dairy farm operation and conventional stanchion barn for dairy cattle were found as the risk factors (Karttunen & Rautiainen, 2013b). A total of 217 farm-related fatalities occurred in Finland between 1988 and 2000. Of these, 120 were tractor-related, and 97 were other fatal injuries. The tractor overturns during driving on a road or working in a field were the most typical fatalities with tractors (Rissanen & Taattola, 2003).

Virtanen and his co-workers (2003) analyzed 11,657 occupational injuries among 69,629 full-time farmers during 1996-1997. The dairy farming and hog farming were the riskiest farm activities and men had a higher injury rate than women, except with regard to injuries caused by animals. Thus animals caused 77% of women's farm injuries in Finland (Kallioniemi et al., 2011). A computer-assisted telephone interview of 1,182 self-employed full-time farmers showed that male gender, younger age, cooperation with other farmers, perceived high injury risk, and stress symptoms were the risk factors for occupational injuries (Taattola et al., 2012). The incident rates in 1996 were 7.4/100 farmers for injuries and 0.61/100 for occupational diseases. The mean cost was € 1340 for injuries and € 6636 for occupational diseases, which means 0.7% of the national gross farm income and 2.2% of the net farm income (Rautiainen et al., 2005). The speciality in the Polar Circle area was reindeer herding. Gathering for separation and separation caused most of reeindeer injuries (Pekkarinen, 2006). I can conclude that agriculture has been one of the main topics in Finnish injury studies. Most of injuries occurred in working with the cattle and cow was among them the most dangerous animal.

5.2. Construction

Based on the analysis of 99 serious occupational injuries in Southern Finland 1988-1989, it was shown that subcontractors' workers at construction sites had 1.7 times higher risk of injury than main contractor's workers (Salminen, 1995). A study of 215 Finnish construction injuries showed that there were more injuries at construction sites for blocks of flats than at construction sites for terrace houses (Niskanen & Saarsalmi, 1983). A comparison of 69 concrete reinforcement employees and 91 painters indicated that the injury rate for musculoskeletal system was four times higher among the reinforcement employees (124) than among painters (30) (Niskanen, 1985). An analysis of 422 construction accidents showed 64% of them occurred during construction of the framework (Niskanen & Lauttalammi, 1989b). The injury rate was highest in building repair and renovation (Niskanen & Lauttalammi, 1989c). Eliminating the hazard of falling was the most important factor in improving occupational safety on industrial building sites (Niskanen & Lauttalammi, 1989a).

The Finnish contruction employees (n = 3,500) built the town of Kostomuksha in the Soviet Union during 1974 to 1982. The injury rate in this construction site was double compared to the Finnish construction sites (Pekkarinen & Anttonen, 1989). A Finnish driven Cochrane review showed that both a safety-campaign study and a drug-free-workplace study reduced significantly the level and the trend of injuries (Lehtola et al., 2008). A Job Load and Hazard Analysis investigated in Finland generated more suggestions to improve safety than the older methods (Mattila, 1989) and according to the employees increased safety (Mattila & Kivi, 1991).

5.3. Forestry

An analysis of 228 Finnish loggers showed that the main causes of their 44 injuries were losing of one's balance, a small flying object, and the chain saw (Salminen et al., 2001). An earlier analysis of the same data set indicated that risk taking was not significantly related to injuries (Salminen et al., 1999). In the Western Black Sea region of Turkey, personal factors (32%) and organisational factors (22%) were identified as the reasons for fatal forest harvesting injuries (Melemez, 2015). The analysis of 470 forestry injuries in Australia showed that they occurred most often during harvesting (37%) and forest management (30%) (Ghaffariyan, 2016). In a Finnish study, 95% of loggers reported the same injuries both on self-reporting and company records (Klen & Ojanen, 1998). In the other Finnish study, loggers less than 40 years old with a low back pain had learned a new work technique and they used it even four years later

(Väyrynen & Könönen, 1991). The use of personal protectors reduced injury rates among Finnish loggers (Klen, 1997). Safety boots prevented the greatest number of injuries (Klen & Väyrynen, 1984). These studies indicated that forestry is an important industry in Finland and has been a focus of many studies. We had also successfully prevented injuries of Finnish forest workers.

5.4. Firefighters

Among the 543 Finnish male firefighters 103 occupational injuries were suffered. Those working over 70 hours per week were involved in injuries almost four times more often than those working less than 50 hours per week (Lusa et al., 2002). There were 66 fatal fighter suppression injuries in the Netherlands since 1946 and till 2006. High time pressure was related to 75% of the fatalities (Rosmuller & Ale, 2008). The analysis of 8,518 injuries to Polish fire fighters showed that sporting activities at the fire stations caused about 41% of the injuries. During rescue operations one out of five injuries occurred (Pawlak et al., 2016). Among Swedish firemen 1468 injuries occurred during fitness training from 1992 to 1998. Most of them (75%) occurred during contact team sports such as soccer and floorball (de Loës & Jansson, 2001). Burn injuries are the special risk for the fire fighters. The analysis of 20 American fire fighters suffering work-related burns showed that face was the site most commonly burned, representing 29% of injuries. The hand/wrist (23% of injuries) and ears (16% of injuries) were the next largest groups (Kahn et al., 2012). It is interesting that sporting activities caused more injuries to firefighters than proper work tasks of fire fighting.

5.5. Seafarers

The injury rate among Finnish seafarers in 1986 was lower (42.3 per million workhours) than that of the whole wage-earning population (49.4).

More than half (52.9%) of the injuries among seafarers were related to the working environment and this percentage is about 10 per cent higher than in the manufacturing industry (Saarni, 1989). The analysis of 942 Finnish sea pilots showed that 262 of them had died between 1956-1985. Violence, accidents or poisoning caused every tenth death. This study did not indicate that the sea pilots in Finland formed a special occupational risk group (Saarni et al., 1996). An international questionnaire study in 11 countries with 6,461 seafarers showed that 9.1% of them were injured. Low self-perceived health, lack of use of personal protection and lack of occupational safety on board were significantly associated with an increased risk of injury (Jensen et al., 2004a). Another international questionnaire study from Finland, Denmark, the Philippines, Croatia and Spain (n = 1,068) showed that the injury risk of seamen was 2.43 times higher than that of officers (Jensen et al., 2004b). However, based on the Danish International Ship Register in 2010-2012, 1,453 occupational injuries were found. The relative risk of occupational mortality for a seafarer was found to be 11.5 times higher than that of Danish male ashore workers (Ádám, 2013). Western Europe seafares had an overall injury rate of 17.5 per 100.000 person-days, whereas seafarers from Eastern Europe (0.53), South East Asia (0.51) and India (0.74) had significantly lower rates (Àdám et al., 2014). Accidents caused 91 deaths among the British seafarers between 1976 and 1995 (Roberts, 2003). Between 1986 and 1995, the relative risk of mortality due to injuries at work among seafarers (96 fatalities) was 23.9 times higher than for all workers in Great Britain (Roberts & Hansen, 2002). The results from Finland differs from those from other countries, which is perhaps due to small number of seafarers in Finland.

CONCLUSION

The occupational safety work in Finland had focused on agriculture, construction and forestry. This is a right decision, because these industries are also the most dangerous industries. These studies have also helped to eliminate occupational injuries at the first steps of research.

Although the number of occupational injuries has decreased significantly from 1970's to nowadays (Salminen, 2009), there are new challenges to injury prevention. For example, fixed-term work contracts and subcontracting have increased the risk of occupational injury. In future especially violence at workplaces will increase (Salminen & Seo, 2015).

Funding of occupational safety research has decreased in Finland as in many other countries. Thus the number of Finnish studies in international journals will decrease in the future. However, the number of occupational injuries is still high in Finland.

REFERENCES

Abas, A. B. L., Said, A. R. B. M., Mohammed, M. A. B. A. & Sathiakumar, N. (2011). Non-fatal occupational injuries among non-governmental employees in Malaysia. *International Journal of Occupational and Environmental Health*, *17*, 38-48.

Ádám, B. (2013). Association between nationality and occupational injury risk on Danish non-passenger merchant ships. *International Maritime Health*, *64*, 121-125.

Ádám, B., Rasmussen, H. B., Pedersen, R. N. F. & Jepsen, J. R. (2014). Occupational accidents in the Danish merchant fleet and the nationality of seafarers. *Journal of Occupational Medicine and Toxicology*, *9*, 35.

Beaton, A. A., Williams, L. & Moseley, L. G. (1994). Handedness and hand injuries. *Journal of Hand Surgery*, *19B,* 158-161.

Bena, A., Giraudo, M., Leombruni, R. & Costa, G. (2013). Job tenure and work injuries: a multivariate analysis of the relation with previous experience and differences by age. *BMC Public Health*, *13*, 869.

Bhushan, B. & Khan, S. M. (2006). Laterality and accident proneness: A study of locomotive drivers. *Laterality*, *11*, 395-404.

Breslin, F. C., Tompa, E., Zhao, R., Pole, J. D., Amick, B. C. III, Smith, P. M. & Hogg-Johnson, S. (2008). The relationship between job tenure and work disability absence among adults: A prospective study. *Accident Analysis and Prevention, 40*, 368-375.

Carter, N. & Menckel, E. (1985). Near-accident reporting: A review of Swedish research. *Journal of Occupational Accidents*, *7*, 41-64.

Cha, S. & Cho, Y. (2014). Fatal and non-fatal occupational injuries and diseases among migrant and native workers on South Korea. *American Journal of Industrial Medicine*, *57*, 1043-1052.

Champoux, D. & Brun, J.-P. (2003). Occupational health and safety management in small size enterprises: an overview of the situation and avenues for intervention and research. *Safety Science, 41*, 301-318.

Chau, N., Wild, P., Deahaene, D., Benamghar, L., Mur, J. M. & Touron, C. (2010). Roles of age, length of service and job in work-related injury: a prospective study of 446 120 person-years in railway workers. *Occupational and Environmental Medicine*, *67*, 147-153.

Clarke, S. (2012). The effect of challenge and hindrance stressors on safety behavior and safety outcomes: A meta-analysis. *Journal of Occupational Health Psychology*, *17*, 387-397.

Coeugnet, S., Naveteur, J., Antoine, P. & Anceaux, F. (2013). Time pressure and driving: Work, emotions and risks. *Transportation Research, Part F, 20*, 39-51.

de Loës, M. & Jansson, B. R. (2001). Work-related injuries from mandatory fitness training among Swedish firemen. *International Journal of Sports Medicine*, *22*, 373-378.

EVA (2017). Yrittäjyysaste eräissä EU-maissa 2010 [Degree of self-employment in some countries in European Union 2010]. http://www.eva.fi/tyotjatekijat/yrittäjien-maara-eussa/Downloaded 6.2.2017.

Fort, E., Chiron, M., Davezies, P., Bergeret, A. & Charbotel, B. (2013). Driving behaviors and on-duty road accidents: A French case-control study. *Traffic Injury Prevention, 14*, 353-359.

Ghaffariyan, M. R. (2016). Analysis of forestry work accidents in five Australian forest companies for the period 2004 to 2014. *Journal of Forest Science, 62*, 545-552.

Hinkka, K., Kuoppala, J., Väänänen-Tomppo, I. & Lamminpää, A. (2013). Psychosocial work factors and sick leave, occupational accident, and disability pension. A cohort study of civil servants. *Journal of Occupational and Environmental Medicine*, *55*, 191-197.

Hintikka, N. (2011). Accidents at work during temporary agency work in Finland – Comparisons between certain major industries and other industries. *Safety Science*, *49*, 473-483.

Hägg, S. A., Torèn, K. & Lindberg, E. (2015). Role of sleep disturbances in occupational accidents among women. *Scandinavian Journal of Work, Environment and Health*, *41*, 377-383.

Jensen, O. C., Sörensen, J. F. L., Canals, M. L., Hu, Y. P., Nicolic, N. & Thomas, M. (2004a). Indidence of self-reported occupational injuries in seafaring – an international study. *Occupational Medicine*, *54*, 548-555.

Jensen, O. C., Sörensen, J. F. L., Kaerlev, L., Canals, M. L., Nicolic, N. & Saarni, H. (2004b). Self-reported injuries among seafarers: Questionnaire validity and results from an international study. *Accident Analysis and Prevention*, *36*, 405-413.

Jolkkonen, A. & Koistinen, P. (2001). Pätkätyö -askel vai este pysyvään työllisyyteen? [A fixed-term work contract - a step or obstacle for permanent contract?]. *Kansantaloudellinen Aikakauskirja*, *97*, 556-572.

Kahn, S. A., Patel, J. H., Lentz, C. W. & Bell, D. E. (2012). Firefighter burn injuries: predictable patterns influenced by turnout gear. *Journal of Burn Care Research, 33*, 152-156.

Kallioniemi, M. K., Raussi, S. M., Rautiainen, R. H. & Kymäläinen, H.-R. (2011). Safety and animal handling practices among women dairy operators. *Journal of Agricultural Safety and Health, 17*, 63-78.

Karttunen, J. P. & Rautiainen, R. H. (2013a). Occupational injury and disease incidence and risk factors in Finnish agriculture based on 5-year insurance records. *Journal of Agromedicine, 18*, 50-64.

Karttunen, J. P. & Rautiainen, R. H. (2013b) Characteristics of and risk factors for compensated occupational injury and disease claims in dairy farmers: A case-control study. *Journal of Agricultural Safety and Health, 19*, 191-206.

Kessler, R. C., Berglund, P. A., Coulouvrat, C., Fitzgerald, T., Hajak, G., Roth, T., Shahly, V., Shillington, A. C., Stephenson, J. J. & Walsh, J. K. (2012). Insomnia, comorbidity, and risk of injury among insured Americans: Results from the America Insomnia Survey. *Sleep, 35*, 825-834.

Kim, H.-C., Min, J.-Y., Min, K.-B. & Park, S.-G. (2009). Job strain and the risk of occupational injury in small- to medium-sized manufacturing enterprises: A prospective study of 1,209 Korean employees. *American Journal of Industrial Medicine, 52*, 322-330.

Klen, T. (1997). Personal protectors and working behaviour of loggers. *Safety Science, 25*, 89-103.

Klen, T. & Ojanen, K. (1998). The correspondence of self-reported accidents with company records. *Safety Science, 28*, 45-48.

Klen, T. & Väyrynen, S. (1984). The role of personal protection in the prevention of accidental injuries in logging work. *Journal of Occupational Accidents, 6*, 263-275.

Kronholm, E., Partonen, T., Laatikainen, T., Peltonen, M., Härmä, M., Hublin, C., Kaprio, J., Aro, A. R., Partinen, M., Fogelholm, M., Valve, R., Vahtera, J., Oksanen, T., Kivimäki, M., Koskenvuo, M. & Sutela, H. (2008). Trends in self-reported sleep duration and insomnia-related symptoms in Finland from 1972 to 2005: a comparative review and re-analysis of Finnish population samples. *Journal of Sleep Research, 17*, 54-62.

Laflamme, L. & Menckel, E. (1995). Aging and occupational accidents: A review of the literature of the last three decades. *Safety Science, 21*, 145-161.

Laitinen, H. (1982). Reporting noninjury accidents: A tool in accident prevention. *Journal of Occupational Accidents, 4*, 275-280.

Laitinen, H. (1984). Estimation of potential seriousness of accidents and near-accidents. *Journal of Occupational Accidents, 6*, 167-174.

Lander, L., Eisen, E. A., Stentz, T. L., Spanjer, K. J., Wendland, B. E. & Perry, M. J. (2010). Near-miss reporting system as an occupational injury preventive intervention in manufacturing. *American Journal of Industrial Medicine*, *54*, 40-48.

Lehtola, M. M., van der Molen, H. F., Lappalainen, J., Hoonakker, P. L. T., Hsiao, H., Haslam, R. A., Hale, A. R. & Verbeek, J. H. (2008). The effectiveness of interventions for preventing injuries in the construction industry: A systematic review. *American Journal of Preventive Medicine*, *35*, 77-85.

Lusa, S., Häkkänen, M., Luukkonen, R. & Viikari-Juntura, E. (2002). Perceived physical work capacity, stress, sleep disturbance and occupational accidents among firefighters working during a strike. *Work & Stress*, *16,* 264-274.

Margolis, K. A. (2010). Underground coal mining injury: A look at how age and experience relate to days lost from work following an injury. *Safety Science, 48,* 417-421.

Mattila, M. (1989). Improvement in the occupational health program in a Finnish construction company by means of systematic workplace investigation of job load and hazard analysis. *American Journal of Industrial Medicine, 15*, 61-72.

Mattila, M. & Kivi, P. (1991). Hazard screening and proposals for prevention by occupational health service: An experiment with job load and hazard analysis at a Finnish construction company. *Journal of Society of Occupational Medicine*, *41*, 17-22.

Mattila, S. & Salminen, S. (2013). Työtapaturmat [Occupational Injuries]. In Kauppinen T. et al., (Eds.), Työ ja terveys Suomessa 2012 [Work and Health in Finland 2012], (pp. 149-158). Helsinki: Työterveyslaitos. (in Finnish).

Melemez, K. (2015). Risk factor analysis of fatal forest harvesting accidents: A case study in Turkey. *Safety Science*, *79*, 369-378.

Mirabelli, M. C., Loomis, D. & Richardson, D. B. (2003). Fatal occupational injuries among self-employed workers in North Carolina. *American Journal of Industrial Medicine*, *44*, 182-190.

Morassaei, S., Breslin, F. C., Ibrahim, S. A., Smith, P. M., Mustard, C. A., Amick, B. C., Shankardass, K. & Petch, J. (2013). Geographic variation in work injuries: a multilevel analysis of individual-level data and area-level factors within Canada. *Annals of Epidemiology, 23*, 260-266.

Nenonen, N., Hämäläinen, P., Heikkilä, J., Reiman, T. & Tappura, S. (2015). Corporate managers' perceptions of safety and its value: an interview study of five internationally operating Finnish companies. *Policy and Practice in Health and Safety, 13*, 3-15.

Niskanen, T. (1985). Accidents and minor accidents of the musculoskeletal system in heavy (concrete reinforcement work) and light (painting) construction work. *Journal of Occupational Accidents, 7*, 17-32.

Niskanen, T. & Lauttalammi, J. (1989a). Accident prevention in materials handling at building construction sites. *Construction Management and Economics, 7*, 263-279.

Niskanen, T. & Lauttalammi, J. (1989b). Accident risks during handling of materials at building construction sites. *Construction Management and Economics, 7*, 283-301.

Niskanen, T. & Lauttalammi, J. (1989c). Accidents in materials handling at building construction sites. *Journal of Occupational Accidents, 11*, 1-17.

Niskanen, T. & Saarsalmi, O. (1983). Accident analysis in the construction of buildings. *Journal of Occupational Accidents, 5*, 89-98.

Nolting, H.-D., Berger, J., Schiffhorst, G., Genz, H. O. & Kordt, M. (2002). Psychischer stress als risikofaktor für arbeitsunfälle bei pflegekräften im krankenhaus. *Gesudheitswesen, 64*, 25-32.

Pawlak, A., Gotlib, J. & Galazkowski, R. (2016). The analysis outlining the occurrence and consequences of accidents in the work environment of the firefighters employed by the State Fire Service in Poland in 2008-2013. *Medycyna Pracy, 67(1)*, 1-9.

Pegula, S. M. (2004). Occupational fatalities: self-employed workers and wage and salary workers. *Monthly Labor Review, March*, 30-40.

Pekkarinen, A. (2006). Changes in reindeer herding work and their effect on occupational accidents. *International Journal of Circumpolar Health, 65*, 357-364.

Pekkarinen, A. & Anttonen, H. (1989). The comparison of accidents in a foreign construction project with construction in Finland. *Journal of Safety Research*, *20*, 187-195.

Pekkarinen, A., Salminen, S. & Järvelin, M.-R. (2003). Hand preference and risk of injury among the Northern Finland birth cohort at the age of 30. *Laterality*, *8*, 339-346.

Personick, M. E. & Windau, J. A. (1995). Self-employed individuals fatally injured at work. *Monthly Labor Review, 118(8),* 24-29.

Pukkila, P. (1998). Yrittäjillä selvästi suurempi tapaturmariski kuin työntekijöillä [Self-employed had a clearly higher risk of injury than employees]. *Tapaturmavakuutus*, *71(3),* 10-11. (in Finnish).

Rautiainen, R. H., Ledolter, J., Donham, K. J., Ohsfeldt, R. L. & Zwerling, C. (2009). Risk factors for serious injury in Finnish agriculture. *American Journal of Industrial Medicine*, *52*, 419-428.

Rautiainen, R. H., Ohsfeldt, R., Sprince, N. L., Donham, K. J., Burmeister, L. F., Reynolds, S. J., Saarimäki, P. & Zwerling, C. (2005). Cost of compensated injuries and occupational diseases in agriculture in Finland. *Journal of Agromedicine*, *10*, 21-29.

Reiman, T. & Oedewald, P. (2004). Measuring maintenance culture and maintenance core task with CULTURE-questionnaire – a case study in the power industry. S*afety Science, 42*, 859-889.

Rissa, K. & Sysi-aho, J. (2012). Nuorilla suurin tapaturmariski [Young employees have the highest risk of injury]. *Tapaturmavakuutus, 85(1),* 12-15. (in Finnish).

Rissanen, M. & Kaseva, E. (2014). Menetetyn työpanoksen kustannus [Cost of lost work contribution]. Helsinki: Sosiaali- ja terveysministeriö, työsuojeluosasto, toimintapolitiikkayksikkö, strateginen suunnittelu -ryhmä. (in Finnish).

Rissanen, P. & Taattola, K. (2003). Fatal injuries in Finnish agriculture, 1988-2000. *Journal of Agricultural Safety and* Health, *9,* 319-326.

Roberts, S. E. (2003). Work-related mortality among British seafarers employed in flags of convenience shipping, 1976-95. *International Maritime Health, 54*, 1-4.

Roberts, S. E. & Hansen, H. L. (2002). An analysis of the causes of mortality among seafarers in the British merchant fleet (1986-1995) and recommendations for their reduction. *Occupational Medicine, 52,* 195-202.

Rosmuller, N. & Ale, B. J. M. (2008). Classification of fatal firefighter accidents in the Netherlands: Time pressure and aim of the supression activity. *Safety Science, 46,* 282-290.

Runyan, C. W. & Zakocs, R. C. (2000). Epidemiology and prevention of injuries among adolescent workers in the United States. *Annual Review of Public Health, 21,* 247-269.

Saarni, H. (1989). Industrial accidents among Finnish seafarers. *Travel Medicine International, 7,* 64-68.

Saarni, H., Niemi, L., Koskela, R.-S., Pentti, J. & Kuusela, A. (1996). Mortality among Finnish sea pilots 1956-85: a retrospective cohort study. *Occupational Medicine, 46,* 281-284.

Saha, A., Kulkarni, P. K., Chaudhuri, R. & Saiyed, H. (2005). Occupational injuries: Is job security a factor? *Indian Journal of Medical Sciences, 59,* 375-381.

Saha, A., Ramnath, T., Chaudhuri, R. N. & Saiyed, H. N. (2004). An accident-risk assessment study of temporary piece rated workers. *Industrial Health, 42,* 240-245.

Salminen, S. (1993). The specific accident factor of older employees. *Accident Analysis and Prevention, 25,* 99-102.

Salminen, S. T. (1994). Epidemiological analysis of serious occupational accidents in Southern Finland. *Scandinavian Journal of Social Medicine, 22,* 225-227.

Salminen, S. (1995). Serious occupational accidents in the construction industry. *Construction Management and Economics, 13,* 299-306.

Salminen, S. (1996). Work-related accidents among young workers in Finland. *International Journal of Occupational Safety and Ergonomics, 2,* 305-314.

Salminen, S. (2004). Have young workers more injuries than older ones? An international literature review. *Journal of Safety Research, 35,* 513-521.

Salminen, S. (2009). Työtapaturmat [Occupational injuries]. In K. Tiirikainen (Ed.), Tapaturmat Suomessa [Injuries in Finland], (pp. 103-109). Helsinki: Edita. (in Finnish).

Salminen, S. (2011). Are immigrants at increased risk of occupational injury? A literature review. *Ergonomics Open Journal*, *4*, 139-144.

Salminen, S. (2012). Handedness and occupational injuries. In: T. Dutta et al., (Eds.), Bias in Human Behavior, (pp 191-197). New York: Nova Science Publishers.

Salminen, S., Heinonen, A. & Sysi-Aho, J. (2016). Retirement age and occupational injury. Helsinki: Finnish Workers' Compensation Center.

Salminen, S., Kivimäki, M., Elovainio, M. & Vahtera, J. (2003). Stress factors predicting injuries of hospital personnel. *American Journal of Industrial Medicine*, *44*, 32-36.

Salminen, S., Klen, T. & Ojanen, K. (1999). Risk taking and accident frequency among Finnish forestry workers. *Safety Science*, *33*, 143-153.

Salminen, S., Klen, T. & Ojanen, K. (2001). Epidemiology of occupational accidents of Finnish forestry workers. *Journal of Forest Science*, *47*, 42-44.

Salminen, S. & Lähdeniemi, E. (2002). Risk factors in work-related traffic. T*ransportation Research F: Traffic Psychology and Behaviour*, *5*, 375-384.

Salminen, S., Oksanen, T., Vahtera, J., Sallinen, M., Härmä, M., Salo, P., Virtanen, M. & Kivimäki, M. (2010). Sleep disturbances as a predictor of occupational injuries among public sector workers. *Journal of Sleep Research*, *19*, 207-213.

Salminen, S, Perttula, P., Hirvonen, M., Perkiö-Mäkelä, M. & Vartia, M. (2017). Link between haste and occupational injury. *Work: A journal of prevention, assessment and rehabilitation, 56*, 119-124.

Salminen, S. & Räsänen, T. (2003). Nuorten naisten työtapaturmat kasvussa [The number of occupational injuries among young women are increasing]. *Työ ja ihminen, 17*, 248-256. (in Finnish with English summary).

Salminen, S. & Saari J. (1995). Measures to improve safety and productivity simultaneously. *International Journal of Industrial Ergonomics*, 15, 261-269.

Salminen, S., Saari, J., Saarela, K. L. & Räsänen, T. (1992). Fatal and non-fatal occupational accidents: identical versus differential causation. *Safety Science, 15,* 109-118.

Salminen, S. & Saloniemi, A. (2010). Fixed-term work and violence at work. *International Journal of Occupational Safety and Ergonomics, 16,* 323-328.

Salminen, S. & Seo, D. (2015). Future of occupational injuries. *International Journal of Asian Social Science, 5,* 341-354.

Salminen, S., Vartia, M. & Giorgiani, T. (2009). Occupational injuries of immigrant and Finnish bus drivers. *Journal of Safety Research, 40,* 203-205.

Saloniemi, A. & Salminen, S. (2010). Do fixed-term workers have a higher injury rate? *Safety Science, 48,* 693-697.

Saloniemi, A., Virtanen, P. & Koivisto, A.-M. (2004). Is fixed-term employment a new risk for adverse physical working conditions? *International Journal of Occupational Safety and Ergonomics, 10,* 33-40.

Schwatka, N. V., Butler, L. M. & Rosecrance, J. R. (2012). An aging workforce and injury in the construction industry. *Epidemiological Reviews, 34,* 156-167.

Serinken, M., Turkcuer, I., Cetin, E. N., Ylimaz, A., Elicabuk, H. & Karcioglu, O. (2013). Causes and characteristics of work-related eye injuries in western Turkey. *Indian Journal of Ophthalmology, 61,* 497-501.

Sinisalo, A. (2012). Expected injury cost indices on Finnish farms. *Journal of Agricultural Safety and Health, 18,* 31-43.

Taattola, K., Rautiainen, R. H., Karttunen, J. P., Suutarinen, J., Viluksela, M. K., Louhelainen, K. & Mäittälä, J. (2012). Risk factors for occupational injuries among full-time farmers in Finland. *Journal of Agricultural Safety and Health, 18,* 83-93.

Taras, J. S., Behrman, M. J. & Degnan, G. G. (1995). Left-hand dominance and hand trauma. *Journal of Hand Surgery*, *20A,* 1043-1046.

Thu, K., Lasley, P., Whitten, P., Lewis, M., Donham, K. J., Zwerling, C. & Scarth, R. (1997). Stress as a risk factor for agricultural injuries: comparative data from the Iowa Farm Family Health and Hazard Survey (1994) and the Iowa Farm and Rural Life Poll (1989). *Journal of Agromedicine, 4,* 181-191.

Tiagi, R. (2015). Are immigrants in Canada over-represented in riskier jobs relative to Canadian-born labor market participants? *American Journal of Industrial Medicine, 58*, 933-942.

TVK. 2017. Työtapaturmat [Official statistics of occupational injuries]. http://www.tvk.fi/fi/Tilastot-/Tilastojulkaisut. downloaded 6.4.2017.

Uehli, K., Mehta, A. J., Miedinger, D., Hug, K., Schindler, C., Holsboer-Trachsler, E., Leuppi, J. D. & Künzli, N. (2013). Sleep problems and work injuries: A systematic review and meta-analysis. *Sleep Medicine Reviews, 18,* 61-73.

Uusitalo, T. & Mattila, M. (1989). Evaluation of industrial safety practices in five industries. In: Mital, A. (Ed.), *Advances in Industrial Ergonomics and Safety I,* (pp. 353-358). London: Taylor & Francis.

Vassie, L., Tomas, J. M. & Oliver, A. (2000). Health and safety management in UK and Spanish SMEs: A comparative study. *Journal of Safety Research, 31*, 35-43.

Virtanen, M., Kivimäki, M., Joensuu, M., Virtanen, P., Elovainio, M. & Vahtera, J. (2005). Temporary employment and health: a review. *International Journal of Epidemiology*, *34*, 610-622.

Virtanen, S. V., Notkola, V., Luukkonen, R., Eskola, E. & Kurppa, K. (2003). Work injuries among Finnish farmers: A national register linkage study 1996-1997. *American Journal of Industrial Medicine, 43,* 314-325.

Väyrynen, S. & Könönen, U. (1991). Short and long-term effects of a training programme on work postures in rehabilitees: A pilot study of loggers suffering from back troubles. *International Journal of Industrial Ergonomics, 7*, 103-109.

Yrjänheikki, E. & Savolainen, H. (2000). Occupational safety and health in Finland. *Journal of Safety Research, 31*, 177-183.

Österlund, A. H., Lander, F., Nielsen, K., Kines, P., Möller, J. & Lauritsen, J. (2017). Transient risk factors of acute occupational injuries: a case-crossover study in two Danish emergency departments. *Scandinavian Journal of Work, Environment & Health, 43*, 217-225.

Öz, B., Özkan, T. & Lajunen, T. (2013). An investigation of professional drivers: Organizational safety climate, driver behaviours and performance. *Transportation Research, Part F, 16*, 81-91.

In: Advances in Business and Management
Editor: William D. Nelson

ISBN: 978-1-53612-615-0
© 2017 Nova Science Publishers, Inc.

Chapter 6

FIRMS AS POLICY ADVOCATES AND INSTITUTIONAL FRAMERS: UNDERSTANDING THE IMPACT OF ETHNIC AND POLITICAL STRATIFICATION ON BRICS MNEs

Luis Alfonso Dau[1,], Elizabeth M. Moore[1,†], James Figgins[1,‡] and Joshua K. Ault[2,§]*

[1]Northeastern University, Boston, MA, US
[2]Thunderbird School of Global Management, Glendale, AZ, US

ABSTRACT

The purpose of this chapter is to invigorate a research program aimed at understanding the impact of ethnic and political stratification on MNE

---

[*] Email: L.Dau@northeastern.edu.
[†] Email: moore.el@husky.neu.edu.
[‡] Email: figgins.j@husky.neu.edu.
[§] Email: Josh.Ault@thunderbird.asu.edu.

growth and activity in the BRICS countries. Using contextual data from India, this inter-disciplinary chapter highlights the link between systemic political conditions and MNE strategy and success. Through the lens of intergroup contact theory, from international relations, and institutional theory, we argue that it is advantageous for BRICS MNEs to adopt a strategy of social activism, to avoid their profit being curtailed by ethnic and political conflict. By examining BRICS MNEs at the firm level, in conjunction with national-level political and ethnic factors that must be overcome before these firms can expand beyond their respective borders, this study aims to understand and highlight unique characteristics that propagate the proliferation and success of these MNEs in a globalizing world.

Keywords: institutional theory, intergroup contact theory, BRICS, MNEs, firm strategy, social activism, India

INTRODUCTION

Globalization has allowed both people and companies to move across and between borders at an unprecedented rate (Lechner & Boli, 2005; Mahtaney, 2013). As a result, the multinational enterprise (MNE) has received increased scholarly attention (Narula & Dunning, 2010; Ramamurti, 2004). Moreover, there has been increased intellectual curiosity surrounding the BRICS countries (Wilson et al., 2011; Wilson & Purushothaman, 2003). Brazil, Russia, India, China, and South Africa have experienced rapid growth and development despite less than ideal home country conditions (Radulescu et al., 2014). As such, scholars continually seek to understand what has motivated this growth, including the effects of MNEs operating in these countries. Understanding how to motivate growth can help bridge the economic gap between developed and developing countries (Hou, 2013). Thus, it is critical that scholars examine the different toolkits that MNEs have at their disposal to bolster economic growth and development.

Political science scholars suggest that ethnic and political stratification – or the categorization and division of individuals based on ethnicity, race, economic status, or other criteria – leads to inequality and violence (Horowitz, 2011). Both types of stratification create hierarchical societal structures that are formed out of either ethnic or political differences (Horowitz, 2011). Often a result of colonialism, these scholars note that social and political hierarchies are extremely difficult to remove as they are often solidly entrenched (Bakwesegha, 2004). They have also noted the impact that this stratification has on individuals, communities, and the nation-state as a whole (Kanbur et al., 2011). Surprisingly, less attention has been given to understanding the impact that ethnic and political stratification has on firms and vice versa. Thus, it is critical to understand how these societal structures and divisions interact with firm strategy and behavior. What role do these hierarchies have on firm strategy and profitability? What pressures do they place on firms? Moreover, what strategies can firms adopt when they exist under unfavorable conditions of political and ethnic tensions to survive and enhance their performance? Can firms influence their environment in a mutually symbiotic way?

This chapter draws on a case study of Infosys from India to add to the literatures on the BRICS (Brazil, Russia, India, China, and South Africa) countries (Vijayakumar et al., 2010), MNE strategy (Ramamurti, 2004), and ethnic and political conflict (Kanbur et al., 2011). We argue that although the BRICS countries are diverse, a commonality among them is societal stratification (Ocampo, 2011; Wilson et al., 2011). Further, contrary to the belief that governments are proactive and firms are reactive, we invite a research program to understand if MNEs with headquarters in countries impacted by ethnic and political conflict can proactively influence domestic institutional quality. We explore whether or not these MNEs can do so by utilizing their ability to self-regulate and incorporate their experiential knowledge from operating in international markets. By introducing intergroup contact theory from international relations, we add to the literature on MNEs' global strategy by examining the role that MNEs can play as policy-advocates and norm-setters. Moreover, through this discussion we extend institutional theory by parsing out the ways that

MNEs can change existing institutional structures. Thus, this chapter cultivates a research program on MNEs as institutional framers that can be augmented in forthcoming research.

The remainder of this chapter is structured as follows. Section two provides a brief background on political and ethnic stratification, MNE strategy, and performance. It also includes a logical justification for the examination of the intersection between BRICS MNE's strategy and political and ethnic stratification. Section three offers the logic and arguments for the future research program suggested by this chapter. Section four utilizes a case study of India to provide evidence in support of this research program. Section five dissects the theoretical and practical importance of the findings and provides the conclusion for the chapter.

POLITICAL AND ETHNIC STRATIFICATION, MNE PERFORMANCE, AND BRICS COUNTRIES

Political and Ethnic Stratification

Within both the political science and sociology literatures, there is a large body of work focusing on social stratification (Ellingsen, 2000; Kofman, 2004). In this framework, society is categorized into different strata based on social status, wealth, ethnicity, and religion (Kuper & Horowitz, 1986; Lebow, 2007). Further, the strata cut society both horizontally and vertically (Kanbur et al., 2011). Vertical stratification relates to the hierarchy of citizens based on socio-economic factors (such as income, education, or occupation), whereas horizontal stratification is based on religious and ethnic groupings (Cederman et al., 2011; Ostby, 2008). Each of the strata can be further subdivided, but the key is that each of the strata is organized into an over-arching, and set, hierarchy that encompasses the entire society and is set in place (Ostby, 2008; Piazza, 2006).

Moreover, extant literature suggests that this social stratification results in and from inequalities among people (Harvey, 2008; Ostby, 2008). This inequality can lead to political and ethnic violence in the form of intergroup fighting (Hagendoorn, 1993; Seinen & Schram, 2006). Ethnic conflict scholars suggest that there are both ranked and unranked ethnic groups that result from this political stratification and the hierarchy of resources and power that it creates (Horowitz, 2011). Further, this hierarchy is often exacerbated by the lasting institutional structures left in place by colonialism (Bakwesegha, 2004). Additionally, prior literature suggests that the prime psychological motivation for ethnic conflict is resentment (Horowitz, 2011). Resentment often arises when one group has increased access to resources at the expense of the other groups (Peterson, 2002). As a result, an "us vs. them" mentality is formulated.

The result of the conflict and tension is a hostile social environment, which bleeds across all segments of society (Kanbur et al., 2011; Karmel, 1995). It impacts individuals, firms, and the national government (Hjort, 2014; Kuper & Horowitz, 1986). Oftentimes, this conflict can cripple government capacity and prevent positive institutional reform (Kanbur et al., 2011). As the tension increases, it exerts pressure on the government and forces it to utilize time and resources to solve the conflict (Ellingsen, 2000). However, these conflicts are difficult to resolve because they are highly entrenched (Alesina et al., 2016; Castles, 1995; Esteban & Ray, 2008). Therefore, a playbook of strategies that helps burgeoning firms thrive under such conditions is necessary and appropriate for the literatures of ethnic conflict and global strategy.

In this chapter, we examine the utility of increased interactions between firms, domestic actors, and international actors through the lens of intergroup contact theory from international relations. This theory suggests that to bridge societal cleaves, groups must encounter each other (Ropers, 2004). Moreover, the theory suggests that this process is facilitated with increased knowledge and experience in operating in diverse environments (Pettigrew, 2008). In other words, it is easier for one actor to increase contact with another group, thus reducing the "us vs. them" mentality, if that actor has prior experience operating in diverse situations (Pettigrew, 2008; Pettigrew et al., 2011).

Institutional Theory and MNE Strategy

Globalization has an impact on the strategy and performance of MNEs (Narula & Dunning, 2000). The recent global financial crisis served as a realization for both individuals and companies that financial resilience, and navigating institutional voids, is critical (Dau et al., 2016a). MNE scholars suggest that these firms benefit from increased institutional quality (Cantwell et al., 2010). Institutions serve as the guidelines that shape firm behavior (Dimaggio & Powell, 1983; North, 1990). Institutions are made up of three key elements that each has an impact on the country's overall institutional profile: regulatory, cognitive, and normative (Busenitz et al., 2004; Dau, Moore, & Bradley, 2015). When institutions are clear and codified, they are easier for firms to follow (Dau, 2011, 2012, 2013, 2016, 2017; North, 1991). However, because of globalization and the changing face of the international community, domestic institutions are experiencing shifts in all three institutional spaces (Dau et al., 2017; Dau, Moore, & Soto, 2016a, 2016b).

Moreover, extant literature suggests that markets may have both institutional voids and supports (Castellacci, 2015; Prokopovych, 2011). Institutional supports are market intermediaries that help overcome inefficiencies (Castellacci, 2015). These include codified tax systems, secure infrastructure, transportation systems, and secure research and development policies (McCarthy & Puffer, 2016). Conversely, institutional voids are the absence of such intermediaries (Palepu & Khanna, 2005). These include faulty or lacking infrastructure systems, unclear labor rights, and insecure innovation policies (Mair & Marti, 2009). Scholars suggest that these voids create obstacles for firms, particularly in emerging markets (Ge & Carney, 2016; Palepu & Khanna, 2005). When institutional voids are extreme, firms must replicate or adapt existing business models, navigate the voids, fill the voids, or exit (Palepu & Khanna, 2010). In other words, to survive and remain profitable, MNEs and firms within these markets must identify the voids and strategize how to address or exploit them.

Ethnic conflict, political tension, and societal stratification strangle the capacity of national governments (Kanbur et al., 2011; Stepanov, 2000). These tensions tie up resources, time, and energy to mitigate social resentment before it erupts. As resentment increases from power and resource hierarchies, national institutions suffer and voids are either created or exacerbated (Horowitz, 2010). While the exact way we study institutional voids has come under some scrutiny, a consensus has emerged that MNEs and firms cannot simply ignore these voids, but rather they must identify them and strategize about how to address or exploit them. As such, it is critical that scholars understand how MNEs from areas prone to political and ethnic tension navigate the voids generated by political and ethnic stratification.

Theoretical Justification for Examining BRICS MNEs and Political and Ethnic Stratification

As the world continues to globalize and firms increasingly expand across borders at an unprecedented rate, it is critical that scholars identify and understand the different toolkits that MNEs can utilize in divergent home and host environments (Narula & Dunning, 2000). Moreover, ethnic tension has perpetuated throughout many parts of the world (Ostby, 2008). As such, firms can benefit greatly from learning to operate under the conditions of this tension and its associated institutional voids. Even under unfavorable conditions, businesses need to prosper for the micro-level success of individuals, as well as the macro-level success of the economy at large (Falvey, Foster, & Greenaway, 2012). Surprisingly, there has been scant scholarly attention focused on the role that MNEs from areas impacted by political and ethnic tension can have as policy advocates and institutional framers. Thus, we examine how BRICS MNEs can enhance their likelihood of survival and performance potential by cultivating mutually beneficial norms of inclusion and accessibility in the institutional environments in which they operate.

BRICS MNEs: INSTITUTIONAL FRAMERS TO SURVIVE AND PROSPER AMIDST ETHNIC AND POLITICAL TENSION

Despite the differences among the BRICS countries, one critical similarity is the social stratification experienced in each of their societies (Ocampo, 2011; Wilson et al., 2011). Unlike other countries, BRICS countries tend to experience higher levels of political and ethnic stratification that both feed into, and result from, social inequality (Jacobs & Van Rossem, 2014). This often leads to increased pressure and social conflict in these countries (Kanbur et al., 2011).

Scholars have noted the subsequent impact this has on both individuals and national governments (Horowitz, 2011). Literature suggests that this stratification leads to a struggle for power and creates the opportunity space for violence (Kanbur et al., 2011; Lebow, 2007). Moreover, it is important to note that social strata, or cleaves, can be both lateral and vertical (Cederman et al., 2011; Ostby, 2008). Vertical cleaves are those that create hierarchy of citizenship, as exemplified through the creation of wealth based social classes (Komarraju & Cokley, 2008). For example, lower, middle, and upper classes are hierarchical (or vertically) structured. Horizontal cleaves are those between religious and ethnic groups that are not necessarily clearly hierarchical (Komarraju & Cokley, 2008). Together, these cleaves stratify citizens into cultural groups. When these cleaves are combined, labor becomes divided on cultural lines.

These conditions create 'winners' and 'losers', but more importantly they concentrate resources within the 'winning' groups (Horowitz, 2010). The result is increased resentment and a hostile environment and condition (Esteban & Ray, 2008; Igwe, 2012). This creates a challenge for the national government that must bridge these cleaves (Chandra, 2005; Ellingsen, 2000). Further, we posit that it creates institutional voids, as evidenced by of the lack of capacity of the national government in junction with the disparate concentration of resources between groups. In other words, individuals at the bottom of the social strata are often dissatisfied and respond violently in response to the lack of ability for social mobility.

As previously noted, global strategy scholars have long studied the MNE and the different ways the firm interacts with its home and host environments (Dunning, 2000; Ramamurti, 2004). Even in disadvantageous conditions, businesses need to survive and remain profitable, or they must exit the country. Extant literature suggests that firms have several options when responding to institutional voids. They can replicate or adapt an existing business model, they can collaborate with domestic partners, they can navigate around the voids or try to fill them, or they can exit the market (Palepu & Khanna, 2005, 2010).

It is worth reiterating that ethnic and political tension presents a unique challenge and exacerbates the hostility of the environment in which firms must operate, thus representing an institutional void (Castles, 1995; Collier & Hoeffler, 1998; Kanbur et al., 2011). Moreover, this fragility impacts all stages of the business cycle (Ault, 2016; Ault & Spicer, 2009, 2014, 2016). As a result, firms operating within these environments must create and employ strategies for bridging the unique types of voids created by the resulting insecurity and tensions to survive. Previous research has identified some advantages that multinationals may possess to overcome existing institutional gaps. For instance, unlike domestic firms that have only operated under this set of conditions, MNEs have increased levels of experiential market knowledge from operating both internationally and amidst the institutional voids created by ethnic and political tensions (Cantwell et al., 2009; Dunning & Pitelis, 2008). As such, MNEs that survive and continue to operate internationally and domestically, despite being from home countries that have high levels of ethnic and political tensions, often have a greater international strategic 'toolkit' from which to draw to fill this void and cultivate a more favorable home environment. In other words, these MNEs have increased market knowledge from operating in external markets that can help them navigate their home country institutional voids (Palepu & Khanna, 2005). Additionally, the skills and knowledge they acquire from operating amidst the institutional voids found in their domestic market allow them to operate in other markets with institutional voids. As such, MNEs benefit from exposure to different institutional environments, since it allows them to accrue knowledge to mitigate the impacts of institutional voids and partake in social activism. In this way, we posit that MNEs have tools to be proactive in filling institutional voids by shifting existing regulatory and normative institutions in areas impacted by political and ethnic tension.

More specifically, in arenas that predate regulation, MNEs can create standards that promote inclusion and accessibility across the horizontal and vertical cleaves (Stone Sweet, 2006). For example, firms can adopt policies of representative hiring to reduce the perception of preferential treatment of certain groups over others, a common view that can perpetuate resentment. Moreover, firms can develop investment projects in different communities and select locations for infrastructure in areas where it is most needed (Boddewyn, 2016; Dunning, 1977). Additionally, firms can use inclusive marketing tactics that comprise all groups within the society (Constantinides, 2006; George et al., 2012). In this way, consistent with intergroup contact theory, MNEs can utilize intergroup contact to foster a positive environment across different societal cleaves (Ropers, 2004). Within this framework, it is suggested that increased interaction will mitigate resentment and lessen the "us vs. them" mentality that is typically present among these groups, through the use of interpersonal connection and understanding (Crisp et al., 2008; Pettigrew, 2008; Pettigrew et al., 2011). By employing this strategy, MNEs can help shift the existing normative institutions that exacerbate the institutional voids within the country.

Additionally, MNEs can employ strategies to alter existing regulatory institutions of the country. Unlike many domestic firms without an international presence, MNEs from BRICS countries have leverage and power (Vijayakumar et al., 2010). As such, they can leverage governments into fairer policies and regulations that focus on inclusivity and accessibility (Chin, 2014; Hou, 2013). Unlike the disenfranchised social groups that have been stripped of resources, MNEs have both capital and capacity. Since they represent an economic lifeline for the country as a whole, governments are more likely to respond to their demands (Hill & Mudambi, 2010; Marano & Tashman, 2012). Once more, employing the strategies suggested within intergroup contact theory (Pettigrew, 2008), we argue that MNEs have the ability to construct cooperative channels through policy structures that allow for the reduction of intergroup conflict. We assert that MNEs can fill the regulatory institutional voids left by political and ethnic tension by acting as institutional framers. They can do so by acting as policy advocates and creating dialogue projects that structure cooperation and intertwined goals between the firm, the community, and the government (Hillman & Wan, 2005; Pettigrew et al., 2011). The result is a potentially mutually symbiotic relationship that mitigates existing conflict. It is important to note, however, that much of this work focuses on the advantages MNEs possess in overcoming institutional voids in the regulatory domain of the state, such as in the absence legal systems or contract-enforcing mechanisms. Yet, burgeoning research has suggested that voids in security can often present firms with a completely different set of challenges that may need to be addressed (Ault, 2016; Khoury & Prasad, 2015). Despite the previously outlined advantages that MNEs possess, there has been surprisingly scant literature on the voids that emerge from ethnic tension and political violence. Given the limited amount of research, although this chapter outlines the advantages MNEs can employ to operate in one type of institutional void, we cannot be certain that these strategies will work with equal effectiveness in environments characterized more by conflict and tension that may present security or social-welfare voids. As such, we utilize the preceding logic to call for a research program that invites future scholarship to better understand the intersection between BRICS MNEs and ethnic and political tension. We present the following case study as a starting point to illustrate the utility of such a research agenda.

CASE STUDY EVIDENCE: INDIA

Ethnic and Political Tension in India

The natural starting place is to recognize India's identity as a post-colonial state. As such, many of its structures of state are holdovers, or offshoots of its colonial administrators (Smith, 1979). These structures were formed in order to benefit the dominant insurgent powers and to appease their interests, resulting in further entrenchment of hierarchical strata of conflict (Alesina et al., 2016; Cederman et al., 2011). Even at the height of colonial power, more than 60 million Indians lived outside the jurisdiction of the British administrators (Varshney, 1997). This led to an uneven distribution of resources and a lack of equal representation in the post-colonial government that favored the regions under colonial rule and disadvantaged those in regions beyond their reach (Doner, 2009). Because of this asymmetric governance and unequal application of policies, some scholars argue that areas that operated under British administration suffer more caste and tribal violence, whereas those regions that existed outside of colonial administration experience more religious violence (Verghese, 2016). Colonial censuses also crystalized what were previously more fluid identities into salient casts that drive conflict (Verghese, 2016).

India is thus faced with the considerable task of developing its economy amidst fragile social conditions fraught with ethnic and political conflict (Varshney, 1997, 2001). The major horizontal, and unranked, source of ethnic tension is that between the Hindu majority and the Muslim minority. The Hindu/Muslim cleavage, perhaps the most visible manifestation of ethnic conflict, often erupts in violence and embroils the country in political tumult that threatens to drive the wedge deeper into society (Mitra & Ray, 2014; Young, 2006). This conflict receives the most outside attention but remains only one of the many issues India faces. But even within the Hindu majority, ethnic differences derived from linguistic, regional, cultural, and historical domains complicate the landscape and present challenges for firms to overcome (Mitra & Ray, 2014; Varshney, 1997). Delving even deeper into the fabric of Indian society, a pervasive Urban/Rural divide creates new fissures in unity (Jha, 2013).

Though it would be impossible to comprehensively describe every fault in Indian ethnic conflict, it serves to list some of the more visible and enduring conflicts to provide insight into the breadth of the problem. Small scale attacks on individuals and religious riots highlight the lack of trust and cooperation between the two largest religious groups in India: Hindus and Muslims (Young, 2006). In the Assam region of northeastern India, the Assamese and Bengali have been the cause of bloodshed, due to protracted disagreements over territorial entitlement and disputes with neighboring Bengal (Cultural Survival, 2017). This conflict highlights a struggle for ethnic dominance rather than religious, as both Assamese and Bengali have elements of Hindu and Muslim in their demographics. The Sikh and Hindu conflict in the Punjab region illustrates another glaring conflict. Though draped in religious trappings, this conflict contains strong economic components quartered with secessionist sentiment (Cultural Survival, 2017).

The most pervasive of the stratified conflicts stems from the caste system (Olcott, 1944). The Hindu caste system divides people into four major classes (with thousands of subdivisions) based on circumstances of birth with a lower strata or *Dalit* existing below the established castes (Ali, 2002; Vaid, 2014). Like the ethnic divisions, it has been argued that colonial influences have ossified the caste divisions in such a way that artificially exacerbated social mobility (Vaid, 2014; Varshney, 1997). The Indian government has taken steps in the public sector to mitigate the disadvantages associated with the *Dalit* (a term embraced by the group in defiance of those who would use it as a pejorative), by establishing employment and education quotas while pressuring the private sector into similar policies (Vaid, 2014). Despite these efforts, members of the lowest castes remain poor due to discrimination in other areas.

MNEs and the Mitigation of Conflict

Indian tech giant Infosys (and its associated charity, the Infosys Foundation) is on the forefront of inclusive policies adopted with a view to limit the cleaves of both vertical and horizontal discrimination (Marketline, 2013; Narus & Seshadri, 2007). The following information, drawn from the Infosys Foundation public relations page, provides insight into the motivations and exigencies of its programs. By investing in rural areas of the region of Madhya Pradesh with development initiatives through the

Infosys foundation, Infosys seeks to improve education and economic conditions in disadvantaged areas. Investments in regions neglected by the government help to even the economic landscape. By devoting resources to these rural areas, MNEs can elevate disadvantaged groups in conjunction with government policies. The program includes a skill development program for tribal youth, establishment of village libraries, and technical training aimed at increasing social and economic mobility. The Infosys foundation has also endeavored to combat malnutrition and aid education by providing lunches for public school children in Kandi near Hyderabad. As one of the key organizers of the project stated, "We thank the Government of Telangana for giving us the opportunity to bring in this biggest social investment to Telangana. This will bring a meaningful change in the lives of school children. We are honored to partner with The Infosys Foundation to build this mega kitchen." This synergy between the government and private sector for the public good demonstrates how MNEs can preempt the government on social programs to promote inclusive benefits. These projects illustrate several important characteristics of this MNE's dedication to improving conflict lines across India. First, this spread of project locations and topics works to bridge the urban-rural divide (Dave, 2015). Despite the tech industry's reliance on urban infrastructure, a philanthropic investment into the rural areas increases the connectivity between MNEs and poor communities.

For instance, Infosys has a crosscutting program that provides a special seven-month training (partnered with the International Institute of Information Technology, IIIT) to assist low-caste engineering graduates who could not find employment in the field (Infosys, 2016). Infosys even hires many of the program's subjects, demonstrating its adherence to its social values and capitalizing on a vastly untapped source of human resources (Infosys, 2016). There is some debate over the motivation for programs such as these. There has been political discussion over enforcing hiring quotas for low-caste and tribal sectors, showing that many corporations have taken their own ideas of affirmative action that preempt such quotas (Balasubramanian & George, 2012). By having MNEs create and adopt their own systems, they can build a socially conscious program that mutually benefits disadvantaged individuals and the corporations themselves (Economist, 2007). Admittedly, such a program only benefits a small sliver of the population and many of those partaking in the course were less disadvantaged than others in their caste. However, it is a demonstrable effort to fill an institutional void that promotes mobility and opportunity for traditionally overlooked groups.

DISCUSSION AND CONCLUSION

The purpose of this chapter is to discuss the intersection between political and ethnic stratification and the strategies that BRICS MNEs can implement to survive and thrive amidst such tension. That is, this chapter examines MNEs from BRICS countries with regards to the strategic choices they make to survive the institutional voids created by ethnic and political conflict. As such, it adds to the growing dialogue on MNE strategy (Narula & Dunning, 2010), BRICS MNEs (Radulescu et al., 2014), and ethnic and political conflict (Kanbur et al., 2011). We assert that MNEs from BRICS countries have unique knowledge and capacity from international market experience that potentially allows them to serve as policy advocates and institutional framers. Further, we argue that by employing tactics outlined in intergroup contact theory (Pettigrew et al., 2011), these MNEs have the ability to fill national level institutional voids left by societal cleaves by shifting both the regulatory and normative institutional structures given their political and social leverage. Moreover, this chapter adds critical insights to the burgeoning study of BRICS countries, specifically the success of the MNEs from these countries. Thus, this chapter builds upon extant literature while highlighting a new avenue for future research.

By examining the relationship between the strategy of BRICS MNE, and ethnic and political tension, this chapter offers several pertinent theoretical contributions. Literature on national governments and institutions suggests that governments create policies and firms follow them (Autio & Fu, 2015; North, 1991). Moreover, global strategy scholars have noted that in the presence of institutional voids, firms can respond by either adapting their business model, navigating the void or filling it, or exiting the country (Khanna & Palepu, 2005; 2010). Limited attention, however, has been given to ethnic and political violence as a void. We argue that in response to the regulatory and normative institutional voids left by ethnic and political violence, MNEs from BRICS countries may be able to use their international knowledge to fill the institutional voids. We invite future research to examine whether these firms can fill normative institutional voids through the use of intergroup contact strategies and inclusive hiring, marketing, and location selection techniques to foster positive interpersonal connections (Pettigrew & Tropp, 2008; Shelton & Richeson, 2005; Tajfel & Turner, 1979). Further, future research could corroborate our preliminary logic that these MNEs can also use their leverage to fill regulatory institutional voids by encouraging inclusive and accessible policies at the national level. Thus, we contribute to the literature on BRICS MNEs, institutional theory, and ethnic and political conflict.

The logical assertions and case study evidence provided by this chapter also have implications for both practitioners and policy makers. As ethnic tension, political conflict, and social stratification continue to plague countries across the world (Ellingsen, 2000; Igwe, 2012), it is essential that managers and CEOs understand the best strategies available. This study suggests that MNEs have knowledge and capacity from international experience (Mudambi & Swift, 2011) that allows them to serve as policy advocates and institutional framers. Further, it suggests that MNEs can help fill institutional voids and create a more positive home country environment. Thus, managers can leverage the position and knowledge held by BRICS MNEs and translate it into their own strategies, if they are operating under similar conditions. Moreover, this research offers insights for policy makers and national governments. This research dissects the relationship between MNEs from BRICS countries and national level institutions. Literature suggests that ethnic and political conflict strangles government capability and capacity (Horowitz, 2011). By understanding the ways in which national governments can work with MNEs to foster a mutually symbiotic relationship, this chapter highlights how policy makers can mitigate the detrimental effects of ethnic and political tension.

Although the research and logical arguments put forth in this chapter were carried out rigorously, the limitations inherent with a single country case study mandate acknowledgement. By examining a single country and firms within it, this study captures nuance, attention to detail and provide meaningful contextualization, while highlighting an opportunity space for future scholarship. Thus, this chapter serves as a launching point for future theoretical and empirical efforts. This chapter would benefit from complementary case studies on the four other BRICS countries. As previously noted, the BRICS countries are all unique, despite all suffering from ethnic and political tension (Nayyar, 2016; Wilson & Purushothaman, 2003). By carrying out case studies on the other four countries, further insights into the strategies that BRICS MNEs employ could be provided, as well as a deeper understanding of differences across those countries. Additionally, the research program could be augmented by large-n quantitative work that would provide generalizability and identify patterns of MNE behavior and the impact that these patterns of behavior have on levels of ethnic and political tension.

Ethnic and political tension continues to threaten equality and accessibility of populations all across the globe (Alesina et al., 2016; Kuper & Horowitz, 1986). Moreover, as scholars continue to search for an answer to the question of economic development, there has been an increased interest into the success of BRICS MNEs (Atale, 2012; Jacobs & Van Rossem, 2014; Wilson & Purushothaman, 2003). The BRICS nations and the firms within them, despite their success, suffer from ethnic and political tension and conflict. As such, this chapter serves as a preliminary study aimed at understanding the divergent ways that MNEs from BRICS countries respond to and navigate the institutional voids created by ethnic and political tension.

REFERENCES

Alesina, A., Michalopoulos, S., & Papaioannou, E. (2016). Ethnic Inequality. *Journal of Political Economy*, *124*(2), pp.428–488.

Ali, S. (2002). Collective and elective ethnicity: Caste among urban Muslims in India. *Sociological Forum*, *17*(4), pp.593–620.

Atale, N. (2012). A Decade of BRICs: Prospects and Challenges for the Next Decade. *Vidwat: The Indian Journal of Management*, *5*(2), pp.16–21.

Ault, J. K. (2016). An institutional perspective on the social outcome of entrepreneurship: Commercial microfinance and inclusive markets. *Journal of International Business Studies*, 47(8), pp. 951-967.

Ault, J. K., & Spicer, A. (2009). Does one size fit all in microfinance? New directions for academic research. *Moving Beyond Storytelling: Emerging Research in Microfinance*, pp. 271-284. Emerald Group Publishing.

Ault, J. K., & Spicer, A. (2014) The institutional context of poverty: State fragility as a predictor of cross-national variation in commercial microfinance lending. *Strategic Management Journal, 35(12),*pp. 1818-1838.

Ault, J. K., & Spicer, A. (2016). Measuring the political context of entrepreneurship: lessons from the state fragility literature. *Academy of Mangement Proceedings.* 1, p. 17750.

Autio, E., & Fu, K. (2015). Economic and political institutions and entry into formal and informal entrepreneurship. *Asia Pacific Journal of Management*, *32*(1), pp.67–94.

Bakwesegha, Christopher J. (2004) Ethnic Conflict and the Colonial Legacy. *Facing Ethnic Conflicts: Toward a New Realism*. Lanham (Conn.): Rowman and Littlefield. 53-60.

Balasubramanian, N., & George, R. (2012). Corporate governance and the Indian institutional context: Emerging mechanisms and challenges. In conversation with K. V. Kamath, Chairman, Infosys and ICICI Bank. *IIMB Management Review*, *24*(4), pp.215–233.

Boddewyn, J. J. (2016). Political aspects of MNE theory. In *The Eclectic Paradigm: A Framework for Synthesizing and Comparing Theories of International Business from Different Disciplines or Perspectives*, pp. 85–110.

Cantwell, J. A., Dunning, J. H., & Lundan, S. M. (2010). An evolutionary approach to understanding The co-evolution international business activity: environment of MNEs and the institutional. *Journal of International Business Studies*, *41*(4), pp.567–586.

Cantwell, J., Dunning, J. H., & Lundan, S. M. (2009). An evolutionary approach to understanding international business activity: The co-evolution of MNEs and the institutional environment. *Journal of International Business Studies*, *41*(4), pp.567–586.

Castellacci, F. (2015). Institutional Voids or Organizational Resilience? Business Groups, Innovation, and Market Development in Latin America. *World Development*, *70*, pp.43–58.

Castles, S. (1995). How nation- states respond to immigration and ethnic diversity. *Journal of Ethnic and Migration Studies*, *21*(3), pp.293–308.

Cederman, L.-E., Weidmann, N. B., & Gleditsch, K. S. (2011). Horizontal Inequalities and Ethnonationalist Civil War: A Global Comparison. *American Political Science Review*, *105*(3), pp.478–495.

Chandra, K. (2005). Ethnic Parties and Democratic Stability. *Perspectives on Politics*, *3*(2), pp.235–252.

Chin, G. T. (2014). The BRICS-led Development Bank: Purpose and Politics beyond the G20. *Global Policy*, *5*(3), pp.366–373.

Collier, P., & Hoeffler, A. (1998). On economic causes of civil war. *Oxford Economic Papers*, *50*(4), pp.563–573.

Constantinides, E. (2006). The Marketing Mix Revisited: Towards the 21st Century Marketing. *Journal of Marketing Management*, *22*(3–4), pp.407–438.

Crisp, R. J., Stathi, S., Turner, R. N., & Husnu, S. (2008). Imagined intergroup contact: Theory, paradigm, and practice. *Social and Personality Psychology Compass*, *2*, pp.1–18.

Cultural Survival. (2017). Ethnic and Religious Conflicts in India. *Cultural Survival*. 27.

Dau, L. A. (2011). Reforms, multinationalization, and profitability. In L. Toombs (Ed.), *Academy of Management Best Paper Proceedings*.

Dau, L. A. (2012). Pro-market reforms and developing country multinational corporations. *Global Strategy Journal,* 2(3), pp. 262-276.

Dau, L. A. (2013). Learning across geographic space: Pro-market reforms, multinationalization strategy, and profitability. *Journal of International Business Studies,* 44(3), pp. 235-262.

Dau, L. A. (2016). Knowledge will set you free: Enhancing the firm's responsiveness to institutional change. *International Journal of Emerging Markets*, 11(2), pp. 121-147.

Dau, L. A. (2017). Contextualizing international learning: The moderating effects of mode of entry and subsidiary networks on the relationship between reforms and profitability. *Journal of World Business* (in press).

Dau, L. A., Moore, E. M., & Bradley, C. (2015). Institutions and international entrepreneurship. *International Business: Research, Teaching, and Practice*, 9(1), pp. 1-20.

Dau, L. A., Moore, E. M., & Soto, M. (2016a). The Great Recession and Emerging Market Firms: Unpacking the Divide Between Global and National Level Sustainability Expectations. In *Lessons from the Great Recession: At the Crossroads of Sustainability and Recovery*, pp. 165–187. Emerald Group Publishing.

Dau, L. A., Moore, E. M., & Soto, M. (2016b). Informal Transnational Political Actors and Emerging Markets: Understanding Entrepreneurship in a Changing Normative Atmosphere. In A. Walsh (Ed.), *Entrepreneurship and Firm Performance*, pp. 19-41. NOVA Science Publishers.

Dau, L. A., Moore, E. M., Soto, M., & LeBlanc, C. (2017). How globalization sparked entrepreneurship in the developing world: The impact of formal economic and political linkages. In B. Christiansen, F. Kasarci (Eds.), *Corporate Espionage, Geopolitics, and Diplomacy Issues in International Business*, pp. 72-91. IGI Global. (in press).

Dave, Paresh. (2017). Indian Immigrants Are Tech's New Titans. Los Angeles Times. Los Angeles Times, 11 Aug. 2015.

Dimaggio, P. J., & Powell, W. W. (1983). The Iron Cage Revisited: Institutional Isomorphism and Collective Rationality in Organizational Fields. *American Sociological Review*, *48*(2), pp.147–160.

Doner, R. F. (2009). *The Politics of Uneven Development. Review of International Studies*, 12.

Dunning, J. H. (1977). Trade, Location of Economic Activity and the MNE: A Search for an Eclectic Approach. In *The International Allocation of Economic Activity*, pp. 395–418.

Dunning, J. H. (2000). The eclectic paradigm as an envelope for economic and business theories of MNE activity. *International Business Review*, *9*(2), pp.163–190.

Dunning, J. H., & Pitelis, C. N. (2008). Stephen Hymer's contribution to international business scholarship: an assessment and extension. *Journal of International Business Studies*, *39*(1), pp.167–176.

Economist. (2007). With Reservations. *The Economist*. The Economist Newspaper, 06 Oct. 2007.

Ellingsen, T. (2000). Colorful Community or Ethnic Witches' Brew? *Journal of Conflict Resolution*, *44*(2), pp.228–249.

Esteban, J., & Ray, D. (2008). On the salience of ethnic conflict. *American Economic Review*, *98*(5), pp.2185–2202.

Falvey R., Foster N., & Greenway D. (2012). Trade Liberalization, Economic Crises, and Growth. *World Development*, 40(11), pp. 2177-2193.

Ge, J., & Carney, M. (2016). Who Fills the Institutional Voids? Utilization of Political and Family Ties in Emerging Markets. *Academy of Management*.

George, G., Mcgahan, A. M., & Prabhu, J. (2012). Innovation for Inclusive Growth: Towards a Theoretical Framework and a Research Agenda. *Journal of Management Studies*, *49*(4), pp.661–683.

Hagendoorn, L. (1993). Ethnic categorization and outgroup exclusion: Cultural values and social stereotypes in the construction of ethnic hierarchies. *Ethnic and Racial Studies*, *16*(1), pp.26–51.

Harvey, D. (2008). *Spaces of neoliberalization: towards a theory of uneven geographical development. Progress in Human Geography*, 32.

Hill, T. L., & Mudambi, R. (2010). Far from Silicon Valley: How emerging economies are re-shaping our understanding of global entrepreneurship. *Journal of International Management*, *16*(4), pp.321–327.

Hillman, A. J., & Wan, W. P. (2005). The determinants of MNE subsidiaries' political strategies: evidence of institutional duality. *Journal of International Business Studies*, *36*(3), pp.322–340.

Hjort, J. (2014). Ethnic divisions and production in firms. *Quarterly Journal of Economics*, *129*(4), pp.1899–1946.

Horowitz, Donald L. (2011). *Ethnic Groups in Conflict: With a New Preface*. Berkeley: U of California.

Hou, Z. (2013). The BRICS and Global Governance Reform: Can the BRICS provide leadership? *Development*, *56*(3), pp.356–362.

Igwe, D. O. (2012). Social Movements, Sustainable Development and the Problem of Ethnicity in Nigeria. *International Journal of Sustainable Society*, *4*(4), pp.405–418.

Infosys. (2016). Sustaintable Development Investment Report.

Jacobs, L. M., & Van Rossem, R. (2014). The BRIC Phantom: A comparative analysis of the BRICs as a category of rising powers. *Journal of Policy Modeling*, *36*(S1).

Jha A, Saumitra. (2013). Trade, Institutions, and Ethnic Tolerance: Evidence from South Asia. American Political Science Review, 107(4), 806-832.

Kanbur, R., Rajaram, P. K., & Varshney, A. (2011). Ethnic Diversity and Ethnic Strife. An Interdisciplinary Perspective. *World Development*, *39*(2), pp.147–158.

Karmel, S. M. (1995). Ethnic tension and the struggle for order: China's policies in Tibet. *Pacific Affairs*, *68*(4), pp.485–508.

Khoury, T. A., & Prasad, A. (2015). Entrepreneurship Amid Concurrent Institutional Constraints in Less Developed Countries. *Business & Society*, 55, pp. 934–969.

Kofman, E. (2004). Gendered Global Migrations. *International Feminist Journal of Politics*, *6*(4), pp.643–665.

Komarraju, M., & Cokley, K. O. (2008). Horizontal and vertical dimensions of individualism-collectivism: A comparison of African Americans and European Americans. *Cultural Diversity and Ethnic Minority Psychology*, *14*(4), pp.336–343.

Kuper, L., & Horowitz, D. L. (1986). Ethnic Groups in Conflict. *Contemporary Sociology*.

Lebow, R. (2007). Coercion, Cooperation and Ethnic in International Relations. *International Relations*.

Lechner, F., & Boli, J. (2005). *Globalization Reader*. Malden, MA: Blackwell Publishing Company.

Mahtaney, P. (2013). *Globalization and Sustainable Economic Development: Issues, Insights, and Inference*. New York: Palgrave Macmillan.

Mair, J., & Marti, I. (2009). Entrepreneurship in and around institutional voids: A case study from Bangladesh. *Journal of Business Venturing*, *24*(5), pp.419–435.

Marano, V., & Tashman, P. (2012). MNE/NGO partnerships and the legitimacy of the firm. *International Business Review*, *21*(6), pp.1122–1130.

Marketline. (2013). Infosys Limited. *Market Line*, (May), pp.1–38.

McCarthy, D. J., & Puffer, S. M. (2016). Institutional Voids in an Emerging Economy: From Problem to Opportunity. *Journal of Leadership & Organizational Studies*, *23*(2), pp.208–219.

Mitra, A., & Ray, D. (2014). Implications of an Economic Theory of Conflict: Hindu-Muslim Violence in India. *Journal of Political EconomyJournal of Political Economy*, *122*(4), pp.719–765.

Mudambi, R., & Swift, T. (2011). Leveraging knowledge and competencies across space: The next frontier in international business. *Journal of International Management*, *17*(3), pp.186–189.

Narula, R., & Dunning, J. H. (2000). Industrial Development, Globalization and Multinational Enterprises: New Realities for Developing Countries. *Oxford Development Studies*, *28*(2), pp.141–167.

Narula, R., & Dunning, J. H. (2010). Multinational enterprises, development and globalisation: Some clarifications and a research agenda. *Oxford Development Studies*, *38*(3), pp.263–287.

Narus, J. A., & Seshadri, D. V. R. (2007). Infosys Technologies Ltd.: Growing Share of a Customer's Business. *Vikalpa: The Journal for Decision Makers*, *32*(2), pp.83–92.

Nayyar, D. (2016). BRICS, developing countries and global governance. *Third World Quarterly*, *37*(4), pp.575–591.

North, D. C. (1991). Institutions. *Journal of Economic Perspectives*.

North, D. C. (1990). *Institutions, Institutional Change and Economic Performance*. Cambridge: Cambridge University Press.

Olcott, M. (1944). The Caste System of India. *American Sociological Review*, *9*(6), pp.648.

Ostby, G. (2008). Polarization, Horizontal Inequalities and Violent Civil Conflict. *Journal of Peace Research*, *45*(2), pp.143–162.

Palepu, K. G., & Khanna, T. (2005). Spotting Institutional Voids in Emerging Markets. *Harvard Business School Cases*.

Palepu, K. G., & Khanna, T. (2010). Winning in Emerging Markets: A Road Map for Strategy and Execution. *Harvard Business School Press Books*, *46*(2), p.1.

Petersen. (2002). *Understanding Ethnic Violence*. Cambridge University Press.

Pettigrew, T. F. (2008). Future directions for intergroup contact theory and research. *International Journal of Intercultural Relations*.

Pettigrew, T. F., & Tropp, L. R. (2008). How does intergroup contact reduce prejudice? Meta-analytic tests of three mediatorsy. *European Journal of Social Psychology*, *38*(6), pp.922–934.

Pettigrew, T. F., Tropp, L. R., Wagner, U., & Christ, O. (2011). Recent advances in intergroup contact theory. *International Journal of Intercultural Relations*.

Piazza, J. A. (2006). Rooted in Poverty?: Terrorism, Poor Economic Development, and Social Cleavages. *Terrorism and Political Violence*, *18*(1), pp.159–177.

Prokopovych, B. (2011). Creating markets under institutional voids: The case of small-scale renewables in Tajikistan. In *Academy of Management Annual Meeting Proceedings*, 8, pp. 1–6.

Radulescu, I. G., Panait, M., & Voica, C. (2014). BRICS Countries Challenge to the World Economy New Trends. *Procedia Economics and Finance*, *8*, pp.605–613.

Ramamurti, R. (2004). Developing Countries and MNEs: Extending and Enriching the Research Agenda. *Journal of International Business Studies*, *35*(4), pp.277–283.

Ropers, Norbert. (2009). From Resolution to Transformation: Assessing the Role and Impact of Dialogue Projects. *Facing Ethnic Conflicts: Toward a New Realism*. Lanham (Conn.): Rowman and Littlefield. 174-88.

Seinen, I., & Schram, A. (2006). Social status and group norms: Indirect reciprocity in a repeated helping experiment. *European Economic Review*, *50*(3), pp.581–602.

Shelton, J. N., & Richeson, J. A. (2005). Intergroup Contact and Pluralistic Ignorance. *Journal of Personality and Social Psychology*, *88*(1), pp.91–107.

Smith, T. (1979). The Underdevelopment of Development Literature: The Case of Dependency Theory. *World Politics*, *31*(2), pp.247–288.

Stepanov, V. (2000). Ethnic tensions and separatism in Russia. *Journal of Ethnic and Migration Studies*, *26* (May 2015), pp.305–332.

Stone Sweet, Alec. (2006) The new Lex Mercatoria and transnational governance. *Journal of European Public Policy*, 13(5), 627-646.

Swank, D. (2002). *Global Capital, Political Institutions, and Policy Change in Developed Welfare States*. New York: Cambridge University Press.

Tajfel, H., & Turner, J. (1979). An integrative theory of intergroup conflict. In *The Social Psychology of Intergroup Relations* (pp. 33–47).

Vaid, D. (2014). Caste in Contemporary India: Flexibility and Persistence. *Annual Review of Sociology*, *40*(1), pp.391–410.

Varshney, A. (1997). Postmodernism, Civic Engagement, and Ethnic Conflict: A Passage to India. *Comparative Politics*, *30*(1), pp.1–20.

Varshney, A. (2001). Ethnic Conflict and Civil Society: India and Beyond. *World Politics*, *53*(3), pp.362–398.

Verghese, Ajay. (2016). Colonial Origins of Ethnic Violence in India. Stanford UP.

Vijayakumar, N., Sridharan, P., & Rao, K. C. S. (2010). Determinants of FDI in BRICS countries: A panel analysis. *International Journal of Business Science and Applied Management*, *5*(3), pp.1–13.

Wilson, D., Burgi, C., & Carlson, S. (2011). The BRICs Remain in the Fast Lane. *BRICs Monthly*, pp.4–7.

Wilson, D., & Purushothaman, R. (2003). Dreaming with BRICs: The Path to 2050. *Goldman Sachs Economic Research - Global Economics Paper*, *99*, pp.1–24.

Young, M. (2006). Votes and Violence: Electoral Competition and Ethnic Riots in India. *Nations and Nationalism*, *12*, pp.179–180.

In: Advances in Business and Management ISBN: 978-1-53612-615-0
Editor: William D. Nelson © 2017 Nova Science Publishers, Inc.

Chapter 7

SOCIAL ENTREPRENEURSHIP IN RURAL DEVELOPMENT OF LITHUANIA: POTENTIAL OF YOUNG ENTREPRENEURS

Jolita Greblikaite[*]

Institute of Business and Rural Development Management,
Faculty of Economics and Management,
Aleksandras Stulginskis University, Kaunas, Lithuania

ABSTRACT

The chapter analyses the problems and challenges of social entrepreneurship in rural areas of Lithuania in order to further the development of this part of the country. The research problem of this chapter is based on the importance of social entrepreneurship for and its role in the rural development of Lithuania, emphasising social cohesion and job creation. Special attention is paid to other activities besides the agriculture in rural areas of Lithuania because of specific situation in villages and small towns. Raising unemployment, emigration, socially disintegrated groups, poor small business development are the main problems in these areas. In this chapter, recent changes in Lithuanian

---

[*] Corresponding Author Email: jolita19@gmail.com; jolita.greblikaite@asu.lt.

rural areas in terms of social entrepreneurship are presented. Situational analysis reveals both specific problems and some insight on young entrepreneurs in Lithuania. Workable solutions and recommendations on how to improve the situation for better development of rural areas are presented. The main findings reveal that Lithuania still lacks the implementation of social innovation, especially in rural areas. Some conditions and aspects such as culture of social innovation and entrepreneurship, appropriate legislation, different financial sources, national and international networking of social innovators, partnership between public sector, private sector and NGOs, involvement of target social groups, infrastructure for social innovation, effective control and monitoring of social innovation, sufficient administrative skills should be developed in appropriate way in favour of social entrepreneurship.

INTRODUCTION

Social entrepreneurship in European Union (EU) countries has been existing and developing for more than twenty years. The different aspects of social entrepreneurship were analysed in the works of Swanson L. A., Zhang D. D. (2010), Zhang D. D., Swanson L. A, (2013), Azmat F. et al. (2013, 2015), Haugh E. (2005, 2007), Kabir M. et al. (2014), Konda I. et al. (2015), Ney S. et al. (2014), Machdu V. et al. (2012, 2014). The objective that this chapter aims to solve is based on the analysis of said works and other research in this field. Of course, the situation of social entrepreneurship is different in each country. Lithuania is one of those countries where social business and social enterprises are just starting to gain first experience and trust [13]. In more urban areas, citizens are more acquainted with innovative forms of business, with various social activities. In rural areas, "social" is related mostly with some free services or goods for people who live in difficult conditions and need extra support from the government. The most important fact is that the number of such people in rural areas is not going down. The research problem of this chapter is based on revealing the importance of the role of social entrepreneurship for the rural development of Lithuania, emphasising the social cohesion and job creation aspects, especially in transforming agribusiness farms to multifunctional ones and focusing on the role of family farms in social entrepreneurship. The aim of the research is to analyse the situation of social entrepreneurship in Lithuania, especially taking into account rural areas, and propose the possible directions for inclusive and smart development of this phenomena in the country in order to help farmers and land owners to become more successful. Research tasks remain on theoretical and analytical points of social entrepreneurship issues concerning rural areas and their development in Lithuania.

The objectives of the chapter are as follows:

- To reveal the importance of social entrepreneurship for and its role in the Lithuanian rural economy;
- To conduct a situation analysis of the phenomena in the country and to reveal related problems and main challenges;
- To present some of the results from the GUESS survey carried out in Lithuanian higher education institutions;
- To give practical solutions and recommendations on how to improve the situation in developing social enterprises and raising social entrepreneurs in Lithuanian rural areas.

The research methodology of the chapter is based on an in-depth analysis of scientific literature, statistical data analysis, document analysis, comparative analysis and analysis of specific examples of social entrepreneurship in Lithuanian rural areas. Some data will be used from the GUESS survey of the students of Lithuanian higher education institutions regarding their entrepreneurial intentions.

LITHUANIAN RURAL ECONOMY: FROM AGRICULTURE TO SOCIAL ENTREPRENEURS?

Lithuanian rural economy was always one of the most important economic sectors in the country. The latest statistical data reveal that in Lithuania at the beginning of 2017 [27]:

- 44 percent of households weregrowing crops;
- 7.1 percent of households were growing livestock;
- 15.3 percent of households were having mixed agriculture;
- 33.4 percent of households were involved in other activity than agriculture.

The numbers reveal that the main economic activity in the Lithuanian rural areas is agriculture, but 33.4 percent of households are involved in other kind of activities. Possibly some of them could be partly social (data from personal experience). The intentions are positive but the realisation is gaining progress just now.

The roots of family business go back only 20 years and its traditions are still rather modest in Lithuania. It is tightly related to rural areas, especially the agriculture economy, where it takes the form of family farms and businesses. There is little research on family business in the country. Some traditions might be discovered concerning agriculture and villages.

It is stated that family farming (family farms) is dominant and constitutes more than 500 million farms in the world [7]. Farms are the social base of many developing countries and are the main form of agricultural organisations around the world [1]. According to farm Register data, on July 1, 2016 122,588 family farms were registered in Lithuania: of which 74,140 registered farmers were men and 48,448 were women. Women as farmers are more positive to implementation of social ideas in their business. That is also very important for the development of social entrepreneurship.

Farmers' land area in Lithuania is 1,148,143.69 ha, the average farm size – 9.37 ha. So it means that farm size in Lithuania remains small. It should be emphasised that in Lithuania there are more than 200 households where the land area is more than 1000 ha. For such a country as Lithuania, the number of big farmers remains high compared with other countries.

According to the data of July 1, 2016, compared with January 1, 2016 the number of Lithuanian farms increased by 75 [27]. But the statistics are not kept as to how many of these statistical data consist of family farms. This form of testing is important to Lithuania because family farms

Social Entrepreneurship in Rural Development of Lithuania 211

contribute to the agricultural development of both the domestic and international markets. It is argued that the family-owned farms account for nearly 80% of global food production [1].

The main problems concerning agriculture in Lithuania are:

- Lack of innovation in farming; Farmers are mostly oriented to traditional agricultural activities such as crop growing (wheats, corn). The innovations which are implemented in the farms most often are related to purchase of new equipment which allows to raise the effectiveness of work. Some investments are made to new buildings but the implementation of process innovations is mostly dependant on the EU support and is not well developed.
- Low managerial competence of farmers; most farmers in Lithuania have agronomy-based education and little management knowledge. That becomes an obstacle for innovative managerial decisions and even financial plans. Lack of competence in managing household farms leads to ineffective and old-fashioned business decisions.
- Lack of financial resources in small farms (10–50 ha); as it was mentioned before in the article, in Lithuania there are mostly small farms. Farmers lack financial resources for very innovative substantial changes. If needed, they use EU funds support. But mostly they are oriented to direct payments from EU. There are some regions, for example, Šilutė region, where there are a lot of land owners having 2–3 ha of land area. Land owners are not interested in farming, agriculture, so they just keep their land hoping to rent or sell when the prices rise.
- Non-diversified activities and unused lands or other territories in rural areas. As mentioned previously, some land are currently still not being unused in Lithuanian rural areas. Another issue is that because of fulfilled traditional activities and other problems mentioned above farmers are not very interested in the diversification of their activity. Some farmers and householders are more progressive and are seeking challenges, and their examples could be inspirational for the others.

Does it mean that in Lithuania agriculture is economically week and maybe unnecessary? It would be a wrong assumption to make. Agriculture is very important in rural areas as it was many years before. But the situation in Lithuanian villages and small towns became quite critical because of emigration, small business problems causing unemployment, family farms creating insignificant amounts of added value in their products, lack of innovation in agriculture [14]. Any solutions that could make the situation better are worth to try. That is why social entrepreneurship in rural areas might be an additional stimulus that would be interesting.

The main support from the national programmes of the Government was allocated precisely to young farmers (89.5 percent) in 2012 [18]. Family business is exceptionally entrepreneurial and it might be the area to express oneself in. Now there are upcoming calls for local action groups in the autumn concerning the involvement in social business. It means that for some people it can become an alternative of their current activities, if they do not want to continue. For the others, it can be an additional activity that would involve them in new challenging and profitable activities if properly done.

SITUATIONAL ANALYSIS OF THE SOCIAL ENTERPRISES AND ENTREPRENEURSHIP ENVIRONMENT IN LITHUANIAN RURAL AREAS

The research of social entrepreneurship is relevant due to two groups of reasons. They could be identified as intrinsic and extrinsic reasons. Intrinsic reasons are those arising from the general economic situation both in the European Union and in Lithuania. Economy's growth rate of the EU is rising not as fast as expected, and population employment is insufficient. Competition is high. It acts as stimulus to business to look for new markets, new products or services and new models of entrepreneurship performance. Entrepreneurship problems in Lithuania are like those in other countries of the EU, and some of them are even more significant, e.g., lack of funding sources, bureaucratic obstacles, activities lacking innovation, challenges posed by small market, etc. Social entrepreneurship is one of the possible alternatives for solving these problems, and the benefit of it is undeniable. Social economy comprises over 50 percent of some countries' budget. In Lithuania, the potential of social entrepreneurship has not been fully utilised, and social innovations have just started being implemented. Without social entrepreneurship, economic development in the EU and welfare society are inconceivable, and this only increases relevance of the research intended by this project.

Another group of reasons which encourages further research into social entrepreneurship is extrinsic or initiated reasons. It covers all political and other initiatives which appeared based on the first group of reasons, i.e., encouraging social entrepreneurship at the strategic level starting from the Lisbon Strategy 2000 and to the Entrepreneurship 2020 Action Plan at the EU level, which clearly articulates and emphasises the need for development of such entrepreneurship, establishment of social entrepreneurship and supporting social entrepreneurs. The Concept of Social Entrepreneurship in Lithuania approved in April 2015 is the most recent politically-legislative initiative in the sector of social entrepreneurship development.

For better understanding of the issues of social entrepreneurship and social enterprises in Lithuania it is worth analysing the environment of their activities [13].

Legal Environment

The Lithuanian government has made some steps towards development of social enterprises, social entrepreneurship, and social innovation, but the essential one has been made just in 2015. The Lithuanian government confirmed the concept of social entrepreneurship adopted in April 2015 [19]. According to the definition accepted by the Ministry of Economy, "social entrepreneurship is a business model according to which the use of market mechanism and the pursuit of profit are related to social aims and priorities. It is based on corporate social responsibility and public and private sectors' partnership. Social entrepreneurship applies social innovation. Such entrepreneurship involves three main aspects: entrepreneurial based on casual business activity, social based on social aims, and managerial based on profit sharing and fair public management."[19, p. 3]. The essence of social entrepreneurship according to the adopted concept is based on attracting existing models for this kind of business and changing NGOs activity through adapting existing business models.

The concept has three objectives [19, p. 6]:

1. To create favourable legal environment for social entrepreneurship;
2. To create favourable financial and tax support system;
3. To reach the visibility and awareness of the phenomena in the society.

The Lithuanian Ministry of Economy (see www.ukmin.lt) is now consulting public entities, businesses including those in rural areas for the preparation of the Law on Social Enterprises. The consultation especially focuses on co-operation in revealing criteria for the evaluation of social entrepreneurship. In the autumn of this year some special meetings will be announced for businesses in rural areas. It will be based on supporting social entrepreneurship in rural areas. A lot of special teaching courses will be made available for businesses situated in rural areas, seeking to invite family business representatives and local action groups to participate in the upcoming meetings.

The coherence of the above-mentioned dimensions provides successful model of social enterprises operating in various countries of the EU. Social entrepreneurship is not the only and the best solution for the traditional business, but it suits the political and social model of the EU and the conditions are favourable or become favourable for the creation of such business and social enterprises. It is very important to integrate EU laws with Lithuanian legislation and specifically define what is considered a social enterprise and what criteria social business should meet.

Source: [4].

Figure 1. Spectrum of social enterprises in Lithuania.

As it can be seen from Figure 1, the real actors in the Lithuanian social entrepreneurship and social business are NGOs and SMEs. The social concept provides a quite similar understanding of what entities should be implementing the social mission in business or, to be more precise, create added value with very specific social dimension. But legislation regulates social services providers therefore the situation must be improved in terms of appropriate legislation.

Economic Environment

To better understand the above-mentioned situation in Lithuanian rural areas, current problems should be discussed deeper. Emigration is a problem not only in Lithuanian rural areas. It is one of the biggest problems in the entire country. Lithuania has the highest emigration numbers in the EU (see http://www.migracija.lt/ index.php?1357390560). There are various causes for this but the essential ones are economic and social. A lack of job places in various sectors remains the most important problem in rural areas. Diversity of activities and business could theoretically provide the conditions for citizens to build their life in native country.

Social economy in the biggest EU countries is very important and creates significant amount of income for their budget. As the statistical data reveal, the United Kingdom, Germany, Spain, France, Finland experienced a boost in social economy (see Figure 2). But, for example, such countries as Denmark, Malta, Cyprus, Latvia were not interested in developing their social enterprises and boost social economy. Slovakia, Romania, Ireland, Bulgaria, Slovakia, and Lithuania were in quite similar situation in terms of the size of their social economy [21].

Ney et al. [23, p. 60; 11] mention that, first of all, value creation refers to the design and delivery of products and services. Some social entrepreneurs will introduce entirely new practices to the provision of public goods and social services. Secondly, value creation also involves the financing practices, human resource management and marketing regimes to deliver products. Some social entrepreneurs may provide a rather common product or service, say health care, but are radically innovative in their financing, managing and marketing practices. In this way, the framework captures social innovations that create value in terms of the services or products, in terms of management and in terms of both. Social innovations aim to create value for society. In some EU countries, for example Slovenia, the greatest difficulty with the implementation of social innovation into the social setting is the weak supportive environment, lack of funds and the unwillingness of the state and other important actors to take risks and make changes [6]. In Lithuania the situation is quite similar, some of the key factors remain a lack of legislation, tax regulation, weak knowledge about social entrepreneurship and social innovation. Such conditions lead to insufficient development of innovative social enterprises. Unemployed people lack inspiration and support for successful entrepreneurial social start-ups.

The data reveal that the motives and preconditions for social economic activity in different countries remain different and can still remain different

Social Entrepreneurship in Rural Development of Lithuania   217

in the future. But strong economies are generally more involved in social entrepreneurship than weaker ones. In the European countries, more than 99% of enterprises are small and medium-sized (SMEs) ones (see http://ec.europa.eu/eurostat/web/structural-business-statistics/structural-business-statistics/sme?p_p_id=NavTreeportletprod_WAR_ NavTreeportletprod_INSTANCE_vxlB58HY09rg&p_p_lifecycle=0&p_p_ state=normal&p_p_mode=view&p_p_col_id=column-2&p_p_col_   pos= 1&p_p_col_count=4). In Lithuania the situation is the same. The problems that arise for such enterprises are still related to bureaucratic procedures, high taxes, poor management skills, non-innovative activities and low added-value created because of a lack of innovative technologies and decisions. SMEs also operate in rural areas. And the situation there is even more difficult because of a small market and lack of consumers.

Family business is also related to SMEs, but the legal basis for it is not well developed in the country. Another important scientific discourse stems from the same family farm profile (Table 1) Namely, the Agriculture Business Register Division, which administers the Farm Register, provides information system development and information delivery to users, summarises and analyses the collected registration data of farms in Lithuania.

Therefore, from the legal economic criteria perspective, some preparations for appropriate classification of family farms have already been made. That is a step forward in Lithuanian agriculture making conditions more favourable for farmers and family householders.

Social Environment

In Lithuania, the population declines faster than in any other EU country (see www.stat.gov.lt). The emigration flows from the country have already been mentioned. Despite economic reasons, said social problems could be the cause of such a situation. During 25 years the corruption index in Lithuania remained almost at the same level (approximately 55) (see www.transparencyinternational.org). People do not trust their public and governmental institutions.

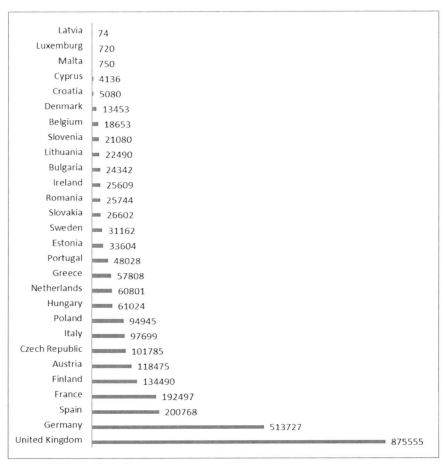

Source: OECD, 2013 [21].

Figure 2. The size of the social economy in 28 European countries.

The reasons are obvious. Public management stayed at quite a poor level, that caused ineffective solutions from the strategic to the tactical levels. That always disappoints people because it creates more social problems, such as insufficient education system, medical services, tax system ineffectiveness, inequality and overall disappointment in the development

Social Entrepreneurship in Rural Development of Lithuania 219

of the country. Lithuania has the biggest number of suicides per country in the EU (see http://ec.europa.eu/eurostat/web/products-eurostat-news/-/DDN-20170517-1?inheritRedirect=true&redirect=%2Feurostat%2F). That leads to very sad social climate and critical thinking about what is happening in the country. Even in the world Lithuania is in the 8th place after such countries as Sri Lanka, Guyana, Kazakhstan (see https://en.wikipedia.org/wiki/List_of_ countries_by_suicide_rate). Those facts are even more disappointing when considering Lithuania's place in the overall context of the world.

Table 1. Family farm profile assessment indicators

Statistical indicators	Family farm	All farms
Number of agricultural holdings		
Number of holdings and updated holdings		
Total holdings' land area and average holding size, ha		
Holding distribution by land ownership and land use		
Farms' land area by property right		
Farms' land structure by land purpose		
Farm distribution by Farms' land area		
Holding distribution by economic activities		
Number of holdings by county		
Average holding size by county, ha		
Distribution of holding owners – legal persons – by land owned		
Distribution of holding owners by age and gender		
Distribution of holding owners by age group		
Distribution of holding owners by age and land owned		
Number of young farmers by county		
Holding owners' educational status		
Economic size of holdings		
Economic size of holdings expressed in standard output		
Number of holdings and holdings registered on partnership basis	-	
Additional statistical indicators of family farms to identify		
Employed family members		-
Which generation of farms		-
Family relationship		-

Source. [27, 22, 2, 7].

Responsibility of the public sector is a quite complicated issue because of the complexity of public organisations and institutions, variety of their functions. Today responsibility of public organisations has a lot in common with CSR as much as some business philosophy and management principles are addapted for implementing social responsibility. In this case, public organisations' responsibility is analysed through accountability and publicity implementation taking into consideration social marketing as a helpful tool [15].

In rural areas, social climate is worse than in the towns because of higher unemployment, poverty, social exclusion, closing schools. The situation is even more different in the so-called third-world countries where poverty is high (but EU countries are also not immune to it – about 20 percent of population live below the poverty line in such countries as Lithuania and Latvia (Eurostat data)). Let's look at another part of the world for comparison. In such countries as Bangladesh, in order to ensure a balanced socio-economic development of the country, emancipation of women with a change in their status is a precondition which can be achieved only when there is an increased participation of women in development activities. However, many income-generating activities related to livestock and poultry, fisheries, social forestry, nursery, vegetable cultivation, sericulture, carpentry, handicraft, etc. are being attempted by women of rural areas [20]. Sustainable agriculture, rural development and food security cannot be achieved through efforts that ignore or exclude more than half of the rural population – women. Women constitute more than half of the agricultural labour force and are responsible for most of the household food production in low-income countries suffering from food deficit. Many social entrepreneurs operate in developing countries that have no structures or resources that would enable and support traditional entrepreneurship. Therefore, social entrepreneurs must create novel business models and organisational structures, and unique strategies for brokering between very limited, disparate and often dynamic resources to create social value [11]. The difference in economic development of the countries does not deny the fact that social entrepreneurship is powerful tool for synergy of different regions and environments especially seeking to diminish poverty and social exclusion.

The example of Bangladesh can prove that, on one hand, the existing problems in Lithuanian rural areas have to be solved by public institutions, but on the other hand that is also an area for social entrepreneurs and their actions. Every social problem could become a great business plan with a positive solution. That is why social entrepreneurship could be a tool for improving not only the economic but also the social situation.

THE POTENTIAL OF YOUNG ENTREPRENEURS IN LITHUANIA

Entrepreneurial Intentions of Lithuanian Students

As it was mentioned in the introduction of the chapter, the potential of substantial changes depends on many conditions and factors, but in this chapter the focus is made on young people as potential entrepreneurs in rural areas, willing and capable to take the initiative in creating perspective and innovative businesses. If we look to the data of the latest survey of Lithuanian students of higher education institutions (see www.guesssurvey.org. The research was carried out by Aleksandras Stulginskis University in Lithuania), it is possible to find out some considerations of young people in terms of entrepreneurial intentions in rural areas (among other places). The research was carried out in all of the higher institutions of Lithuania: colleges and universities. Family business was one of the focuses of the detailed survey. In the family business, the following trends could be mentioned [14]:

- The number of employees is no more than 10;
- 56.78% of respondents have never worked in their family business despite that their families have one (n = 100);

- International data about students from 50 countries show that those students who have been working in their family business are prepared to take over it in 5 years (7.86% of respondents);
- In Lithuania, this number is very similar – 7.46%.

Table 2. Data on family business in Lithuania according to the GUESS survey

Question	Response	Respondents	
		N	%
Do your parents have a business? (n = 112)	No	27	24.11
	Yes	85	75.89
Is your family a shareholder of this business? (n = 100)	0–25%	20	20.00
	26–50%	10	10.00
	51–99%	12	12.00
	100%	58	58.00
Are you one of the shareholders of this business? (n = 110)	0%	83	75.45
	1–25%	13	11.82
	26–50%	4	3.64
	51–99%	4	3.64
	100%	6	5.45
Do you think about this business as a family one? (n = 115)	No	61	53.04
	Yes	54	46.96

Source. GUESS survey data from Lithuania Report, 2016 [8].

Even if the families of the respondents (students) hold a family business, 53.04% of respondents (n = 115) think about this business as not a family one (see Table 2). These statistical survey data are very interesting and need to be analysed in more detail for interconnections between different answers to find correlation and clusters. These data are important for discussing the social entrepreneurship issues in Lithuanian rural areas because family business is directly related to family farms and households. The diversification of activities in these entities is possible and it is already happening. At the moment it is mostly related to EU financial support but later it could be seen as a positive change providing personal motivation to be in this kind of business.

Development of Entrepreneurial Skills and Abilities at University

Entrepreneurial education is very important for developing new entrepreneurs and creating new start-ups. Some research about this was made before and part of the results can be discussed in this chapter to better present the analysed problem. When researching the opinion of Lithuanian students on entrepreneurship (listeners of the Entrepreneurship course), the development and improvement of their skills and abilities, it became obvious that students agree that the teaching process can reinforce their desire and provide opportunities to become entrepreneurs [16]. According to the opinions of student target group A (Lithuanian students), the main characteristics, such as confidence, risk-taking, courage, creativity, seeking adventure, opportunity creation, leadership, flexibility, originality, innovativeness, spontaneity, communicativeness, capability of decision-making, competitiveness, and persistence, might be developed in the study process. The means t how to develop such characteristics could be situation and case study analysis, discussions, teamwork, model creation and decision-making, listening to success stories, as well as various improvisations.

After analysing the results of target group B (Polish students) (the same questionnaire was applied in a Polish university) it should be mentioned that just three of the students were attending the course of entrepreneurship. None of them declared to have knowledge about social entrepreneurship. The respondents emphasised that potentially significant measures for raising young entrepreneurs could be practical examples. Such features of character as imagination and adaptiveness was also mentioned as important.

The respondents from target group C (group C was students from various universities studying in Erasmus in Mendel university, Brno, Czech Republic) indicated the following character features as the most important for entrepreneurial activity: open-mindedness, social ability, management skills, financial and economic knowledge, creativity, responsibility, reliability, leadership, communication skills, languages, self-confidence, risk-taking, positivity, and flexibility. These characteristics could be supported at university by special courses, as well as scientific literature on entrepreneurship.

During the study process, certain entrepreneurial skills and abilities might be introduced and developed as well. According to group A, analytical thinking, adaptiveness to innovation, well-grounded decision-making, situation and environmental analysis, knowledge of modern technologies, organisational skills, communication skills, creativity, responsibility, teamwork, and effective knowledge management might be introduced and/or developed during tertiary studies. Target group B named knowledge gained at university and teamwork as potential means for the development of personal features to become an entrepreneur.

The most effective means for developing an impetus for young people to become entrepreneurs might be: analysis of examples of success; cooperation between the science and business sectors; teamwork; encouragement of competition; generation of ideas; meeting real entrepreneurs; work experience at entrepreneurial enterprises; and innovative projects. In turn, the respondents from group C indicated management skills, strategic and marketing skills, accounting, organisational skills, communication skills, teamwork, leadership, negotiation skills, analytical thinking, forecasting, networking, flexibility, and encouragement of "free thinking" as entrepreneurial skills and abilities which should be developed during tertiary studies.

According to the students, the most important conditions and/or measures for strengthening the entrepreneurial potential at university are lectures from current entrepreneurs, practical examples, internships, and project-based activity. Target group B students emphasised the importance of time management, creativity development and internships provided by university.

In terms of the most crucial factors for developing young entrepreneurs, respondents from target group.

Social Entrepreneurship in Rural Development of Lithuania   225

Table 3. Development of entrepreneurial skills and abilities at university

Group A	Group B	Group C	Comment
Means for developing personal entrepreneurial features			
• situation and case analysis; • discussions, teamwork; • model creation and decision making; listening to success stories; • various improvisations.	• teamwork; • gaining appropriate knowledge.	• special courses; • scientific literature on entrepreneurship.	Lithuanian students, after completing the entrepreneurship course, indicated further measures on how to develop entrepreneurial features at university.
Means for developing entrepreneurial skill and abilities at university			
• analysis of examples of success; • cooperation between science and business sectors; • teamwork; • encouragement of competition; • generation of ideas; • meeting real entrepreneurs; • work experience at entrepreneurial enterprises; • innovative projects.	• tight schedule with additional activities; • creativity development; • internships.	• lectures from current entrepreneurs; • practical examples; • internships; • project-based activity.	Group A and Group C had a similar attitude to the question; it means that they proposed similar measures. Group B showed a lack of comprehension of deeper suggestions.
Means for developing young entrepreneurs			
• systematic approach to developing entrepreneurs at primary education and high schools, and later at college and university; • real stories of successful entrepreneurs in Lithuania; • cooperation between business and university; • entrepreneurs' involvement in the study process; • interdisciplinary education.	• involving real entrepreneurs in education process; • strong character development; • practice; • imagination; • adaptiveness.	• managerial skills; • simulations; • traineeships; • good ideas; • planning; • teamwork; • decision making; critical thinking.	Group B and C (non-students of the special course) mostly were focused on character and managerial skills development and did not demonstrate a complex view of the problem.

Source: [16].

A emphasised a systematic approach in developing entrepreneurs at primary education and high schools, and later at college and university; real stories of successful entrepreneurs in Lithuania; cooperation between business and university; entrepreneurs' involvement in the study process, and interdisciplinary education. Such measures might help to develop social entrepreneurs as well, given the emphasis on social value. Young people are interested in social activities, which might be the first step towards social enterprise creation. Interdisciplinary study programmes have started to be implemented in Lithuania, which may be considered entrepreneurial opportunities for developing social entrepreneurs. These results are compared in Table 3.

The students' research disclosed one of the most significant aspects pertaining to the role of education in the development of social entrepreneurs. Students, being young people and potential young entrepreneurs, strongly believe that entrepreneurial skills and abilities might be strengthened or even acquired at university and could be leading to entrepreneurial possibilities. They are interested in finding out more about social entrepreneurship and its characteristics. It reaffirms the main conclusion that education institutions and the study process might be an appropriate place and an effective instrument for raising and enhancing young social entrepreneurs in Lithuania.

The disclosed interests of students highly imply a deeper correlation between the studies and start-ups at universities which have technology parks or similar spaces where very valuable experience and motivation to start own business can be gained.

CONCLUSION

Lithuania still lacks the implementation of social innovation, especially in rural areas. Such preconditions as a culture of social innovation and entrepreneurship, appropriate legislation, different financial sources, national and international networking of social innovators, partnership between public sector, private sector and NGOs, involvement of target groups, infrastructure for social innovation, effective control and monitoring of social innovation, sufficient administrative skills are essential for successful implementation of social innovation policy and development of social enterprises in Lithuania, including rural areas.

Young people have the most potential of social entrepreneurship in Lithuania. The research implies that Lithuania can be regarded as a country in which entrepreneurship is driven by external factors (unemployment, income loss) more than internal motivations (goals, dreams). However, research suggests that young entrepreneurs in Lithuania were more likely to start their activity as opportunity-based rather than out of necessity. It seems very promising and allows having positive expectations in the future. The latest research about entrepreneurial potential puts Lithuania in a very high seventh place. Rural areas are not an exception because they can be regarded as unexplored territory for young social entrepreneurs.

REFERENCES

[1] Agence Française De Développement Family. *Family farming*, 2016 at http:// www.afd.fr/ webdav/site/afd/ shared/PUBLICATIONS/ THEMATIQUES/AFD-agriculture-familiale-VA.pdf/.

[2] Slesinger, DP; Whitaker, JJ. *A Portrait of Family Farmers in Wisconsin*, 2016, at https://www.ssc.wisc.edu/cde/cdewp/98-30.pdf/.

[3] Zhang, D; Swanson, LA. Social Entrepreneurship in Nonprofit Organizations: An Empirical Investigation of the Synergy Between Social and Business Objectives, *Journal of Nonprofit & Public Sector Marketing*, 25, p.105–125 (2013)

[4] EC, *Social enterprises: report presents first comparative overview*, 2014 at: http:// ec.europa.eu/social/ main.jsp?langId=en&catId =89 &newsId=2149.

[5] Azmat, F; Ah. Sh. Ferrous, P. Couchman, Understanding the Dynamics Between Social Entrepreneurship and Inclusive Growth in Subsistence Marketplaces, *Journal of Public Policy & Marketing*, 34 (2), pp. 252–271 (2015).

[6]   Azmat, F; Samaratunge, R. Exploring Customer Loyalty at Bottom of the Pyramid in South Asia, *Social Responsibility Journal*, 9 (3), pp. 379–94 (2013).

[7]   Food and Agriculture Organization of the United Nations, *Towards Stronger Family Farming*, 2014, at http://www.fao.org/3/a-i4306e.pdf/.

[8]   GUESS survey results, *Lithuania Report* (primary data), 2016, report at: htttp://www.guesssurvey.otg.

[9]   Haugh, H. A Research Agenda for Social Entrepreneurship, *Social Enterprise Journal*, 1 (1), pp. 1–12 (2005).

[10]   Haugh, H. New strategies for a sustainable society: the growing contribution of social entrepreneurship, *Business Ethics Quarterly*, 17(4), pp. 743-749 (2007).

[11]   Konda, I; Stare, J; Rodica, B. Social challenges are opportunities or sustainable development: tracing impacts of social entrepreneurship through innovations and value creation, *Ekonomske teme*, 53 (2), pp. 215-233 (2015).

[12]   Greblikaitė, J. Development of Entrepreneurship in Lithuania: Becoming Social Entrepreneurs, Entrepreneurship and Firm Performance. New York: Nova Science Publisher's, pp. 81-92 (2016)

[13]   Greblikaitė, J; Rakštys, R. *Socialaus verslumo aplinka Lietuvoje*, Vadyba, kooperacija, inovacijos. Tarptautinės mokslinės-praktinės konferencijos medžiaga, (*International Conference, Book of Abstracts*), pp. 16-17 (2016)

[14]   Greblikaite, J; Rakstys, R; Caruso, D. Social Entrepreneurship in Rural Development of Lithuania, *Management Theory and Studies for Rural Business and Infrastructure Development*, 39(2), pp. 69–85 (2017).

[15]   Greblikaitė, J; Tamulienė, V. *Responsibility of public sector: CSR implementation through social marketing*, Публічне управління та адміністрування в умовах інформаційного суспільства: вітчизняний і зарубіжний досвід: монографія. Запоріжжя: РВВ ЗДІА, pp. 521-540, (2016).

Social Entrepreneurship in Rural Development of Lithuania 229

[16] Greblikaitė, J; Sroka, W; Gerulaitienė, N. Involving Young People in Polish and Lithuanian Social Enterprises by Fostering Entrepreneurial Skills and Abilities as Entrepreneurial Opportunity at University, Entrepreneurial Business and Economics Review. *Krakow: Cracow University of Economics*, vol. 4, no. 3, pp. 131-152 (2016).

[17] Swanson, LA; Zhang DD. The Social Entrepreneurship Zone. *Journal of Nonprofit & Public Sector Marketing*, 22, pp. 71–88 (2010).

[18] LR Finansų ministerija/Lithuanian Ministry of Finance, *Jaunimo verslumą skatinančių priemonių vertinimas.*, 2012 at http:// www. pwc.lt, www.vini.lt.

[19] LR Ūkio ministerija/Lithuanian Ministry of Economy, *Socialinio verslo koncepcija/ The concept of social entrepreneurship*, 2015 at http://www.ukmin.lt/uploads/documents/Verslo%20aplinka/Smulkus %20verslas/Socialinio_verslo_koncepcija_2015_%C4%AFsakymas. pdf.

[20] Kabir, MS; et al., Social capital in rural poor women entrepreneurship: The Case of Bangladesh, *Journal of Advanced Research in Law and Economics*, 1(9), pp. 4 – 14 (2014).

[21] OECD, Ed. By Antonella Noya and Emma Clarence, The Social Economy. *Building inclusive economies* 2007 at https:// www.scribd. com/document/93901305/OECD-the-Social-Economy-Building-Inclusive-Economies.

[22] Helfand, SM; Moreira, ARB; Bresnyan, EW. *Agricultural Productivity and Family Farms in Brazil: Creating Opportunities and Closing Gaps*, 2016, at http:// economics.ucr.edu/people/faculty/ helfand/Helfand%20Ag%20Productivity%20and%20Family%20Far ms%20in%20Brazil%202015.pdf/.

[23] Ney, S; et al., Social entrepreneurs and social change: tracing impacts of social entrepreneurship through ideas, structures and practices, *Journal Entrepreneurial Venturing*, 6(1), pp. 51-60 (2014).

[24] Madhu, V; Raj, E; Srinivas, V; Jung, K. Marketing Interactions in Subsistence Marketplaces: A Bottom-Up Approach to Designing

Public Policy, *Journal of Public Policy & Marketing*, 31, pp. 159–177 (2012).

[25] Madhu, V; Raj, E; Srinivas, V; Srinivas, S. Subsistence Entrepreneurship, Value Creation, and Community Exchange Systems: A Social Capital Explanation, *Journal of Macromarketing*, 34 (2), pp. 213–226 (2014).

[26] Žemės ūkio informacijos ir kaimo verslo centras, *Lietuvos žemės ūkis faktai ir skaičiai*, 2016 m, Nr. *2* (18) at http://www.vic.lt/?mid=108/.

INDEX

#

20th century, 40, 94
21st century, 2, 31, 39

A

accident prevention, 172
accreditation, 111
activism, xi, 182, 190
administrators, 105, 192
adulthood, 12, 15, 101
affective experience, 8, 9
affirmative action, 194
Afghanistan, 42
Africa, 95, 98
African Americans, 203
aggression, 69
agriculture, x, xi, 155, 162, 164, 165, 168, 171, 175, 207, 210, 211, 212, 217, 220, 227
alcohol consumption, 67
alertness, 61, 64
altruism, 39
ambidexterity, 140, 145, 152
American Psychological Association, 47

amputation, 161
amygdala, 68, 92
anthropology, 101
antibody, 65
anxiety disorder, 72, 76, 91
apnea, 75
At the Crossroads, 200
attention to task, 21

B

back pain, 166
Bangladesh, 203, 220, 221, 229
bankruptcy, 109
basic needs, 17, 19
behaviors, 80, 170
benchmarking, 150
benefits, ix, 24, 36, 81, 93, 112, 194, 195
Black Sea region, 166
blood, 76
body mass index (BMI), 66, 67, 88
bottom-up, 61
brain, 62, 85, 92
Brazil, 76, 182, 183, 229
breakdown, 7, 99
breathing, 80

BRICS, vi, vii, xi, 181, 182, 183, 184, 187, 188, 190, 191, 195, 196, 197, 199, 202, 204, 205, 206
Britain, 3
Brno, 223
Bulgaria, 216
Burkina Faso, 104, 118
burnout, 75, 90
business cycle, 189
business environment, 3, 40
business ethics, 4, 39
business model, 103, 110, 115, 129, 130, 134, 142, 148, 186, 189, 196, 213, 220

C

caffeine, 71, 79
cardiovascular disease, 65, 66
catastrophes, 94, 100, 106, 116
causal relationship, 13
Central Asia, 98
challenges, vii, viii, xi, 2, 4, 39, 40, 149, 153, 169, 191, 192, 198, 207, 209, 211, 213, 228
chemical industry, 153
children, 100, 111, 112, 113, 114, 194
China, 98, 182, 183, 202
circadian rhythm, 65, 79
civil servants, 160, 171
civil war, 199
classification, 138, 217
cleavage, 192
climate, 180, 219, 220
clusters, 14, 222
cognitive domains, 63, 64, 88
cognitive function, 63
cognitive load, 64
cognitive performance, viii, 60, 61, 62, 63, 64, 65, 69, 70, 71, 72, 82, 83
cognitive tasks, 61, 62
cognitive theory, 3

cognitive variables, 88
cognitive-behavioral therapy, 82
collaboration, 143
collectivism, 203
college students, 67, 68, 69, 89, 92
colonial rule, 192
communication skills, 224
comorbidity, 172
comparative analysis, 202, 209
compassion, 102, 111, 125
competitive advantage, 137, 141, 145
competitive markets, 97
competitiveness, 94, 223
competitors, 131, 132, 137, 143
comprehension, 12, 225
conceptualization, 134, 146
conflict, xi, 4, 20, 21, 22, 39, 77, 82, 85, 94, 182, 183, 185, 187, 188, 191, 192, 194, 195, 196, 197, 201, 205
congruence, 21
conscientiousness, 24
construction, x, 109, 120, 147, 155, 156, 157, 160, 164, 165, 166, 168, 173, 174, 175, 176, 178, 201
contextualization, 197
controlled trials, 76
convergence, 28
conviction, 17
cooperation, 152, 165, 191, 192, 224, 225, 226
coronary heart disease, 66
correlation, 222, 226
corruption, 217
cost, 11, 72, 76, 90, 91, 117, 137, 148, 165, 178
country of origin, 67
creativity, 11, 13, 27, 223, 224, 225
credit rating, 108
crisis management, 95, 102, 104
critical thinking, 219, 225
Croatia, 168
crop production, 164

Index

cultivation, 220
currency, 111, 112, 113, 114
Cyprus, 216
Czech Republic, 223

D

data analysis, 209
data set, 63, 157, 163, 166
database, 162
death rate, 162
deaths, 82, 102, 168
Denmark, 168, 216
depression, 67, 69, 75, 76, 77, 83, 84, 86, 88, 89, 90, 91, 92
depressive symptoms, 67
deprivation, 61, 62, 63, 64, 70, 71, 73, 75, 83, 86, 88, 92
developed countries, 96
developing countries, 96, 98, 104, 182, 204, 210, 220
developing country(ies), 94, 96, 98, 104, 182, 200, 204, 210, 220
diabetes, 65, 66, 88
diffusion, 147
direct cost, 76
direct payment, 211
disability, 73, 76, 162, 170, 171
discrimination, 27, 193
disturbance variables, 73
duality, 202
durability, 145

E

earthquakes, 95
East Asia, 98, 168
Eastern Europe, 98, 168
e-commerce, 4
economic activity, 94, 98, 210, 216

economic development, 3, 95, 96, 97, 119, 197, 213, 220
economic growth, 182
economic landscape, 194
economic status, 183
education, 81, 184, 193, 194, 211, 218, 223, 225, 226
educational institutions, 32
egocentrism, viii, 1
emerging markets, 186
emigration, xi, 207, 212, 215, 217
emotion regulation, 68, 69, 77, 82, 85, 89, 91
emotional disorder, 76, 86
emotional exhaustion, 10
emotional state, 11
emotional stimuli, 63
empathy, 75, 90, 111
empirical studies, vii, 1, 3, 7, 9, 10, 11, 13, 14, 15, 17, 18, 19, 21, 24, 26, 27, 29, 30, 32, 33, 35, 36, 37, 39
employment, 14, 76, 91, 95, 98, 162, 178, 179, 193, 194, 212
employment opportunities, 95
encouragement, 224, 225
energy, 61, 94, 120, 187
engineering, 124, 194
entrepreneurs, ix, xi, 93, 103, 105, 106, 119, 122, 208, 209, 213, 216, 220, 221, 223, 224, 225, 226, 227, 229
entrepreneurship, vii, xi, 98, 152, 153, 198, 200, 202, 207, 208, 209, 210, 212, 213, 214, 215, 216, 217, 220, 221, 222, 223, 224, 225, 226, 227, 228, 229
environment, 20, 68, 80, 106, 109, 111, 115, 116, 168, 183, 188, 189, 190, 196, 199, 213, 214, 215, 216, 217
environmental influences, 150
environments, 185, 187, 189, 191, 221
equality, 197
ethical issues, 4, 39
ethnic diversity, 199

Index

ethnic groups, 100, 185, 188
ethnicity, 182, 184, 198
European Union, 98, 170, 208, 212
everyday life, 82
executive function, 64
executive functioning, 65
exercise, 18, 35, 79, 81
expenditures, 132
explicit knowledge, 140
exploitation, 134, 139, 140, 141, 144, 147, 148, 150, 152
exposure, 79, 189
extrinsic motivation, 13, 14, 15, 16, 17, 18, 38
extrinsic rewards, 16, 18

F

factor analysis, 173
farm size, 164, 210
farmers, 159, 164, 165, 172, 178, 179, 209, 210, 211, 212, 217, 219
farms, 162, 164, 178, 208, 210, 211, 212, 217, 219, 222
FDI, 206
financial crisis, 186
financial incentives, 4
financial institutions, 109, 117
financial performance, 148
financial resources, 114, 116, 211
financial support, 103, 113, 222
Finland, 155, 157, 158, 161, 162, 163, 165, 166, 167, 168, 169, 171, 172, 173, 175, 176, 177, 178, 180, 216
fire fighting, 167
firm strategy, 182, 183
fisheries, 220
flexibility, 80, 104, 223, 224
flooding, 94, 105, 113, 115
floods, ix, 93, 104, 112
flour, 109

food industry, 152
food production, 211, 220
food products, 114
food security, 220
forecasting, 224
forest management, 166
formal education, 108
formal sector, 95
France, 120, 125, 216
friendship, 109
funding, 213
funds, 109, 113, 114, 211, 216

G

GDP, 98
general knowledge, 12, 13
Germany, 216
global markets, 95
globalization, 186, 200
goal setting, 8
God, 112, 113
governance, 30, 38, 124, 148, 192, 198, 204, 205
Great Britain, 168
Great Recession, 200
group membership, 25
growth, vii, ix, xi, 13, 34, 93, 182, 212
growth rate, 212
guidelines, 186
Guyana, 219

H

health care, 73, 80, 88, 216
health care costs, 73
health condition, 90
health problems, 20, 72
health services, 67
heterogeneity, 101
high blood pressure, 66

Index

high fat, 162
high school, 225, 226
higher education, 209, 221
history, 4, 103, 118, 150, 164
homogeneity, 26, 28
housing, 117
human behavior, 16
human capital, 30
human development, 94, 95
human nature, 4, 31, 36, 39
human resource management, 49, 52, 53, 54, 56
human resources, 194
hygiene, 78, 79, 88

I

immigrants, 163, 177, 179
immune system, 65
immunity, 83
inbound knowledge flows, ix, 127, 129, 131
income tax, 119
increased access, 185
India, xi, 168, 182, 183, 184, 191, 192, 194, 198, 199, 203, 204, 205, 206
Indians, 192
individual character, 32
individual characteristics, 32
individual differences, 23, 24
industrial revolution, 3
industrialized countries, 3
inequality, 183, 185, 188, 218
inertia, 79
informal sector, vii, ix, 93, 94, 95, 96, 97, 98, 99, 101, 102, 104, 105, 106, 107, 110, 111, 116, 118, 119, 120
information sharing, 136
information technology, 4
infrastructure, xii, 186, 190, 194, 208, 227
injuries, vii, x, 74, 82, 87, 91, 155, 156, 157, 158, 159, 160, 161, 162, 163, 164,
165, 166, 167, 168, 169, 170, 171, 172, 173, 175, 176, 177, 178, 179, 180
injury prevention, 156, 169
insomnia, 60, 62, 67, 72, 73, 74, 81, 87, 88, 89, 91, 159, 172
institutional change, 200
institutional theory, xi, 182, 183, 196
institutions, 31, 32, 95, 108, 186, 187, 190, 195, 196, 198, 209, 218, 220, 221, 226
integration, 16, 17, 38
intellectual capital, 150
intellectual property, ix, x, 127, 128, 136, 138, 142, 143
intellectual property rights, ix, x, 127, 128, 136, 138, 142, 143
interdependence, 28
intergroup contact theory, xi, 182, 183, 185, 190, 195, 204
internalization, x, 16, 17, 128, 140, 143
international relations, xi, 182, 183, 185
interpersonal conflict, 77
intervention, 82, 170, 173
intrinsic motivation, 13, 16, 21, 22
intrinsic rewards, 12
investment, 153, 190, 194
investments, 30, 211
Iowa, 159, 179
Ireland, 216
Israel, 71, 81, 92
Ivory Coast, 111

J

Japan, 95, 98
job characteristics, 32
job creation, xi, 207, 208
job performance, 16, 88
job satisfaction, 10, 27, 33
job strain, 158
jurisdiction, 192
justification, 33, 108, 184

K

Kazakhstan, 219
knowledge economy, 39

L

labor force, 76
labor force participation, 76
labor market, 179
labour force, 220
Latin America, 98, 199
Latvia, 216, 220
leadership, 30, 33, 103, 129, 151, 202, 223, 224
left-handers, 161
lens, xi, 182, 185
less developed countries, 202
level of education, 32
lifestyle behaviors, 81
Lisbon Strategy, 213
Lithuania, vi, vii, xi, 207, 208, 209, 210, 211, 212, 213, 215, 216, 217, 220, 221, 222, 225, 226, 227, 228
locus, 16
longitudinal study, 68
long-term memory, 62
Louisiana, 59

M

machinery, 156
magnitude, 82
major crisis, 94, 96, 99, 100, 118, 120
majority, 60, 72, 82, 118, 157, 192
Malaysia, 163, 169
malnutrition, 194
management, 3, 4, 5, 33, 39, 81, 101, 103, 110, 115, 116, 118, 119, 122, 125, 129, 131, 132, 140, 145, 156, 170, 179, 211, 214, 216, 217, 218, 220, 223, 224
manpower, 108
manufacturing, 74, 149, 158, 168, 172, 173
marital status, 74
marketing, 131, 160, 190, 196, 216, 220, 224, 228
marketplace, 107, 115
mellitus, 87
memory performance, 63
mental health, viii, 60, 61, 65, 67, 68, 73, 75, 76, 82, 86
merchandise, 109, 112, 117
meta-analysis, 14, 63, 65, 67, 84, 88, 90, 91, 159, 170, 179
metabolic syndrome, 88
methodology, ix, 93, 97, 102, 209
MNEs, vi, xi, 181, 182, 183, 186, 187, 188, 189, 190, 191, 193, 194, 195, 196, 197, 199, 205
models, 2, 3, 8, 83, 134, 139, 212, 214
mood disorder, 86
moral development, 34, 35
moral judgment, 4, 39
mortality, 168, 175, 176
motivation, vii, 1, 2, 3, 4, 5, 7, 8, 9, 10, 11, 14, 15, 16, 18, 19, 20, 21, 22, 24, 25, 26, 27, 28, 29, 31, 33, 34, 36, 37, 38, 39, 40, 72, 133, 153, 185, 194, 222, 226
multidimensional, 102
multinational corporations, 200
multivariate analysis, 169
musculoskeletal system, 166, 174
music, 80
Muslims, 193, 198
mythology, 100

N

natural disaster, 94, 95, 100, 106
negative emotions, 10, 68

Index

negative influences, 28
negative mood, 63
negative outcomes, 9
negative relation, 13
Netherlands, 167, 176
networking, xi, 208, 224, 226
neural function, 83
New Zealand, 52, 91, 95, 98
NGOs, xii, 208, 214, 215, 226
nicotine, 79
Nigeria, 1, 202
nodes, 106
nurses, 14, 70, 71, 85, 86, 90, 159

O

obesity, 65
obstacles, 105, 186, 213
obstructive sleep apnea, 75
occupational health, 156, 164, 173
occupational injury, x, 70, 75, 86, 155, 157, 158, 159, 160, 162, 163, 164, 169, 171, 172, 173, 177
OECD, 218, 229
open innovation processes, ix, x, 127, 128, 142, 149
open-mindedness, 223
opportunities, 9, 14, 103, 107, 109, 123, 223, 226, 228
optimism, 69
organizational behavior, 2
organizational learning, 140, 150
organizational membership, 25
organizational tenure, 33
OSHA, 162
outbound knowledge flows, v, vii, ix, x, 127, 128, 130, 135, 138, 139, 144
ownership, 30, 219

P

painters, 166
participants, 62, 63, 64, 65, 67, 68, 70, 71, 72, 73, 134, 179
payback period, 115
peer review, 5, 7
perceived health, 168
performance ratings, 11
performance related pay, 33
perinatal, 100
personal goals, 8, 16, 30
personal identity, 25, 34
personality factors, 24
personality traits, 19
pharmaceutical, 145
physical activity, 67, 82, 85
physical exercise, 80
physical health, 65, 67, 73, 75
physical well-being, 69, 86
physicians, 71
pilot study, 179
pneumonia, 65, 89
Poland, 174
policy makers, 196
political parties, 32
population, 60, 74, 89, 100, 159, 167, 172, 195, 212, 217, 220
Portugal, 148
positive correlation, 159
positive emotions, 10, 11
positive mood, 30
positive relationship, 15, 33
poultry, 220
poverty, 94, 198, 220
poverty line, 220
preferential treatment, 190
prefrontal cortex, 62
prejudice, 204
prevention, 75, 85, 172, 173, 174, 176, 177
primary data, 228

private sector, xii, 193, 194, 208, 214, 226

problem solving, 20, 21, 22

procedural fairness, 30

process innovation, 211

production costs, 137

productivity, viii, 2, 4, 7, 11, 15, 60, 72, 74, 75, 82, 84, 88, 90, 145, 178, 229

profit, xi, 18, 19, 39, 111, 182, 213

profitability, 183, 200

project, 80, 96, 100, 106, 112, 145, 147, 153, 175, 194, 213, 224, 225

proliferation, xi, 182

protection, 96, 145, 168, 172

psychiatric disorder, 85, 125

psychological distress, 158

psychological health, 65

psychological processes, 20

psychological resources, 20, 22

psychological stress, 66, 69

psychologist, 85

psychology, 52, 100, 101

psychopathology, 85, 87

public goods, 216

public markets, 109

public sector, xii, 17, 18, 19, 31, 33, 38, 159, 163, 177, 193, 208, 220, 226, 228

public sector employee, 33, 159

public service, 8, 31

Q

qualitative research, 15

quality of life, 60, 77

questionnaire, 160, 168, 175, 223

quotas, 193, 194

R

reaction time, 63, 64

regulations, 190

rehabilitation, 177

REM, 67

reputation, 137

research institutions, 132

researchers, 2, 15, 20, 22, 33, 65, 96, 99, 102, 104, 120

resentment, 185, 187, 188, 190

reservations, 201

resilience, v, ix, 93, 94, 95, 96, 97, 100, 101, 102, 103, 104, 106, 107, 108, 109, 110, 111, 112, 113, 114, 115, 116, 117, 118, 119, 120, 122, 124, 125, 186, 199

resistance, 125

resolution, 34, 103

resource management, 216

resources, ix, 12, 13, 14, 28, 29, 38, 94, 96, 97, 101, 103, 108, 110, 111, 113, 115, 116, 117, 118, 119, 120, 128, 185, 187, 188, 190, 192, 194, 211, 220

right-handers, 160

risk assessment, 176

risk factors, vii, x, 100, 155, 164, 165, 171, 180

risk management, 119

risk-taking, 166, 223, 224

Romania, 216

rural areas, vii, xi, 193, 207, 208, 209, 210, 211, 212, 214, 215, 217, 220, 221, 222, 226

rural development, xi, 207, 208, 220

rural population, 220

S

safety, xi, 70, 71, 72, 88, 137, 155, 156, 166, 168, 169, 170, 174, 178, 179, 180

Safety Management, 156

sanctions, 29

saturation, 105

science, 36, 85, 122, 132, 133, 143, 147, 182, 184, 224, 225

second-class citizens, 119

Index

security, 137, 148, 176, 191
self-concept, 32, 38
self-confidence, 224
self-efficacy, 122
self-employed, 161, 162, 165, 173, 174
self-employment, 170
self-esteem, 25, 77
self-expression, 36
self-interest, 31
sensitivity, 23
separatism, 205
shareholders, 222
shock, 94, 95, 104, 116
short-term memory, 63
showing, 194
Silicon Valley, 202
Singapore, 124
sleep, v, vii, viii, 59, 60, 61, 62, 63, 64, 65,
    66, 67, 68, 69, 70, 71, 72, 73, 74, 75, 77,
    78, 79, 80, 81, 82, 83, 84, 85, 86, 87, 88,
    89, 90, 91, 92, 156, 159, 171, 172, 173,
    177, 179
sleep apnea, 75, 80, 81, 86
sleep deprivation, 61, 62, 63, 64, 65, 67, 69,
    70, 71, 72, 73, 75, 77, 83, 84, 85, 86, 87,
    88, 89, 90, 91
sleep disorders, 62
sleep disturbance, 65, 67, 68, 71, 73, 77, 85,
    89, 171, 173
sleep habits, 88
sleep latency, 67
sleep medicine, 87
sleep physiology, 91
sleeping pills, 73
sleeping problems, x, 155, 159
Slovakia, 216
small business, xi, 94, 207, 212
smoking, 67
snoring, 80
sociability, 69, 82
social activism, xi, 182, 190
social activities, 77, 208, 226

social categorization, 25, 26, 27, 28
social change, 229
social class, 188
social comparison, 25, 26, 27, 28
social development, 94
social entrepreneurship, vii, xi, 207, 208,
    209, 210, 212, 213, 214, 215, 216, 217,
    221, 222, 223, 226, 227, 228, 229
social environment, 185
social exclusion, 220
social group, xii, 25, 26, 190, 208
social identity, 8, 25, 26, 38
social identity theory, 8
social problems, 217
social programs, 194
social relationships, 68
social responsibility, 214, 220
social sciences, 22, 38
social services, 215, 216
social situations, 25
social status, 13, 184
social support, 84
socialization, 140, 141
society, 31, 32, 34, 39, 119, 184, 185, 190,
    192, 213, 214, 216, 228
socioeconomic status, 65, 67
sociology, 101, 184
software, 106, 110, 148, 149, 153
solidarity, ix, 94, 116, 117, 120
solution, 102, 103, 132, 214, 221
South Africa, 182, 183
South Asia, 98, 202, 228
Sri Lanka, 219
stakeholders, 39, 119
state, 4, 9, 10, 21, 38, 102, 106, 110, 113,
    130, 138, 139, 183, 191, 198, 216, 217
states, 9, 10, 16, 21, 23, 24, 28, 31, 36, 38,
    95, 199
statistics, 61, 157, 179, 210, 217
steel, 161
stereotypes, 201
stimulation, 13

stimulus, 212
stock, 30, 109, 114
stratification, xi, 181, 182, 183, 184, 187, 188, 195, 196
stress, x, 60, 66, 69, 76, 79, 82, 83, 84, 91, 92, 100, 148, 155, 156, 159, 165, 173, 174
stress factors, 159
stressors, 66, 77, 159, 170
stretching, 79
stroke, 66
successful aging, 13
suicide, 219
supply chain, 95
suppression, 167
survival, ix, 93, 94, 99, 102, 107, 110, 187
susceptibility, 65, 82, 84
sustainability, 119
sustainable development, 94, 96, 202, 228
Sweden, 162

T

tactics, 190, 195
Tajikistan, 205
target, xii, 114, 132, 134, 135, 136, 142, 208, 223, 224, 226
task performance, 25
tax rates, 109
tax system, 186, 218
team members, 28, 29, 30
team sports, 167
teams, 28, 30, 39, 62
tension, 9, 185, 187, 189, 191, 192, 195, 196, 197, 202, 145, 183, 187, 189, 205
tenure, 158, 169
territory, 99, 100, 227
terrorism, 100
terrorist attacks, 95
theoretical approach, 103
Third World, 204

Tibet, 202
trade union, 32
trade-off, 140
training, 13, 14, 15, 33, 70, 79, 82, 102, 111, 119, 167, 170, 179, 194
transcendence, 34
transportation, 74, 108, 162, 186
traumatic events, 111
treatment, 68, 75, 90
Turkey, 166, 173, 178
type 2 diabetes, 66, 87

U

underlying mechanisms, 68
United Kingdom, 156, 216
United Nations, 95, 228
United Nations Development Program, 95
urban, 117, 194, 198, 208
urban areas, 208

V

valence, 9
variables, 23, 24, 32, 36, 60, 63, 74, 138
vein, 30, 131, 132, 133
venture capital, 132
vertical dimensions, 203
victims, 104, 117, 157, 158
violence, 163, 169, 178, 183, 185, 188, 191, 192, 196
vision, 99, 108
vocabulary, 12
vulnerability, 95

W

waking, 60, 79, 80
Western Europe, 168
Wisconsin, 227

Index

wood, 156
work absenteeism, 35, 84
work activities, 4, 40
work environment, 19, 32, 97, 174
workers, 3, 4, 11, 12, 13, 14, 36, 61, 71, 72, 74, 75, 77, 81, 82, 84, 87, 96, 107, 157, 158, 159, 160, 162, 163, 165, 167, 168, 170, 173, 174, 176, 177, 178
workforce, 60, 76, 162, 178
working conditions, x, 155, 161, 163, 178
working memory, 12, 62, 63, 64, 69, 70, 82, 87, 91
working population, 158, 159, 164

workplace, vii, viii, 35, 59, 60, 61, 68, 69, 73, 74, 77, 80, 82, 84, 85, 86, 87, 110, 159, 166, 173
work-related stress, 76

Y

young adults, 62, 86, 88, 91
young entrepreneurs, xi, 208, 223, 224, 226, 227
young people, 221, 224, 226
young women, 157, 177